O CANADA

THE DOLPHIN

Series Editor: Tim Caudery

25

O CANADA

ESSAYS ON CANADIAN LITERATURE AND CULTURE

Edited by Jørn Carlsen

AARHUS UNIVERSITY PRESS

Copyright: Aarhus University Press, 1995
Printed by The Alden Press, Oxford
ISBN 87 7288 376 6
ISSN 0106 4487

AARHUS UNIVERSITY PRESS
Building 170
University of Aarhus
DK-8000 Aarhus C, Denmark
Fax (+45) 8619 8433

73 Lime Walk
Headington
Oxford OX3 7AD
Fax (+44) 865 750 079

Box 511
Oakville, Conn. 06779
Fax (+1) 203 945 9468

Editorial address:
The Dolphin
Department of English
University of Aarhus
8000 Aarhus C, Denmark
Fax (+45) 8619 1699

Published with financial support from the Aarhus University Research Foundation.

The cover shows a detail from a woodcut of Jens Munk's chart from Cape Farewell to Munkenes Winterhauen at Nova Dania, Churchill, Manitoba. It is taken from Jens Munk, *Navigatio Septentrionalis*, 1624 (reproduced by kind permission of the Royal Danish Library, Copenhagen). The woodcut is shown in full on page 11.

Contents

Preface

The title of *The Dolphin* no. 25 is *O Canada*, since 1980 officially Canada's national anthem. Both melody and words originated a hundred years earlier in Quebec, and the song was translated into English and widely accepted by Anglophone Canada.

This is vividly demonstrated by Margaret Laurence in the novel *The Diviners* (New Canadian Library 1994, McClelland & Stewart 1988, 76), where she brings us into a pre-war classroom in the fictive prairie small-town of Manawaka. The pupils here begin the day by standing up and singing 'O Canada' both in English and, more tentatively, in French. Laurence uses the scene for several purposes; one of them is to show the conscious attempt made by the educational authorities to promote the ideas of a common Canadian identity and the existence of one united Canada.

The title of this volume should be seen as a homage to Canada, to a united Canada whom we have come to respect and admire as a progressive and humane medium-sized power.

The elegiac note which is also discernible in the title we tend to ignore. We cannot accept it as a swan song for a national structure which is good, fair, democratic and under constant improvement.

The study of Canada can be accomplished through many scholarly disciplines. As the *Dolphin* series is produced by a department of English, and as all the contributors except one come from departments of English, it is natural that the component of Canadian literature and culture related to the English language will be emphasized. There is nothing divisive in that, as long as we acknowledge that there are other literatures and cultures in Canada, and that Anglo-Canada is not a *pars pro toto* for all of Canada.

The essays of this volume are intended to constitute a useful introduction to Anglo-Canadian culture. Among our contributors you will not only find some of the best-known Canadianists but also junior scholars such as Charlotte Beyer (Aarhus, Warwick) and Brian Johnson (Manitoba).

My thanks are in particular due to my colleague Tim Caudery, who apart from being the chief editor of the *Dolphin* series, has done all the text layout work related to the production of this volume in the absence of our secretary. I am also indebted to the Aarhus University Research Foundation for their generous financial support for this publication.

Jørn Carlsen

The Story of Canada

Jørn Carlsen

1. Early European Contact

From the Saga of the Greenlanders we know that Leif Eriksson sailed from the newly settled Vesterbygd (986) in Greenland to Vinland around the year 1000. In the late 1960s, after seven archaeological expeditions to L'Anse Aux Meadows at the northernmost tip of Newfoundland, Helge and Anne Stine Ingstad (Norway)[1] finally proved that they had found a Norse settlement in what is now Canada. The Norsemen, who had found Greenland uninhabited when they settled there, found Canada inhabited by Inuits and Indians. No friendly relations were established between these late Vikings and the indigenous population.

Almost 500 years later John Cabot, sailing for Bristol merchants in search of a short route to Asia, made landfall in Newfoundland (1497) and reported a wealth of fish on the Great Banks. In 1583, at a time when hundreds of fishing boats from Europe were already making huge catches on these banks every summer, Sir Humphrey Gilbert claimed St John's, a unique natural harbour, for Elizabeth I and England.

2. The Settling of New France

The French were already operating in the Gulf of St Lawrence, where Jacques Cartier explored the St Lawrence River from 1534 onward, also in search of a short cut to Asia. Although his first impression of Canada was that this was the 'Land God gave to Cain', he did see the potential of the region, especially for fishing and also for profitable fur trading with the Indians; and he led colonizing expeditions up the river to the Iroquois village of Stadacona (Quebec City) (1535) and on to Hochelaga, another Iroquois village on the site of present-day Montreal.

Cartier's expeditions created a French interest in Canada, and these expeditions were followed up by Samuel de Champlain, who from 1603 till his death in 1635 laid the foundations of New France from Acadia to Quebec City, which was founded in 1608. In 1632, as a result of his many exploratory journeys, he published a startlingly accurate map of Canada from Newfoundland to Lake Huron.

Champlain wanted a colony, not just a temporary trading station. He had come to stay. This meant permanent settlement based on farming and trading. From the very beginning Champlain sought Indian allies, whom he believed would strengthen New France. He chose the Hurons and allied tribes as trading partners in preference to the Iroquois and their allies. He took part in their wars, having the great advantage of possession of firearms.

As Champlain wanted to evangelize the Indians, his allies were forced to open their villages to Jesuit missionary zeal. Today we can read about the Indians and their way of life from a Jesuit point of view, since the missionaries meticulously wrote down their experiences in their reports or accounts to their superiors back in France. A huge volume of material from 1632-73 is available about the Indians and their way of life.[2]

The Indians, and the Iroquois in particular, were always against European settlement. In the 1640s the Iroquois defeated the Hurons, and right up to end of New France (1753) the Iroquois would, except for a few peaceful periods, attack and harass French settlements, often alone but also with their new allies the British. It was in the 1640s that a number of Jesuit priests were slaughtered by the Iroquois. Best known among them is Jean de Brébeuf (d. 1649). He and other French Canadian martyrs were canonized in 1930.

3. A Royal French Province

Until 1663 the development of New France was slow, being left to commercial interests and initiative. In that year, however, New France became Louis XIV's royal province, and colonial policies were now shaped by the King and his government right up until the end of French presence in North America in 1763. A Governor General represented the King, and a regiment of French troops was stationed there to defend the colony. Many of the officers stayed on, being encouraged to do so by the King, and they came to form part of the new class of seigneurs in a system of landlords and tenants.

The new class was not as exclusive as in France; the tenants (or 'habitants') had to be treated properly, or they would leave for the 'pays d'en haut' as 'coureurs de bois'. It was really due to these individual traders that France established a presence north and west of the Great Lakes. Soon 'voyageurs' would carry goods by canoe from Montreal to far away places in the Northwest.

The Crown encouraged settlement in New France, and in order to increase the number of women in the colony the King offered free transportation from France. The result was an increase of the population. By 1681, however, when the population was about 10,000, large-scale immigration had stopped. In 1763 the French Canadian population numbered about 60,000.

4. The Hudson's Bay Company

In 1670 something happened which had far-reaching consequences for the Canadian Northwest, the fur trade, and the relations between the British and the French in North America. King Charles II gave the Hudson's Bay Company the right to trade in the drainage basin of Hudson Bay, also called Prince Rupert's Land, a huge area looked upon until then by the French as their hinterland. The idea of a full scale expansion of the fur trade into this area was fostered by two French fur traders and explorers, Médard Chouart Des Groseilliers and Pierre Esprit Radisson, but their idea and expertise had been turned down by the French. British merchants, when they were approached by the two Frenchmen, saw the potential and presented the project to Charles II.

British sea captains had been there before. Henry Hudson gave his name to Hudson Bay, the great inland sea which he had started exploring while

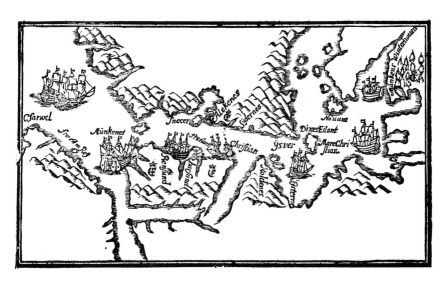

From Jens Munk, *Navigatio Septentrionalis*, 1624. A woodcut of Munk's own chart from Cape Farewell to Munkenes Winterhauen at Nova Dania, Churchill, Manitoba.

The map is drawn from a northerly viewpoint, i.e. the top of the map is the most southerly part. Though disproportionate, the map shows the southern part of Baffin Island, the Hudson Strait, the north coast of Ungava and Hudson Bay. Reproduced by kind permission of the Royal Danish Library, Copenhagen.

11

searching for a Northwest Passage, and where he met his death in 1611. The Dane Jens Munk wintered at the mouth of the River Churchill in 1619-20, with disastrous results.[3] Others had been there since then, all in search of a sea route to China, the Northwest Passage.

The Hudson's Bay Company (HBC) came for the purpose of trading with the Indians. However, one of the conditions for the trade monopoly was that the HBC should continue the search for the Northwest Passage. Before the turn of the century trading posts or factories, as they were called, had been established at the mouths of the great rivers running into the Bay, e.g. York Factory between the Rivers Nelson and Hayes (1684).

The posts were often attacked and taken by the French, who vigorously defended a very lucrative fur trade kept alive by strong European demand. A French Canadian hero, Sieur d'Iberville (1661-1706), should be mentioned here. He was a brilliant sea-captain and military strategist who brought to a halt, at least temporarily, British advances in the Hudson Bay area, Acadia and Newfoundland.

The French were well aware of being squeezed by the British, to the south by the British colonies, to the north-west by the HBC. However, the HBC did not venture far away from the shores of the Bay, leaving it to the French Canadians to explore and establish posts inland. Especially under La Vérendrye, the waterways of the Northwest were explored and opened for fur trade. For a long time Montreal in New France dominated the fur trade in Canada.

5. A Distinct Society

In and around the year 1700 New France was a well-established colony reaching from Port Royal in Acadia (Nova Scotia) to Montreal. From here, a line of posts to the north-west left New France in control of the great inland waterways.

Urban centres developed, and the degree of sophistication in, for example, Quebec City, could often match that of the old world. In most fields New France had become self-sufficient. As early as 1663 Bishop Laval had founded the Séminaire de Québec, a college of fine arts and theology that later became known as Université Laval. It was indeed a distinct society.

It was not due to weakness on the part of the French Canadians that France had to give up in North America. A strong, resourceful people was made a pawn at peace conferences in Europe between the British and the French. At the Treaty of Utrecht, signed in 1713, France gave up to Britain Newfoundland, Hudson Bay and Acadia except for Île-Royale (Cape Breton Island).

The Seven Years' War was fought both in Europe and overseas in India and in Canada. Even though the French lost the great fortress of Louisbourg (1758) in Cape Breton Island and saw the seizure of Quebec City by James Wolfe (1759), the war was actually lost in Europe. At the signing of the Treaty of Paris in 1763, France ceded all her possessions in North America except for the small islands of St Pierre and Miquelon, south of Newfoundland. The defeat of the French in Europe, India and North America was Britain's greatest victory of the 18th century. Within a few years, however, Britain suffered her greatest defeat of the century: the loss of the 13 American colonies.

6. The American Revolution

The causes of the American Revolution are well-known. Paying taxes to Britain without representation in Parliament at Westminster was unacceptable in the long run. When Britain forced the colonies to pay their share of the war expenses, the situation exploded in Massachusetts (1774). The Quebec Act passed at Westminster in 1774 may be seen in the context of the deterioration of the relations between Britain and her American colonies. Although Anglicization of French Canada was no doubt the ultimate aim, the act allowed the Canadians to continue to speak French, to live under French civil law, and to preserve the seigneurial system and the Roman Catholic Church.

The Act pacified the French Canadians and brought loyalty to Britain, but antagonized the Protestant American colonies. In that sense the American War of Independence may be said to have saved French Canadian culture in North America. A few years earlier the British had shown their efficiency in an ethnic cleansing operation when in 1755 and in 1758 they swiftly deported approximately 7,000 French-speaking Acadians from New Brunswick and Nova Scotia.

After the American Revolution the demography of British North America or Canada changed drastically. Refugees from the 13 newly-independent states, the so-called Loyalists, approximately 60,000 in all, settled in Canada from Nova Scotia to the southern part of Ontario.

7. British North America

Over the next hundred years British North America experienced a dramatic growth of population. This was due to extensive immigration from Ireland, Scotland, England and the United States. At a census in 1861, the population was approximately 3.3 million, and of these approximately 1 million were of French origin.[4]

When the USA gained independence from Britain in 1783 the border, which is also the present international border, was drawn from the Atlantic to the Lake of the Woods on the border between Manitoba and Ontario. To begin with the border was challenged by the Americans, who soon found themselves prevented from expanding to the north and north-west.

Strained relations between Great Britain and the USA led to the War of 1812, declared by the USA. The Canadians may well claim that they won the war. Afterwards the country was intact, the borders were not disputed, and the war had given Canada its first sense of nationhood or common purpose. British forces, Loyalists, French Canadians and Indians under Chief Tecumseh had successfully repelled the invasion from the south. The War of 1812 was the last military conflict between the two neighbours.

8. The Durham Report

With an eye on the USA the Constitutional Act of 1791 created the two Canadas, Upper Canada (Ontario) and Lower Canada (Quebec), with governors and elected assemblies. Thus the Canadians got a franchise that most Britons would not enjoy until after the various Reform Laws of the nineteenth century. Even though the War of 1812 had brought some sense of unity to the Canadians, the increasing wealth and vigour of the new democratic, republican USA was attractive to many Canadians and compared favourably with what were after all colonial conditions in Canada. Whatever grievances there were, they were not widespread enough to make an outright rebellion successful. In 1837 William Lyon Mackenzie (Upper Canada) and Louis-Joseph Papineau (Lower Canada) led abortive uprisings, however. The rebellions were put down with severity, and the modern Canadian Left got a set of heroes.[5]

One of the results of the rebellion was the Durham report.[6] The British Government was so worried about the situation that Lord Durham was asked to make a report on Canada, including a thorough analysis of the constitutional situation, and stating fully his recommendations. Most important was his recommendation concerning 'responsible government', i.e. that the government should reflect the composition of the elected assemblies. That had not been the case in, for example, Upper Canada, where the British governors had relied on a corrupt Tory elite representing only a few families. Lord Durham's analysis of Lower Canada has never endeared him to Quebeckers. Here he found 'two nations warring in the bosom of a single state'. His recommendation was a union of the two Canadas and the assimilation of the French-Canadian population into the English-speaking majority.

The Durham Report, however, remains a cardinal document, not only in Canadian history, pointing towards Confederation in 1867, but also in the later stages of the history of the Empire, when its principles could be applied to the relations between Britain and her colonies and dominions.

9. Defining the Borders

Since the American War of Independence British diplomacy had worked hard to reach agreements concerning the undefined border between the two countries from the Lake of the Woods to the Pacific. By 1818 the International Boundary was extended along the 49th parallel to the Oregon Territory, which was occupied jointly by Britain and the USA; and in 1846 the present border[7] was extended to the Pacific.

In the far Northwest, an agreement between Russia and Britain was reached in 1825 as regards the description of the border between the Northwest Territories and Alaska. In 1867 the USA purchased Alaska from the Russians.

Especially in the West, the border was little more than a straight line drawn on a map. It was open to free crossing, a fact which was exploited by the Americans to trade illegally with the Indians. The border remained unpoliced until 1873, when the North West Mounted Police was established. When the Klondike gold rush started in 1896 the NWMP saw to it that Canadian sovereignty in the Northwest was respected.

The massive influx of land-hungry European immigrants into the USA resulted in a westward drive of settlers and a certain pressure on Canada. The idea of uniting the remaining British colonies in a confederation was strongly supported by the British. Especially after the American Civil War there was a certain fear that a well-trained, unemployed American army might go for other objectives than pacifying Indians in the West. Anti-British sentiments prevailed in Washington after the Civil War, and little was done to prevent Irish-American or Fenian raids into Canada. However, the creation of a confederation was not easy. The remaining British colonies had followed different paths of development.

But on 1 July 1867 the Dominion of Canada was created by an act of the British Parliament known as the British North America Act (BNA). John A. Macdonald and George-Étienne Cartier were the most important of the founding fathers. Four colonies, now provinces, joined the Confederation in 1867, namely Ontario, Quebec, New Brunswick and Nova Scotia. Ottawa, on the border between Ontario and Quebec, became the new nation's capital. Three more colonies joined the Confederation within the following decade: Manitoba in 1870, British Columbia in 1871, and in 1873 Prince Edward Island.

10. Canada after Confederation

The first two decades in the life of the Dominion of Canada ('Dominion' was chosen rather than 'Kingdom' in order not to offend republican sensibilities in the United States more than was necessary) were eventful and dangerous for the new country. In 1869 Ottawa secured the possibility of westward expansion through the purchase of Prince Rupert's Land, which was owned and controlled by the Hudson's Bay Company. The price was C$ 1.5 million plus 1/20 of the arable land. The Northwest Territories more than doubled the size of Canada and faced Ottawa with communication problems of a gigantic order.

No roads or railways on Canadian territory connected Ottawa with its new territories in the West. No Canadian coast-to-coast railway was operational until 1885. The promise of a rail link brought British Columbia into the Confederation in 1871. Apart from being a unique financial and engineering achievement, the Canadian Pacific Railway opened the way for mass settlement and in 1905 two new western provinces, Alberta and Saskatchewan, came into existence. The building of a trans-Canada railway not only pointed at national unity, but it also emphasized the top priority that Canada gave to an east-west trade pattern. Sir John A. Macdonald, who was Prime Minister of Canada for almost 50 years, introduced protective tariffs, many of which lasted until the days of the Free Trade Agreement with the USA (1989) and NAFTA (The North American Free Trade Agreement of 1992 between Canada, the USA and Mexico).

11. The Metis Rebellions

As early as 1869 the new Confederation was faced with a serious domestic problem: the Red River Rebellion of 1869-70. Basically it seems that Ottawa was too slow to grant the Metis or half-breeds, who were Roman Catholic and French-speaking, the right to keep the river lots where they had settled as squatters. The land question was of the greatest importance now that these buffalo hunters could foresee the disappearance of the buffalo and already feel the pressure of an ever-increasing number of new settlers. Under Louis Riel they rebelled and founded the province of Manitoba. The execution of an Ontarian prisoner fuelled a dormant animosity between the French and the English in Quebec and Ontario. The Rebellion was put down and Riel went into exile in the USA; and Manitoba was admitted to the Confederation in 1870.

In 1884-5 the story repeated itself. Many of the Red River Metis had moved farther to the northwest along the North Saskatchewan River in the Prince Albert area. Again they felt that rightful grievances related to land rights were being ignored by Ottawa. Riel was brought back from exile to lead the Metis. Ottawa feared a full scale Indian war, so the army was sent in this time on the almost completed Canadian Pacific Railway. Only a few young braves from Big Bear's band of Cree Indians joined the Metis.[8] The North-West Rebellion was put down at Batoche 1885, and a few months later Riel was hanged in Regina for high treason.

Irrespective of the question of guilt, the French Canadians had in Louis Riel obtained a martyr, and many Anglo-Canadians especially Ontarians had acquired a hate object. For both the Indians and the Metis the result of the rebellion was complete marginalization, a situation which lasted into the 1960s. Eventually all the Indians of the West signed treaties with the government and went into reserves.

12. Mass Immigration

In 1873 Prince Edward Island had joined the Confederation without enthusiasm – there was hardly anything else they could do. On the whole the popularity of the Confederation among the provinces was low towards the end of the century. By comparison with the USA, Canada's performance was not impressive. In 1896 the Liberals put an end to the Tory hegemony. The new Liberal Prime Minister, Sir Wilfred Laurier, was a free trader and a continentalist working for reciprocity in trade between Canada and the USA. He authorized, however, the building of the second trans-Canada railway, the Grand Trunk Railway, along a more northerly route than that of the CPR. This meant a better rail service in the new provinces of Saskatchewan and Alberta. In 1911 Laurier was defeated by Robert Borden and the Conservative Party, and by Canadians who were really living quite happily behind the tariffs and on the benefits of an east-west trade, which flourished due to the ever larger numbers of homesteaders pouring into the West.

The immigration flow into Canada, which was supported and encouraged by the government, did not make national unity easy. French immigration had stopped when the French were defeated in 1763. A healthy birthrate helped the French Canadians at first, but later on it declined drastically. The newcomers were either English-speaking or Anglophile, which meant an annual decrease in the percentage of French-speaking Canadians. However, no federal government could secure a majority in the House of Commons without the support of either Conservative or Liberal votes from Quebec. One touchy issue was always the remaining influence of Britain in Canadian politics. Right up to 1931 Canada was legally tied to Britain. In that year the passage of the Statute of Westminster gave Canada, along with the other Dominions, full independence. That Canada (both the Federal Government and the Provincial Government) left its birth certificate (the BNA Act) and the amending powers to the British Parliament at Westminster for another 51 years is an amazing story.

13. Towards Independence

The last British troops left Canada in 1871. Britain, however, expected more than moral support whenever she was involved in imperial crises and wars like the one in Sudan in 1885 and the Boer War in 1899. Whenever the question of sending troops out of the country came up, Quebec would strongly oppose Anglo-Canadian readiness to support the Empire. Towards the end of both World War I and World War II conscription became necessary due to the lack of volunteers. Quebec led the fierce opposition to conscription but Westerners of non-British extraction, pacifists and Labour union officials would join what at times looked like insurrection.

The introduction of conscription despite promises to the contrary made the French Canadians feel even more besieged. As a minority outside Quebec they had been threatened by the introduction of publicly financed, non-denominational English-speaking schools in Manitoba (1890), and now in 1914 Ontario reduced French education in counties bordering on Quebec.

Canada joined World War I and lost no less than 60,661 lives on the battlefields of Europe. As a proportion of the population (approx. 8 million), Canada lost as many men as did Britain. But an utterly inexperienced Canadian army was – despite supercilious and incompetent British generals – turned into an efficient fighting force. The victories at Vimy Ridge and Paesschendaele made Canada an accepted and respected ally and a feared adversary. In 1919 Canada's Prime Minister Borden joined the British delegation at the Paris Peace Conference and signed the Versailles Treaty which ended the war with Germany.

14. Industrialization

The war also brought a higher degree of industrialization to Canada. Shortages of male workers brought women into many of the war-related industries. In 1918 Canadian women got the federal franchise. However, it was not until 1940 that all Canadian women were granted the right to vote in provincial elections. The last province to grant this right was Quebec in 1940. Slowly, organized labour had become a force to be reckoned with. Among workers and veterans dissatisfaction was widespread, and when claims to be compensated for moderation shown during the war were not met, several general strikes broke out, none more fiercely and resolutely met by the Mounted Police than the one in Winnipeg on Bloody Saturday June 21, 1919.

No doubt a fear of a socialist/communist revolution made the authorities react with determination. A small Communist Party of Canada was founded in 1921, and in 1932 a number of Labour and farm groups established a democratic socialist party: the Cooperative Commonwealth Federation (CCF) in Calgary. This party developed into the New Democratic Party (NDP), founded in 1961. None of these parties has had great federal success, but the CCF won the provincial election in Saskatchewan in 1944 and formed the first socialist government in North America. Since then the NDP has won provincial elections in British Columbia, Manitoba and most recently in Ontario (1990).

During the 1920s Canada became the preferred destination for European emigration. Immigration quotas and the fact that there was no more free land in the USA left Canada as the only place where the emigrant's dreams might come true. A very efficient transportation system brought thousands of immigrants from Europe to the Canadian West (Manitoba, Saskatchewan, Alberta).

15. The Depression

As in other countries both industry and agriculture found it difficult to adapt to postwar conditions. Both in 1920 and in 1923 there were cyclical depressions of relatively short duration, but the Great Depression of the 30s was of a very different calibre; it lasted almost a decade. Its causes were many. In 1929 a huge wheat crop at a guaranteed price proved unsaleable on the world market. For support industries the result was inevitable: the loss of thousands of jobs. The Wall Street collapse of the same year made investors hypercautious and pessimistic. Soon 23 per cent of the Canadian work force was unemployed and many more were on reduced time. Protectionist measures or beggar-my-neighbour policies in Canada and other countries made it all worse. The Great Depression hit Canada worse than any other Western country.

The Canadian West was hit with a vengeance. Coinciding with the Great Depression was a change of climate which produced unpredictable agricultural conditions. Throughout the 1930s the West was haunted by plagues of Biblical dimensions. Drought, grasshoppers, rust, and soil erosion left huge areas of the so-called 'bread basket of the world' as an uninhabitable dust-bowl. In a situation like that a vast number of people from both country and town came to rely on relief measures. It is a black chapter in Canadian history that relief was often given under conditions which left the recipient without any dignity. Politicians like the Conservative Bennett, who was Prime Minister from 1930-35, and the Liberal Mackenzie King, leader of the opposition and later Prime Minister from 1935-48, did not understand the depth of the catastrophe.

No wonder that political populism appeared. The population was ready for any remedy. In Alberta William Aberhart ('Bible Bill') was convinced that 'social credit', i.e. the state giving the consumer purchasing power, would pull the country out of what looked like a lasting depression. In his radio sermons he would convey his political message as well: those guilty were the banks and the ruling establishment in Ottawa and Eastern Canada. Aberhart won the provincial election in 1935. Federal laws and economic realities prevented the implementation of Social Credit. The party ruled Alberta from 1935 to 1968. After Aberhart's death in 1943 Ernest Manning became Premier. He was the father of Preston Manning, who in 1992 became leader of the new populistic Reform Party which has spread across Canada and into the House of Commons in Ottawa.[9]

16. Social Turmoil

One relief measure will be remembered in particular. The government established a system of work camps for unemployed single males. They were located across the country in remote and isolated places and kept under military control. It was from these camps that the workers organized the 'On To Ottawa Trek' in 1935 which was meant to draw the attention of the public to the plight of the workers and take their grievances from Vancouver to Ottawa. Because of the huge distance involved, the Trek was made on board freight cars. It was halted at Regina, and when a delegation returned empty-handed from Ottawa, the Regina Riot broke out July 1, which ended the trek. Many of the organizers and leaders of the Left were frustrated at the lack of support from the general public. To many it was quite clear that Canada would never turn socialist, if the country could stomach the conditions as they were. Quite a few found their way as illegal volunteers to the Spanish Civil War, fighting in the Canadian Mackenzie-Papineau battalion against Franco and fascism.

The fact that more than 1200 Canadians had to break Canadian law in order to volunteer in Spain tells us something about Mackenzie King's domestic and foreign policies. To keep the Confederation intact and Canada united were the most important political objectives for King. Unobstructed Canadian participation in a war against fascism in Spain would have antagonised influential French Canadians with a strong admiration for Mussolini and Franco. The rejection of Jews fleeing out of Europe may be seen as another example of the same tendency in King's foreign policy ('None is better than one!'[10]). King was realistic enough, however, to embark upon a modest programme of rearmament, something that might keep the dreaded conscription at bay. When Britain declared war on Germany on September 3, 1939, a united Canada entered the war on Britain's side. A few days later numerous unemployed men volunteered across Canada. Soon the war would pull Canada out of the Great Depression.

17. World War II

It can be said that World War II resulted in a final severance of the colonial ties to Britain, but also that it saw Canada's passage into a USA-dominated sphere of influence. With the Ogdensburg Agreement of 1940, a Joint Board of Defense was established between the two countries. The war did not unite the French-Canadians and the Anglo-Canadians. Again a political war raged concerning conscription. As it became obvious that volunteers could not fill all the gaps that arose as the war went on, Mackenzie King first introduced conscription for military service at home. A request to be released from a pledge given by King that conscripted personnel would not be sent abroad was put to the nation in a plebiscite. The release was granted but the result showed a deep split between the two peoples. In the end very few conscripts were sent into combat, however.

Canada lost 42,042 lives in the war. More than a third of the casualties were in the Royal Canadian Air Force. The navy, too, learnt its much praised convoy techniques the hard way. After the abortive and much criticized Dieppe operation (Aug. 1942) and the heavy action in the Italian theatre, the Canadian army was ready to make a substantial and successful contribution on D-Day 1944 when it landed at Bernières-sur-Mer in Normandy.

The Japanese attack on Pearl Harbour in 1941 brought the USA into the war, a step much welcomed by Canada. Both countries began organizing a common defence of the Pacific coast of the USA, Canada and Alaska. A visible result was the 1600-mile long Alaska Highway built by the Americans from Dawson Creek, B.C. to Fairbanks in Alaska. The internment of Japanese-Canadians that followed the defence preparations in British Columbia still worries many Canadians.

18. Postwar Foreign Policies

Because it was closely tied to the American economy, Canada's economy recovered very quickly during and after the war, and the country found herself in a position to help Europe. Irrespective of French-English grievances, federal Canada was after World War II as strong and united as ever.

Two politicians demand special attention in the first decades after the war: Lester B. Pearson (1897-1972) from the Liberal Party and John G. Diefenbaker (1895-1979) from the Conservative Party. As a minister in the governments of both Mackenzie King and St Laurent, Lester Pearson was responsible for Canada's joining NATO in 1949 and for Canada again having defence obligations abroad. He also led Canada into the Korean War (1950) in support of the United Nations. In the UN he worked hard to give the organization a peacekeeping role, which it fulfilled both in Korea and in Egypt (1956). As a reward Lester Pearson received the Nobel Peace Prize in 1957.

The great neighbour and ally to the south was not always happy with Lester Pearson and especially not when he as a prime minister (1963-68) opposed the US war in Vietnam (1965). The Americans were, however, more displeased with John G. Diefenbaker, who was prime minister from 1957-63. Although he was a Conservative prime minister, being from the Canadian West he was not part of the Conservative establishment, and this rendered him politically weak despite his oratory and charisma. Diefenbaker feared what the Canadian philosopher George Grant called 'the American Empire',[11] and that Canada's ever closer ties to the USA would result in a complete loss of national identity.

Reluctantly, Canada was forced into the missile age when she signed the North American Air Defence Command Agreement (NORAD) in 1957. Even though Canada was dependent on American military strength for her defence, the country was amazingly independent in terms of foreign policy, and was often – due to its UN involvement – looked upon by the world as a neutral power. The recognition of the People's Republic of China was one of the first tasks of the Pierre Elliott Trudeau government in 1968; and huge wheat sales to both Russia and China, and the accommodation of numerous American draft dodgers from the Vietnam War certainly irritated the USA.

Being a member of the Club of Seven means that Canada is an industrialized country with a very important economy. It is rich in nearly all the important minerals; huge oil deposits were found at Leduc, Alberta, in 1947. Only a fraction of Canada's hydro-electric potential has been exploited. The lumber industry and the huge agricultural sector add to the affluence of the Canadian people. To safeguard her economic strength Canada has in recent years reluctantly entered a Free Trade Agreement (1989) with the USA and a North American Free Trade Agreement (NAFTA) with the USA and Mexico (1992).

19. Postwar Domestic Policies

As in most other countries the distribution of wealth is uneven not only among people, but also among provinces. The federal government transfers funds from rich to poor provinces. That was probably why Newfoundland joined the Confederation in 1949 as the tenth province of Canada. In 1968 the government was also responsible for introducing a nationwide health insurance programme (Medicare), which made Canada a welfare state.

In domestic politics the most important development in the 1960s was the Quiet Revolution in Quebec. Maurice Duplessis' death in 1959 led to the collapse of a personal regime which had kept Quebec backward. A new Liberal government under Jean Lesage introduced an impressive programme of reform. Over the next decade Quebec was secularized, and administrative and educational systems were fundamentally changed. What was not clear to begin with, even for the Quebeckers themselves, was the kindling of a strong nationalistic bias that came to regard Quebec as an independent state. If it was not conspicuous already to ordinary Canadians, it became so in 1967, when Canada celebrated its centenary, and President de Gaulle of France greeted Montrealers and TV viewers all over Canada with his 'Vive le Québec libre'. In 1968 René Lévesque, who was a minister in Lesage's Liberal provincial government, founded his own party: Parti Québécois (PQ). In 1980 Lévesque was the first premier to let the question of independence of Canada be decided in a referendum. The pro-independence side won 40.5 per cent of the vote, but a clear majority of 59.5 per cent wanted to stay within Canada.

In 1968 Pierre Elliott Trudeau succeeded Lester Pearson as Prime Minister of Canada. By the passing of the Official Languages Act of 1969, which opened up the way for equal opportunities in both languages and an increased emphasis on bilingualism in public life, Trudeau hoped to deflate an ever stronger Quebec nationalism. All of Canada, Quebec included, was in a state of shock when a small group of extremists ('Front de Liberation du Québec') supported in the streets by radical students, kidnapped a British trade commissioner and killed a Quebec Minister of Labour. Trudeau proclaimed the War Measure Act, brought in the army and detained close to 500 people suspected of complicity.

Even though Quebec Premier Robert Bourassa had asked Ottawa to intervene, the show of federal power in the form of a virtual takeover of Quebec did not improve relations between Ottawa and Quebec. A strong national passion was also reflected in the language laws that were introduced in Quebec to protect the French language. In 1974 Bourassa passed Bill 22 which proclaimed French as the only official language of Quebec and abolished the right of parents to choose between French – and English – language schooling. The unilingualism of Quebec was strengthened by PQ in 1977 when Bill 101 made French the only legal and also the only visible language of Quebec. Signs in English and other languages were prohibited. The English-speaking minority (10%) have pointed out that Quebec violates the Charter of Human Rights and Freedoms in the Constitution Act of 1982.

20. The Constitutional Impasse

One of Pierre Trudeau's objectives as Prime Minister (he was in office for more than 14 years) was to patriate the BNA Act of 1867, Canada's constitution. The fact that the BNA Act was still at Westminster tells us something about the relations between the provinces and the federal government of Canada. After years of constitutional quarrelling, Trudeau made a daring move by letting his government present a new constitution with an amending formula and a new Charter of Rights and Freedoms. The Supreme Court of Canada ruled that the procedure was unusual but not illegal. The result was that Queen Elizabeth gave her royal assent to the new Constitution Act of 1982, accepted by all provinces except Quebec.

Prime Minister Brian Mulroney's landslide victory in 1984 made him confident enough to try to bring his own province Quebec to accept a reformed constitution. It looked like a success when Mulroney announced that the premiers of all 10 provinces had agreed to the Meech Lake Accord (1984) as the basis for a new constitution for all of Canada. Now it was only for the legislatures in the provinces to ratify the agreement within three years. It was during these three years that it dawned upon many that the Meech Lake Accord was based on a very conservative dualistic (English, French) vision of Canada which was out of step with Canadian realities. The Charter of Human Rights and Freedoms (1982) had opened new possibilities for marginalized groups such as the aboriginal people and women. To them and other groups the Meech Lake Accord looked like a step backwards. In Manitoba it was a native leader, Elijah Harper, who blocked the ratification of the Accord; nor could it be accepted by Newfoundland.

The rejection of the Accord in 1990 was felt by Quebec to be a slap in the face. Quebec had been denied a 'distinct society' status by the rest of Canada (ROC). On September 12, 1994 Parti Québécois defeated the Liberal Party in the provincial election. The declared aim of the PQ and its leader Jacques Parizeau is independence for Quebec. Before the summer of 1995 the people of Quebec will once again be asked in a referendum whether they want to stay in Canada or not.

21. Postscript

It should be obvious to the reader that this presentation of selected events in the history of Canada reflects a European/Eurocentric bias. Although Canada is a multicultural country, the great majority of Canadians are white and of European origin. The major schism of the country has so far always been between the two so-called founding nations, the English and the French. Over the years the indigenous population of Indians and Inuits, also called the First Nations, have largely been ignored. It seems, however, that legislation related to the Charter of Human Rights from 1982 has spread optimism concerning land claims and possible home rule. Irrespective of the constitutional impasse which has overshadowed native problems, the Inuits of Canada will be given their own territory, Nunavut, in 1999.

NOTES

1. Helge Ingstad, 'The Norse Discovery of North America', in: Carlsen & Streijffert (eds.), *Canada and the Nordic Countries*. Lund: Lund University Press, 1987.
2. R.G. Thwaites (ed), *The Jesuit Relations and Allied Documents* (73 vols, 1896-1901), with texts in English and French.
3. See Jørn Carlsen, 'Jens Munk's Search for the Northwest Passage in 1619-20 and his Wintering at Nova Dania, Churchill, Manitoba', *The Journal of the Scottish Society for Northern Studies*, Vol. 28, 1992.
4. *Canada Year Book*, 1988
5. Cp. the name of the Canadian Mackenzie-Papineau Battalion consisting of volunteers who fought in the Spanish Civil War (1937-39) for the Republican or the Communist cause.
6. *Report on the Affairs of British North America, 1839*.
7. Described in the Oregon Treaty of 1846.
8. See Beal & Macleod, *Prairie Fire. The 1885 North-West Rebellion*, 1984, and Rudy Wiebe, *The Temptations of Big Bear*, 1973.
9. At the General Election 1993 the newly founded Reform Party won 52 out of 295 seats in the House of Commons in Ottawa.
10. Irving Abella and Harold Troper, *None Is Too Many. Canada and the Jews of Europe 1933-1948*, 1983.
11. George Grant, *Lament For A Nation. The Defeat of Canadian Nationalism. Carlton Library* no. 50, 1965 and 1970.

Identity – Identities: Infamous Canadian Pastime, Venerable Quest, or Trivial Pursuit?

Konrad Groß

Despite frequent statements to the contrary, the problem of a Canadian national identity has survived all attempts at marking it as something that is taken for granted, yet has eluded all recent efforts at politically cementing a pan-Canadian consciousness. The repatriation of the Canadian Constitution (1982) and the signing of the Meech Lake Accord by the premiers of the provinces (1987) were not able to silence the multifarious dissenting voices of both regional and ethnic provenance. The downfall of Meech Lake brought about by the two provincial parliaments of Newfoundland and Manitoba unleashed a new national debate which reached its peak in a referendum on constitutional reform in October 1993. The rejection of the reform proposals by the majority of the Canadian voters was a clear sign that the venerable Canadian virtue of striking a political compromise was no longer seen as a desirable goal and that the centrifugal forces in Canadian society had apparently gained the upper hand. Canadian cultural and in particular literary criticism, which in the past had been frequently in the forefront of Canadian nationalism, had more or less banned the problem of a national identity from critical discourse ever since Frank Davey's anti-thematic diatribe in his famous 'Surviving the Paraphrase' (1974).[1] Nationalist literary quests in the wake of Northrop Frye's influential thesis of the Canadian garrison mentality were suddenly perceived not only as simplistic, but also as ideological and therefore completely misleading explanations of the nation's spirit.[2] Canada seemed to have reached maturity by joining the postmodern era in which national concerns were of lesser importance than international, cosmopolitan, and local concerns.

Davey's attack on all-Canadian models of identity as centrist ideologies was an attack launched from the cultural and geographical periphery (he has his roots in British Columbia). In contrast to the centrist notions with their tacit implications of cultural hegemony, Davey emphasized the existence of multiple Canadian identities embedded in a tight net of cultural and political hierarchies. He rejected the restless search for a pan-Canadian identity as an infamous and ideologically misleading pastime, thus tacitly admitting that many factors have stood in the way of the formation of a Canadian identity:[3] the lack of historical experiences analogous to those which helped to shape an American nationality; the dualism between Francophone and Anglophone Canada; regionalist disparities; and the transformation of Canada into a multicultural society as a result of its immigration history.

1. Canada: An Un-American Nation?

Of the two most popular views on Canadian history one is fact, the other fiction. Fact: unlike the U.S.A., the Canadian nation was not initiated by a revolution, but by a piece of British legislation, the British North America Act (1867). Fiction: in contrast to the violent winning of the American West, Canada's westward expansion was peaceful.

It is true that the creation of the Dominion of Canada in response to a real or imagined threat by the American republic gave birth to an alternative political philosophy and system which was modelled on Britain. Whereas the U.S.A. had developed a political profile in sharp opposition to Europe, the leading political forces in Canada liked to regard their country as a replica of Britain. Oliver Goldsmith, the first English-Canadian poet of importance, expressed this in his long poem *The Rising Village* (1825) in the metaphor of Canada as Britain's obedient child. The colonial heritage, which did not lose its grip on Canadian life even after the country had left its political colonial status behind, was more than a mental stumbling-block to the emergence of a national identity. As late as 1967, when Canada celebrated its centenary in a wave of nationalist euphoria, novelist Hugh Hood put his finger on this dilemma by complaining that Canadian thinking had never developed beyond the Age of Enlightenment and hence had missed out on all important 19th century movements, among them Romanticism, with its strong nationalist impetus.[4] Subsequently, Canada had created neither a Canadian dream nor a nationally distinct mythological hero like the American Westerner, cowboy, or frontiersman. As a matter of fact, the Canadian state was not the result of historical experiences shared by all Canadians, but was imposed on the people from above and was based on the consent of the Anglophone and Francophone conservative elites.[5]

At this point it remains to be asked why the Canadian westward expansion, which like the American Western experience brought about the territorial completion of the nation, did not generate an equally significant national myth. Poet Stephen Scobie has an ironic answer:

... in America West was a shifting frontier, a line to be pushed across the map ... America has never quite reconciled itself to the existence of the Pacific Ocean. It always wants new Wests, and none of them pacific. The Canadian West was never Wild; we take the perverse delight in insisting that the Mounties got there first. Since we never had outlaws, we make do with politicians.[6]

Scobie's witty aphorism plays with the pious legend of Canada's peaceful Western settlement which ignores the two Métis resistances of 1869/70 and 1885. The defeat of the half-nomadic Métis and their culture paved the way for the settlement of the prairies, a process directed and controlled by Ottawa and coloured strongly by Imperialist ideology. Needless to say that against this political background Canadian concepts of wilderness, frontier, and West carried ideological messages completely different from those of the famous Turner thesis, which understood the American Western frontier as the place where the democratic and individualist spirit of the American national character was forged.[7] For Canadian historian Samuel Delbert Clark law and order were never absent on the Canadian frontier where the police, upper class and church, as the power agents of the Empire, held potentially violent conditions in check.[8]

However, Canadian historical developments and historical particularities should not tempt us to call Canada an un-American nation. The Canadian experience can be regarded as strange, anachronistic and alien only if one takes the American development as the one and only legitimate historical process on the North American continent. From the two different North American historical patterns Canadian literary critic Robin Mathews drew the conclusion that Canada's political tradition should be viewed as an alternative to that of the U.S.A. He sees the conflict between 'a balanced communitarianism [Canadian] and an unleashed competitive individualism' [America] as the central dialectic at work in Canadian politics and society. According to Mathews it should be the chief goal of the Canadian communitarians to protect the Canadian way against the destructive impulse of the aggressive individualist ideology.[9] In other words, Canada should remain the North American window to Europe and a potential corrective to the negative aspects of America's political culture.

2. Quebec: One Canada or Two?

One major obstacle to the development of a pan-Canadian consciousness has been Quebec. Novelist Mordecai Richler from Montreal, where Franco- and Anglophone cultures have faced each other without overcoming what Hugh MacLennan once termed the 'two solitudes', summarized Quebec's trauma in his controversial book *Oh Canada! Oh Quebec! Requiem for a Divided Country* (1992) in a polemical way:

Canadian mythology has it that until very recently the true movers and shakers in this country were the dour Scotch Presbyterians of the incomparably affluent Montreal suburb

28

of Westmount. ... a popular French Canadian variation of this theme is enriched by the conviction that, even today, the quintessential Westmount man – a banker – is chauffeured each morning to his office ... where, in need of a daily hee-haw, he will foreclose on an impecunious habitant and then hurry home to mount the ravishing but innocent Francophone maid, throwing her off the roof if she gets preggers. The women shop at Holt Renfrew and they repair to their neighbouring Ritz-Carlton Hotel for drinks and, providing they are not hopelessly frigid, assignations as well. And once a year the Westmount men and women convene at the Ritz in their tribal finery for St.Andrew's Ball, their champagne-laden tables attended by the white niggers of North America, Québecois pure laine, whose parents live in an unheated East End flat, owned by a short fat Jew Slumlord, the mother suffering from consumption and the father bound to die without ever once wintering in Hollywood, Florida, a lifelong dream.[10]

Richler's biting comment suggests that grumbling is second nature to Quebeckers and that their complaints fail to acknowledge realities. Yet French-Canadian resentment has been alive ever since the Quebec Act of 1774, which helped Quebeckers to preserve their language, culture, religion, and identity. In Philip Aubert de Gaspé's novel *Les Anciens Canadiens* published in 1863, precisely one hundred years after the fall of New France, a seigneur's daughter rejects the marriage proposal of a young Scotsman who, during the war, was forced by an English officer to burn her paternal home. Only an English-Canadian novelist, Rosanna Leprohon, in her novel *Antoinette de Mirecourt* (1864) could contemplate a symbolic interethnic marriage as a convincing solution, like Hugh MacLennan eighty years later, who in *Two Solitudes* (1945) offered a similar recipe for overcoming Canadian dualism. For a long time Quebec was able to ward off all attempts at assimilation, due to the overpowering influence of the Catholic Church and the long preservation of the province's backward social structures. Francophone literary critic René Dionne in his essay 'Qu'est-ce qu'un Québecois?' (1984) summed up the ideologies with which the French-Canadian elites explained a distinct French-Canadian identity:

... celui de l'agriculture humanisante, saine physiquement et moralement, celui de la culture qui garantirait la survivance, celui de la mission canadienne-française, spirituelle et intellectuelle, ... celui de la revanche des berceaux qui permettra à la nation de rejoindre démographiquement le groupe Anglophone qui est moins nataliste, celui de la France modèle, celle de l'Ancien Régime. La culture de ces mythes distrait des préoccupations politiques et économiques essentielles ... Une certaine unité nationale provient cependant de ces mythes, une certaine satisfaction aussi: sa langue et sa foi, le Canadien français les conserve comme les biens les plus précieux, et il en a le moyen au Québec (mais au Québec seulement), car l'éducation relève du gouvernement provincial et le clergé a mis la main sur presque tout le système d'enseignement. Celui-ci, patriotique et religieux, est facteur d'homogénéité ... L'on parle du 'bon' peuple canadien-français qui grandit, nation sainte, sous l'oeil de Dieu ...[11]

These mythologies began to crumble when the modernizing process reached the province. From World War II onwards the opportunities of observing what went on in the outside world increased tremendously and helped Quebeckers to put the social and economic backwardness of their province into sharper focus. The transformation of Quebec society reached its zenith in what became known as the Quiet Revolution, when between 1960 and 1966 the Liberals under Jean Lesage carried out reforms (education system, medical insurance, pension plan etc.) which broke the old power structures. The decline of the traditional ideologies was paralleled by the concentration of the identity debate on the language problem, which became a pivot of Quebec's cultural strategies. While the *Official Languages Act* (1969), which turned Canada officially into a bilingual nation, aimed at granting Francophones an equal status within the country, Quebec's language legislation with its separatist *lois 101* (1977) and *178* (1988) deliberately acted against the federal policy. Fears for the future destiny of the Francophone identity were fed by demographic trends which from lower birth rates and the Anglicization of immigrants predicted the eventual disappearance of French-Canadian language and culture from the face of Canada. The policy of Francicization was meant to demonstrate that Quebec is – in the controversial wording of the failed Meech Lake Accord – a distinct society. However, in recent years Quebec has become aware that against the background of immigration the old equation of language = nation has lost its basis and that the mere francicization of the newcomers without their commitment to commonly shared political goals would be insufficient.[12]

Since the rejection of Meech Lake the voices in Quebec demanding separation and sovereignty have multiplied. They have certainly been encouraged by the emergence of smaller independent states in Eastern Europe in the wake of the collapse of the Communist bloc and paradoxically also by the signing of NAFTA (North American Free Trade Agreement). But they have also caused among other Canadians a tremendous amount of irritation and anger, leading to instances of an Anglophone backlash (e.g. the formation of the Reform Party). The 1980 referendum could not swing public opinion in Quebec in favour of a separation. Another referendum in the near future, however, may produce different results.

Quebec's two-hundred-year old trauma is still alive and continues to be a burden, if not a threat, to Canadian national unity.

3. Canada: One Nation or an Assembly of Regions?

Quebec is 1000 km from Halifax and over 5000 km from Vancouver. In view of such distances, the geographical diversity of the country, and different patterns of regional settlements over a vast territory, the existence of Canadian regionalism is no surprise. Regional voices and regional discontent frequently receded into the background on account of the predominance of the dualist texture. Yet Quebec is only one of several regions. To use the most common regional classification we distinguish the Maritimes, Ontario, the West (i.e. the Prairie provinces), British Columbia, and the North. This listing of regions follows pretty divergent criteria: geographical, historical, political, and economic.[13] Politically regionalism was enshrined in the political set-up of the confederation, a union of initially four colonies which were joined by other territories. The fact that the last province to become a member of Canada was Newfoundland (in 1949!) makes it clear that the strength of regional differences should not be underestimated and that in times of crises regional disparities might even become another threat to Canadian unity. In 1969 historian Maurice Careless introduced the phrase of 'Limited Identities in Canada' – this being the title of an essay which spoke of regionalism as a powerful political force.[14] Geographer Cole Harris characterized these limited (regional) identities in the following manner:

> Inside Quebec, French-speaking sentiment readily crystallized around the province. In Newfoundland, where separate dominion status is well remembered, where after the Irish and Southern English migrations of the early nineteenth century there has been little subsequent migration, and where the elemental context of rock, settlement and sea is everywhere apparent, the province corresponds to a strong sense of separate identity. Much the same is true of Prince Edward Island. Elsewhere provincial feeling has been weaker. It has been diluted in New Brunswick and Nova Scotia by ethnicity, isolation and the tension of local metropolitan hinterland relationships; in Ontario by a tendency to equate the centre with the whole – to think of English Canada rather than Ontario; and in the West by recency. British Columbians ... are recent immigrants from different backgrounds who have converged on a complex physiographic realm dominated by different, rapidly changing local economies. Inevitably, their sense of themselves as British Columbians has been inchoate – a surrounding natural magnificence, a certain frontier optimism ... and a certain unconventionality in a new and relatively benign setting, but nothing like the unconscious generational identification of Prince Edward Islanders or Newfoundlanders with their islands, or most Quebeckers with Quebec.[15]

According to this statement different historical patterns have been responsible for the diverging grades of intensity of regional consciousness in Canada. However, one has to remember that the shaping and articulation of regionalist identity has been often based on commonly shared modes of life and on feelings of being economically disadvantaged. The Canadian Prairies are a prime example. Despite their ethnic diversity and despite the recency of their history (in contrast to that of the centre and the East) the prairie provinces developed a kind of Western identity which was the result of shared sufferings during the period of settlement, of a commonly experienced economic way of life and of the growing alienation from the centre. In 1969, after extensive research, a team of journalists from the *Toronto Telegram* summed up the historical reasons for Western resentment against the East in the following way:

... for more than eighty-five ... years the people of the Prairies have been shouting their discontent. First, they complained of the national tariff policy and the monopoly of the C.P.R. By the turn of the century the protest had broadened to envelop 'Eastern' business interests with an alleged propensity to gouge the West. In the 1920s Prairie farmers turned their sights on the Grain Exchange and its reflection of constantly fluctuating prices for their grain. In the 1930s and early 1940s, the Prairie appeal was for federal assistance in providing depression relief. In the last twenty years many of the old grievances have been renewed and new ones born. Bolstered by new-found wealth in oil and potash, the plaintive cries ... are taking on a more confident tone.[16]

The West has always been an arena where contrary perspectives clashed: the national with the regional, and those of the East (here in the sense of the centre) with those of the West. Historian Doug Owram showed in his study on the settlement of the Prairies how the West was sacrificed to expansionist ideologies from the vantage point of nation and British Empire. Here the West was seen as the last and vital link in the completion of the nation and the Empire.[17] Some Canadian nationalists even went so far as to declare the West the future centre of the Empire. The Canadian heartland also provided the images with which settlers were lured, first from Ontario and the U.S.A., and later from Europe. Early images of the prairies as a desert and wasteland were replaced by images of the promised land and a bountiful garden.[18] Politically and economically the West was, however, placed in the position of a useful hinterland. It was furthermore culturally marginalized, as examples from Canadian historiography, literature and literary criticism show. Thus Canada's first internationally acclaimed bestselling novelist Ralph Connor, an Easterner, appropriated the West in many of his adventure romances at the beginning of this century submitting it to Eastern perspectives. In the thirties historian Donald Creighton explained the history of the West with what is generally known as the Laurentian thesis, i.e. he saw Western expansion and the building of the transcontinental railway (1885) as the commercial-national continuation of the metropolitan centres of the St. Laurence area. While Canadian historiography with W.L. Morton replaced the centralist Laurentian concept by a regional one in 1957,[19] the literature of the West had begun to develop a regionally distinct voice in the twenties, when the emerging prairie realism began to question the centralist ideologies at the heart of the adventure romances. Yet this could not prevent the appropriation of the Western self-images by Eastern cultural and literary criticism which transformed these regional images into national mythologies. The concept of a hostile nature so central to prairie fiction fell easy prey to Eastern myths of Canadian victim, Canadian Christ, exile from paradise, and survival.

Separatism is commonly linked to Quebec. Yet separatist tendencies have also been characteristic of the West. The founding of populist regional political parties in the thirties (Social Credit and Cooperative Commonwealth Federation) was the response of Western indignation to the Federal neglect of the widespread social and economic hardship in the prairie provinces, which were severely hit by the Depression and drought. While these political parties did not pursue a separatist course, separatist voices have always been there, as the separatist movement at the end of the seventies whose message of prairie power was the result of the changed economic structure (from farming to oil producer) and an increased political status can prove.[20]

Although one has to be careful when tying political and cultural developments together, it is safe to say that in the case of the West a strong cultural regionalism was paralleled by a growing political regionalist confidence. From the end of the sixties, and perhaps even earlier, Western writers began to resist cultural models which they felt were imposed by the centre and operated with an alien ideology and aesthetics. Novelists such as Margaret Laurence, Robert Kroetsch, and Rudy Wiebe, to name just a few, responded to the hegemonical understanding of the Canadianness of Canadian culture by developing a regionalist aesthetics which placed the ideals of process, openness, and experiment against the notion of a monolithic tradition.[21] Their works provided alternative cultural perspectives in which the experiences of the other were no longer marginalized or ignored. It would, however, be going too far to speak of a cultural separatist movement in the West. For if we look at the history of the rise and distribution of cultural centres in Canada, we can observe a shifting or better expansion of cultural centres from the far East (the Maritimes since the 18th century) via the middle East (the Canadian heartland since the mid-nineteenth century) to the Canadian West and Pacific (since the seventies of this century). We can furthermore assume that the Western cultural regionalism has led to a revision of cultural concepts of the centre and has given new impetus to regionalist cultural voices in the Maritimes.

Despite repeated frictions in the past regional identities and national concerns have not always worked against each other, but have also been mutually supportive. A last question to be asked, yet one which is hard to answer, is whether cultural regionalism is able to defuse political separatism, or whether it reinforces its centrifugal tendencies to the point of threatening national unity.

4. Canada: A Multicultural Nation

Canada had been a multicultural society long before the Trudeau government announced multiculturalism as an official federal policy in 1971. The recognition of Canada's multi-ethnic composition had been long overdue. Paradoxically, the initiative for this came from the Royal Commission on Bilingualism and Biculturalism (the so-called B & B Commission), which was expressly formed in 1963 to help overcome the inequalities existing between Quebec and the rest of the country. Pressed by voices who envisioned the need for a 'Third Force' between the two charter groups, the Commission added a report on 'The Cultural Contribution of the Other Ethnic Groups' to its inquiry.[22] The government's new multicultural directive was an explicit reaction to changed patterns of immigration and demography which had come about since the farewell to racially discriminatory practices in the Immigration Acts of 1962 and 1967.[23] The rising number of non-white immigrants which made the third force group also increasingly visible was perhaps a welcome opportunity of challenging the traditional dualist outlook.

Leaving the special case of Quebec aside, one can with good reason call Canadian immigration up to 1870 (the beginning of Western settlement) fairly homogenous. After the fall of New France, immigration from France ceased. In contrast to British immigration (Loyalists during and after the War of Independence, Scottish settlers in the wake of the so-called Highland Clearances since the 1770s, etc.) non-British settlement was only sporadic (e.g. the Germans in Lunenburg county 1753 or the arrival of Mennonites in 1786). It is true that Scottish and Irish settlers may have possessed an identity of their own and that Catholic Irish settlers were viewed by other Anglophones with suspicion. Yet the gap between the various immigrant groups from the British Isles, the Scots, the Irish, the Welsh, and the English, was never so deep as to render assimilation completely impossible. The ethnic diversification of the country's population began with the settlement of the West, in particular during the second immigration wave after 1896, when the Canadian minister of the Interior, Clifford Sifton, pushed the immigration not only of American and British, but also of a great number of Eastern European settlers whom he defended against racist resentment as 'stalwart peasants in sheep-skin coats'.[24]

Goldwin Smith, one of the leading former exponents of *Canada First,* pleaded in *Canada and the Canadian Question* of 1891, probably under the influence of American 'Anglo-Saxonism', for a political union of the U.S.A. and Canada as a bulwark of Anglo-Saxon civilization.[25] In view of 800,000 newcomers from Central and especially Eastern Europe, it does not come as a surprise that the concept of the mosaic was first used in connection with the Canadian West. Victoria Hayward, an American visitor to the country, spoke in 1922 of the West as 'a mosaic of vast dimensions and great breadth',[26] and in 1938 John Murray Gibbon turned the concept into a metaphor for the whole of Canada.[27] Gibbon's report on the ethnic groups failed to mention the existence of Asian immigrants who, particularly in British Columbia, their logical place of destination, faced an increasingly hostile public climate characterized by a head tax for Chinese immigrants (after 1885), restrictive immigration practices, racist labour legislation, and even open violence (white riots in Vancouver's Chinatown and Japanese district in 1907). On the pretext that Asians were unassimilable, immigration of Japanese was drastically restricted by a mutual agreement with Japan, whereas Chinese immigration was first considerably obstructed and then completely stopped by the federal Chinese Exclusion Act of 1923[28]. Against this background it becomes understandable why the majority of the immigrants until 1965 came from Europe. After that, the picture changed tremendously and the proportion of non-white immigrants turned the tables in favour of the visible minorities. Thus between 1981 and 1986, 43% of all immigrant arrivals were of Asian origin (1988: 50%, 1989: 49%, as against 24% and 27% of European descent).[29]

It is easy to understand that the ideas of Canadian mosaic and multiculturalism have frequently served as a contrast to the American ideology of the melting-pot.[30] George Woodcock even considered 'anti-assimilationism' as an archetypal Canadian tradition and the quintessence of Canadian identity.[31] Nevertheless the concepts of mosaic and multiculturalism have come under fire from various camps. Both concepts are noble ideals enshrined in the Canadian constitution (article 27) and the *Canadian Multiculturalism Act* of 1988. Whether they will form the basis of a widespread Canadian self-image across the various ethnic borders depends on their general acceptability. The *Multiculturalism Act* aims at the disappearance of racial discrimination, respect for ethnic diversity, and the full participation of members of the ethnic communities in the country's social, economic, and political life. Critical voices in Quebec fear that the legal recognition of 'the cultural and racial diversity of Canadian society' in article 3.1 of the *Multiculturalism Act* will hasten the departure of the state from its basically bicultural (not bilingual) orientation. Criticism of multicultural policies is to be found also outside Quebec. As early as in 1965 the sociologist John Porter summed up economic disparities in Canadian society in his famous metaphor of the vertical mosaic with ethnic members at the bottom.[32] More recent warnings concern some unintended implications of the Act. Thus it is feared that multicultural government projects such as the 'Heritage Cultures and Languages' programme will be limited to the cultural sector, lead to ethnic ghettoization, and fail to contribute to the abolition of discrimination in the economic and social sectors of the Canadian polity. Sociologist Gladys Symons is therefore right to point out that the policy of cultural pluralism often served 'to mask the reality of dominant-conformity (with institutional support for folkloric cultures) ... This Anglo-conformity is clearly evident in large work organizations ... where ... adaptation to the (Anglo) organizational culture is the *sine qua non* of a successful working life'.[33]

The concepts of mosaic and multiculturalism have also been challenged by writers and critics. Enoch Padolsky's attempt at replacing the notion of a cultural mainstream by a pluralist cultural model undermines the traditionally privileged position of English-Canadian texts by examining them from the perspective of ethnogenesis, which treats both British and French like any other ethnic group.[34] For similar reasons writer Janice Kulyk Keefer, who has Ukrainian roots, prefers the term 'transculturalism' to multiculturalism and suggests replacing the image of the mosaic by that of the kaleidoscope. According to her, political multiculturalism, with its goal of preserving cultures, would freeze cultures and prevent members from crossing cultural borderlines in a transcultural step. For Keefer the concept of the mosaic would cement the hierarchical relationship between majority and minorities:

> ... the notion of mosaic demands that someone – Artist or authority – decree which figures are accorded more or less power and importance in the overall design. Perhaps a better model would be that of a kaleidoscope ... The user of a kaleidoscope can make out separate pieces, none of which is more privileged than any other, a changing and infinitely variable pattern precisely because the shifting parts are held together by the cylinder that contains them. And that cylinder ... we may liken to Canada.[35]

Keefer's vision is an ideal, the realization of which depends on the proper social and political arrangement of the country so that the transcultural crossing (and the cultural cross-fertilization) becomes the norm rather than the exception. How this will be achieved is hard to predict. Canada has taken well-meant steps towards the creation of a more just society. Yet its multi-ethnic character together with basic dualism and regionalist disparities will severely test the country's ability to stay together.

NOTES

1. See Frank Davey, 'Surviving the Paraphrase', *Canadian Literature* 70, 1976, 5-13.
2. See Paul Goetsch, 'Der literarische Nationalismus in Kanada seit 1960', in: Heinz Kosok, Horst Prießnitz (eds.), *Literaturen in englischer Sprache: Ein Überblick über englischsprachige Literatur außerhalb Englands.* Bonn, 1977, 122-140.
3. See Frank Davey, *Reading Canadian Reading.* Winnipeg, 1988, 1-18.
4. Cf. Hugh Hood, 'Moral Imagination: Canadian Thing', in: K. Groß, W. Pache (eds.), *Grundlagen zur Literatur in englischer Sprache: Kanada.* München, 1987, 113-118.
5. Cf. the excellent analysis of the political tradition by Martin Thunert, 'Zum Verhältnis der politischen Kulturen Kanadas und der Vereinigten Staaten', *Zeitschrift der Gesellschaft für Kanada-Studien* 11, 1991, 63-78.
6. Stephen Scobie, *Ghost: A Glossary of the Intertext.* Toronto, 1990, 63.
7. Cf. Frederick Jackson Turner, 'The Significance of the Frontier in American History', *American Historical Association Annual Report for the Year 1893.* Washington, 1894, 199-227; and *The Frontier in American History.* New York, 1920.
8. See Samuel Delbert Clark, 'The Social Development of the American Continental System', *Culture* 5, 1944, 133-143.
9. See Robin Mathews, *Canadian Identity: Major Forces Shaping the Life of a People.* Ottawa, 1988, 6.
10. Mordecai Richler, *Oh Canada! Oh Quebec! Requiem for a Divided Country.* Harmondsworth, 1992, 72.
11. René Dionne (ed.), *Le Québécois et sa littérature.* Sherbrooke, Paris, 1984, 12-30, 27.
12. Cf. Tom Sloan, 'Immigration and Quebec', *Language and Society/Langue et societé* 39, 1992, 17-18, 17; and Hal Winter, 'Quebec's new language realities', *Language and Society/Langue et societé* 39, 1992, 24-25.
13. A very good introduction to regionalism is William C. Wonders' 'Canadian Regions and Regionalisms: National Enrichment or National Disintegration?', *Canadian Issues/Thèmes canadiens* 5, 1983, 16-53.

14. Maurice Careless, 'Limited Identities in Canada', *Canadian Historical Review* 50, 1969, 1-10.

15. Cole Harris, 'The Emotional Structure of Canadian Regionalism' (1981); quoted by Peter Crabb, 'Regionalism and National Identity: Canada and Australia', in: Reginald Berry, James Acheson (eds.), *Regionalism and National Identity: Multidisciplinary Essays on Canada, Australia and New Zealand*. Christchurch, 1985, 19-29, 25.

16. The Telegram (Toronto) Canada 70 Team, *The Prairie Provinces; Alienation and Anger*. Toronto, Montreal, 1969, 3.

17. Cf. Doug Owram, *Promise of Eden: The Canadian Expansionist Movement and the Idea of the West, 1856-1900*. Toronto, 1980, 125-148.

18. Cf. Douglas Francis (ed.), *Images of the West: Changing Perceptions of the Prairies, 1890-1960*. Saskatoon, 1989, especially chapters 3 and 4.

19. Cf. W.L. Morton, *Manitoba: A History*. Toronto, 1957.

20. See George Melnyk, 'Das Unbehagen am Regionalismus', in: Wolfgang Klooß, Hartmut Lutz (eds.), *Kanada: Geschichte, Politik, Kultur*. Gulliver. Deutsch-Englische Jahrbücher 19, 1986, 88-95, 91.

21. See Wolfgang Klooß, 'Multiculturalism, Regionalism and the Search for a Poetics of Disparity in Contemporary Canadian Writing', in: Wilhelm Busse (ed.), *Anglistentag 1991 in Düsseldorf: Proceedings*. Tübingen, 1992, 346-360.

22. Cf. Hugh R. Innis, 'The Cultural Contribution of the other Ethnic Groups', in: Groß, Pache, 123-129.

23. Cf. Jean-Michel Lacroix, 'Recent Trends in Immigration Policy in Canada: Some Remarks on the 1981 Census', in: Alfred Pletsch (ed.), *Ethnicity in Canada: International Examples and Perspectives*. Marburg, 1985, 147-154, 148f.

24. Cf. *The Canadian Encyclopedia*. Edmonton, 1985, s.v. Sifton.

25. See Goldwin Smith, *Canada and the Canadian Question*. Toronto, 1973, 211 (first 1891). On American 'Anglo-Saxonism' cf. Stephen Thernstrom (ed.), *Harvard Encyclopedia of American Ethnic Groups*. Cambridge, Mass., London, 1980, s.v. American Identity and Americanization.

26. Victoria Hayward, Edith S. Watson, *Romantic Canada*. Toronto, 1922, 187.

27. Cf. John Murray Gibbon, *The Canadian Mosaic: The Making of a Northern Nation*. Toronto, 1938.

28. See Roland Vogelsang, 'Visible Minorities in Canada: Problems in the Investigation and Analysis of Non-White Immigrants', in: Pletsch, 268-285, 276f.

29. Statistics Canada, *Canada Yearbook 1992, 125th Anniversary*. Ottawa, 1991, 91-93.

30. Cf. Allan Smith, 'Metaphor and Nationality in North America', *Canadian Historical Review* 51, 1970, 247-275.

31. See George Woodcock, 'A Plan for the Anti-Nation', in V. Nelles, A. Rotstein (eds.), *Nationalism or Local Control: Responses to George Woodcock*. Toronto, 1973, 4.

32. Cf. John Porter, *The Vertical Mosaic: An Analysis of Social Class and Power in Canada*. Toronto, 1965, part I, chapter III.

33. Gladys Symons, 'The Social Construction of Race and Ethnicity in Canadian Society'. Typescript 1991.

34. See Enoch Padolsky, 'Cultural Diversity and Canadian Literature: A Pluralistic Approach to Majority and Minority Writing in Canada', *International Journal of Canadian Studies/Révue internationale d'études Canadiennes* 3, 1991, 110-128.

35. Janice Kulyk Keefer, 'From Mosaic to Kaleidoscope: Out of the multicultural past comes a vision of transcultural future', *Books in Canada* 20, 1991, No. 6, 13-16, 16.

Double Voicing:
A View of Canadian Poetry

Stephen Scobie

1.

It was a warm summer evening on a boat in Finland when Jørn Carlsen sidled up to me and said "Stephen, how would you like to write an essay on Canadian poetry for a collection I'm editing?"

"Fine," I said, unthinking, taking another swig at my beer. The port city of Turku was fading astern. "Which Canadian poets do you want me to write about?"

"All of them," he said.

"Oh. You mean, like, a survey of contemporary poetry in Canada?"

"Not just contemporary."

"Oh. You mean modern poetry: the whole of the 20th century?"

"All of Canadian poetry," said Jørn, his chin jutting like a Viking into the evening breeze. "From the beginnings." Then he added, generously, "Only in English, of course."

"I see. One short essay, twenty pages say, and I have to cover the entire history of English poetry in Canada, from the beginnings until today, in a comprehensive, balanced, impartial, and fully detailed manner. When did you say you wanted this by?"

A massive, Stena lines ferry glided past. Jørn contemplated the horizon.

"Ah, how about next Tuesday?"

– Well, it may not have happened precisely like that, but you appreciate my predicament. It is of course impossible to write any such essay, comprehensive and detailed yet at the same time judicious and impartial: so the reader should be advised that what follows is both selective and subjective. Exceptions could be found, easily, to all the generalisations I will advance; and my approach will reveal as much about my own aesthetic and ideological biases as it will about the nature of Canadian poetry. All I can do is pick out a few scattered points in the history of Canadian poetry which strike me as having some significance, and offer a few, highly personal, observations which I hope may prove useful, not as definitive statements, but as provocations to more extensive study and more leisured research.

2.

In the beginnings, Canadian poetry always arrived late. In 1825, a Canadian author named Oliver Goldsmith published a poem called 'The Rising Village', in deliberate homage to the English poem 'The Deserted Village', published fifty-five years earlier by the poet's namesake and grand-uncle. The group of poets usually seen as marking the coming of age of Canadian poetry in the 19th century – Charles G.D. Roberts, Bliss Carman, Archibald Lampman, Duncan Campbell Scott – are known collectively as the 'Confederation Poets'. Yet Roberts' first book, *Orion*, was not published until 1880, thirteen years after Confederation; and most of the group's best work was done between twenty and thirty years after the event for which they are named. This curious time-lag is typical of 19th century Canadian poetry (Lampman at the end of the century was writing poems that are at times indistinguishable from Wordsworth at the beginning of the century[1]), and it is an aspect of the essential retrospectiveness of a colonial culture.

The hallmark of a colonial culture is that it always looks *elsewhere* for its criteria of value. Feeling itself to be marginal, it appeals to the centre of Empire to validate its products. (Even to this day, the coverage of literary prizes in the Canadian press pays more attention to the Booker Prize in England than to the Governor-General's Awards in Canada.) For the 19th century Canadian poet, literary excellence was defined in England: and for the greater part of the century, that meant that the dominant mode was Romanticism, and that the overwhelming model was Wordsworth. Yet there are times when the model doesn't quite fit. Perhaps the most interesting way of approaching 19th century Canadian poetry is to read it 'against the grain': to see in it those moments when the particularity of the Canadian experience resists the normative effects of the imported form. Take, for example, Charles G.D. Roberts' poem 'The Skater' (1901).

In this poem, Roberts describes skating, alone, on a wilderness lake surrounded by snow-covered mountains. At first he is exhilarated, and revels in the experience –

My glad feet shod with the glittering steel
I was the god of the winged heel

– but then suddenly he gets spooked. The solitude of the wilderness terrifies him, and abruptly, he turns and flees.

Shapes in the fir-gloom drifted near.
In the deep of my heart I heard my fear;

And I turned and fled, like a soul pursued,
From the white, inviolate solitude.[2]

This poem is very reminiscent of a famous passage in Book I of Wordsworth's *The Prelude*.[3] In that poem, the young Wordsworth 'borrows' a boat and rows out onto a lake. Again, at first he is filled with the joy of the natural environment; and again, he suddenly becomes alarmed and afraid, as a looming mountain seems to chase him back to shore. The narrative line is identical in the two poems, but there is one great difference. *Roberts didn't steal the skates.*

In Wordsworth, the sense of alarm is an expression of moral guilt. A psychological reading would have it that the young Wordsworth felt guilty about his unauthorised borrowing of the boat, and that he projected this feeling of guilt out onto the landscape, so that the mountain became threatening. Wordsworth himself would have been more likely to argue that the moral sense was inherent to the landscape: that nature itself is the source, sanction, and teacher of moral values. But none of this applies in the Canadian poem. There is no guilt (Roberts didn't steal the skates), morality has nothing to do with it. The wilderness is, in and of itself, scary. The setting has no moral lesson to teach; it is, simply, hostile. Roberts' skater gains no sense of a Wordsworthian harmony; for him, nature is something to be wary of, a vast, inimical presence that can, indifferently, kill him.[4] So a certain disjunction, a slippage between two schemes of value, divides the poem. The model seems orthodox and traditional, a good Romantic poem about the encounter with Nature; but the actual import of the text is anti-Romantic, profoundly distrustful of Wordsworthian idealism.

I would argue that moments like this can be found throughout 19th century Canadian poetry: moments where a perception of the Canadian reality does not quite fit the aesthetic and ideological ideals which the colonial poet has been led to suppose are the 'correct' and apposite ways for writing fine literature. (One can see it also in the ways in which Lampman's obsession with death, and with the annihilation of thought, keeps on intruding into his inherited Romantic orthodoxy.) It is at such moments of strain and slippage that an authentic 'Canadian' voice begins to emerge.

Or perhaps it would be more accurate to say 'voices', or 'split voice', or 'double voicing'. For the proposition I would like to advance (in all its outrageous generality) is that the most characteristic mode of Canadian poetry is, in one form or another, a kind of double voicing. In 'The Skater', that is, I hear the voice of Wordsworth, the voice of English tradition, the voice of the colonial poet paying dutiful tribute to empire; but at the same time I hear the other voice which says no, that's not the way it works, I'm scared, I'm getting the hell out of here. These two voices inhabit each other, haunt each other. What I have called the 'slippage' works only because it is a slippage *within* a pre-existing discourse; and that discourse in turn is never simply discarded or denied, but rather retains its force too within the poem. Recall the double voice, and double name, of Oliver Goldsmith. The two 'Village' poems exist, for us now, in a state of parasitical inter-dependency. The Canadian poem is haunted by its English predecessor, but the ghost has been deliberately invoked, and invited to take up residence.[5]

Double voicing takes many forms, of which the presence of a non-Canadian influence or model is only one.[6] But it is one which is worth pursuing a little farther. Of course I know that this whole line of argument is problematic: that to trace a history of Canadian poetry in terms of its outside influences is (or could be seen as) itself a colonial pursuit, complicit with the very forces it seeks to critique. Nationalist critics have reacted strongly, and with justification, against any attempt to read Canadian poetry as the sum of its influences; and they have also reacted strongly, though with less justification, against Canadian poets who have explicitly acknowledged, and paid tribute to, foreign mentors.

A whimsical but not entirely inaccurate way of tracing this history would be to say that the time-lag rapidly diminishes and then disappears. The Confederation poets looked back over several decades to the English Romantics; the Canadian poets of the 1920s, such as A.J.M. Smith and F.R. Scott, looked back only one decade, to the experiments of Imagism and early English Modernism. By the 1930s, politically committed poets like Dorothy Livesay were marching in step with Auden and Spender. In the 40s and 50s, Canadian poets corresponded with their mentors – Raymond Souster with William Carlos Williams; Louis Dudek with the imprisoned Ezra Pound – and by 1963, they were issuing invitations.

The 1963 Poetry Conference in Vancouver was one of the key moments in modern Canadian poetry; and if I choose to stress it here, it is in part as a tribute to one of its organisers, Warren Tallman, who died in 1994. It is in some ways emblematic for the whole question of American influence on contemporary Canadian poetry that I heard about Tallman's death when I was at the Jack Kerouac School of Disembodied Poetics in Boulder, Colorado, attending a week-long tribute to the life and poetry of Allen Ginsberg. The news was announced to the conference by Anselm Hollo, and an audience of some 800 people observed a minute of silence. Later in the week, further tributes were paid to Tallman by Ginsberg himself, and by Robert Creeley, who had worked with Tallman to organise the Vancouver conference. Creeley and Tallman were two out of five members of the organising committee, Creeley recalled, and were initially outvoted by the more conservative members, who wanted to invite more 'established' poets. (At least one of these poets was so 'established' that he was in fact, at the time an invitation was sent to him, dead.) Don't worry about this, Tallman told Creeley; all these people will say no, and then we'll jump in with our list of reserves. And so it happened that the Vancouver Poetry Conference of 1963 brought to Canada Charles Olson, Robert Duncan, Denise Levertov, Allen Ginsberg – a fairly massive influx of foreign and imperial masters.

But the influence of the Vancouver Conference was, paradoxically, to act as one of the most important factors in spurring on the resurgence of Canadian poetry in the 1960s.[7] The most immediate result of the influence of poets like Olson, Duncan, and Creeley was the formation of the school of Vancouver poets grouped around the magazine *TISH*: Frank Davey, George Bowering, Daphne Marlatt, Fred Wah, Jamie Reid. And that influence broadened out in all kinds of directions, to embrace (at least) the three poets whom I would advance as the most important figures in the Canadian poetry of the last thirty years: Phyllis Webb, bpNichol, and Michael Ondaatje. But it also swept up older poets like Dorothy Livesay, who was in Vancouver in the mid-60s, and who had a thing or two to show these youngsters about breath-line poetics. (Livesay's career, which might well have come to an honourable if minor close in the 1950s, rekindled itself with the 1967 publication of *The Unquiet Bed*.) And the poets of the 60s reached back, reclaiming (or perhaps creating) their own lineage, to figures like Souster and Dudek, with their allegiance to the canonical figures of Williams and Pound. After all, Irving Layton had corresponded with Creeley; even Margaret Avison, with her astringent Christian vision, had been published in Cid Corman's *Origin*. Currents and cross-currents here; tracing the lines of poetic 'influence' is no job for a merely two-dimensional map.

The further paradox of the Olson-Creeley 'Black Mountain' influence, often denounced as a late manifestation of American cultural imperialism, is that it advocated a *particularity* of poetic response to the immediate environment ('No ideas but in things', said Williams) that discounted in advance any possibility of subservience to a foreign model. The poets who were willing to come to Vancouver, that is, were the ones who were most prepared to take seriously a localised writing community. Being true to Olson's precepts, the Canadian 'Black Mountaineers' climbed strictly local peaks. The poetry of Davey, Marlatt, or Bowering is fiercely regional, and staunchly Canadian. (Though, since the region was British Columbia, central-Canadian critics sometimes had problems making this equation.) One thinks of Davey's evocations of shipwrecks[8] in the local waters of B.C. (including the virulently anti-American *The Clallam* (1974)); Daphne Marlatt's intense meditations on the fishing community of *Steveston* (1974); or George Bowering's resiting of Rilke in the cosy suburbs of Vancouver in *Kerrisdale Elegies* (1984).

Certainly, from the 60s on, the idea of Canadian poetry as being in any way derivative from, or subservient to, foreign traditions is no longer a problem. For the past few pages, my argument has been that an accounting of English or American influences on Canadian poetry need not be seen as a way of casting Canadian writing in a secondary or inferior position. Rather, an account of the responses and resistances of Canadian poets may be seen as one form of the 'double voicing' which I am advancing as the most characteristic mode of writing in this country. Canadian literature is no longer, nor has it been for quite some time, a project of colonial subservience. Nevertheless, Canadian poets remain alert and open to other voices, and often their most interesting and characteristic work takes the form of a response to such 'influences', in the form of a dialogue, or even an appropriation of the other voice. I have just mentioned George Bowering's *Kerrisdale Elegies*, which can be seen as an extended act of double voicing. When Rilke writes

> Und das Totsein ist mühsam
> und voller Nachholn, dass man allmählich
> ein wenig Ewigkeit spürt

(translated, in rather stilted fashion, by Spender and Leishman as 'And it's hard, being dead,/ and full of retrieving before one begins to espy/ eternity'[9]), and Bowering responds

> Being dead is no bed of roses,
> you have so much work piled up in front of you
> before the long weekend[10]

– then one is dealing with something much more complex than mere 'influence'. The critical terms most often applied to this dialogue are 'intertextuality', and, especially in recent Canadian criticism, 'documentary'.

3.

The term 'documentary', well established in the history of Canadian film due to the influence of the (Scottish) John Grierson, was first applied to Canadian poetry in an influential talk by Dorothy Livesay[11], first delivered to the Association of Canadian University Teachers of English (an organisation with the debatable acronym ACUTE) in 1969, and published in 1971[12]. In her talk, Livesay advanced the idea that the most characteristic form of Canadian writing was a 'documentary' form, that is, one based on factual, documented information, but which nevertheless interpreted that information in an idiosyncratic manner. The resulting poem represents, she said, 'a dialectic between the objective facts and the subjective feelings of the poet' (267).

Livesay's essay itself, one might say, was an example of such a dialectic. At the time she wrote it, the 'objective facts' (that is, existing Canadian texts that would support her argument) were in fact rather few and far between. She could point mainly to her own work, and to the sprawling, epic, idiosyncratic narrative poems of E.J. Pratt, such as 'The Titanic' (1935) and 'Towards the Last Spike' (1952).[13] But in terms of 'subjective feeling', the essay was a remarkable act of poetic intuition, for in the course of the following twenty years, dozens of Canadian poets were to provide, retrospectively, the evidence for Livesay's assertion.

Livesay saw the documentary as the historic articulation of a culture or a collectivity; in her own case, she was thinking of her poem 'Call My People Home' (1950), which attempted to articulate the grievances of the Japanese-Canadians who were persecuted at the time of the outbreak of the war with Japan. There is no single protagonist to this poem; each section in turn is spoken by a representative character. The documentary poem, as Livesay saw it, was a historically-grounded expression of group identity.

But in between Livesay's original delivery of this talk and its eventual publication, there intervened the publication of the two books which established the 'documentary' in its dominant form: Margaret Atwood's *The Journals of Susanna Moodie* and Michael Ondaatje's *The Collected Works of Billy the Kid* (both 1970). Whereas Livesay had insisted that the documentary should have a collective protagonist, both of these books focused on an individual.[14] The 'speaking voice' of both books was, classically, a doubled voice: simultaneously Atwood and Moodie, Ondaatje and Billy.

Atwood's book articulates a contemporary (1970) critique of 19th century colonialism and settlement, from a point of view as much ecological as political. But this critique can never be expressed *directly*, since the ostensible speaking voice of the poem is that of the 19th century persona, Susanna Moodie. Thus the basic 'double voicing' of the poem is Atwood/Moodie, with the contemporary Atwood voice making itself heard in the insinuated tones of irony, and indeed in the verse form itself, with its jagged rhythms and elliptical line-breaks. But even further than this, Atwood finds a 'double voicing' within Moodie herself: 'Two voices/ took turns using my eyes'.[15] In her 'Afterword', Atwood memorably wrote:

> If the national mental illness of the United States is megalomania, that of Canada is paranoid schizophrenia. Mrs Moodie is divided down the middle.... Perhaps that is the way we still live.... This country is something that must be chosen – it is so easy to leave – and if we do choose it we are still choosing a violent duality. (62)

Ondaatje's book shows similar effects, as the voice expresses both author and character, 20th century poet and 19th century outlaw. The title – 'Collected Works' – emphasises the ambiguity of the project, since it refers both to the aesthetic (the 'works' of the poet, the images of beauty he creates) and to the violent (the 'works' of the outlaw, the killings he commits). Other doublings abound in the book: the outlaw Billy against the marshall Pat Garrett; the Billy of historical fact against the Billy of myth and legend; poetry against prose; the very fact that such a quintessentially American legend is being told by a Canadian poet (born in Sri Lanka).

The success of Atwood and Ondaatje's books produced many poems in similar vein in Canada over the following twenty years or so. I would mention Sid Stephen's *Beothuck Poems* (1976); E.D. Blodgett's *Sounding* (1977, on Van Gogh); Jon Whyte's *Homage, Henry Kelsey* (1981); Gwendolyn MacEwen's *The T.E. Lawrence Poems* (1982); Phyllis Webb's 'I Daniel' (1982); my own *McAlmon's Chinese Opera* (1980), *The Ballad of Isabel Gunn* (1987), and *Gospel* (1994); Sharon Thesen's *Confabulations* (1984, on Malcolm Lowry); Bronwen Wallace's *Keep That Candle Burning Bright* (1991, on Emmylou Harris); and many more. Most of these volumes follow the example of the 'double voicing' in Atwood and Ondaatje by adopting a first-person stance for the narrative. Webb's poem, for instance, adopts the voice of the Old Testament prophet Daniel, and finds it too haunted by doubles: 'in the breakdown// of the bicameral mind – wherein I Daniel/ alone saw the vision'.[16]

But there have also been many other works which deal in a 'documentary' fashion, but without this appropriation of another voice, with issues in Canadian history, geography, and society. I am thinking of works as varied as Frank Davey's *The Clallam* (1974), Daphne Marlatt's *Steveston* (1974), or Andy Suknaski's *Wood Mountain Poems* (1976); and the list could clearly be extended into fiction, in the works of Rudy Wiebe, Timothy Findley, or Kristjana Gunnars – and, of course, in the novels of Michael Ondaatje. In these cases, it seems to me that the 'double voicing' is that of fact and fiction, history and imagination, the documented record and the poetic re-creation. Canadian writers seem fascinated by this border-line, and are compelled both to honour and to transgress it. None of these works is pure invention; even when it is taking the most outrageous liberties with the facts (as in George Bowering's *Burning Water* (1980)), the documentary form retains a respect for historical truth, and especially for its written record. The documentary is full of documents: journals, diaries, letters, confessions, maps, photographs, ledgers, account books, mail-order catalogues, libraries, other poems, every imaginable written trace. The poet is always in dialogue with the intertext. And at times, the intertext may take the form of the poet's own previous work.

4.

So far, I have pointed to two areas which I see as characteristic, or at least instructive, of the nature of Canadian poetry: double voicing as a response to the influence and prestige of other poetic traditions, and double voicing in the particular form of the documentary. The third and final area I would like to look at is the Canadian preference for the long poem. Here I would argue that the 'double voicing' takes the form of a dialogue between the lyric impulse of the short poem and more extended forms of discursive strategy and practice; as the 'long poem' becomes longer, it begins to question itself, and, almost inevitably, to turn back on itself, self-reflexive and self-referential.

Several critics have advanced the idea that the Canadian sense of space is too large to be expressed within the limits of the lyric poem. How can you encompass Saskatchewan in a sonnet? Certainly, the long poem seems to be a constant factor in Canadian writing, from as early as the aforementioned 'Rising Village' of the Canadian Oliver Goldsmith, through the narratives of E.J. Pratt, to the long poems of Louis Dudek, such as *Europe* (1955) and *En Mexico* (1958). Most of the 'documentary' poems mentioned in the previous section are book-length poems.[17]

An early example, though a tantalisingly incomplete one, is Isabella Valancy Crawford's *Hugh and Ion*. This project, written in the 1880s but neither finished nor published by the poet herself, set up an open-ended narrative structure in which two young men went on a camping trip in the wilderness. Several fragments which have been published as separate lyric poems (notably the extraordinary 'Said the Canoe') would have found a place in this structure alongside more extended discursive passages in which the two young men carried on earnest philosophical discussions. These various dualities – short lyric poem against extended philosophical debate – are summed up in the title, where the two young men, Hugh and Ion, are clearly You and I, a double voicing of Crawford herself, addressing herself at a careful narrative distance.

Hugh and Ion meet again, as it were, in Leonard Cohen's *Death of a Lady's Man* (1978). As with so many of the books which I am loosely calling 'long poems', this volume transgresses several genres: a book-length poem? a sequence of poems? poems mixed with prose, journal entries, critical essays, self-recriminations? For the past twenty years or more, Cohen has been better known, especially in Europe, as a singer and song-writer[18], but *Death of a Lady's Man* remains perhaps his most intriguing and under-rated work as a poet. In language which ranges from the lyric to the banal, from the brutal to the romantic, Cohen examines the collapse, not only of one man's marriage, but of the whole social and ideological position of 'the male' as it was re-defined in the 1970s. It was a difficult book for Cohen to write; on at least one occasion, he withdrew it from publication even after it had reached the stage of page-proofs. Then, at the last moment, he added to it a whole second layer of self-reflexive commentary. Almost all the sections of *Death of a Lady's Man* are accompanied by a second section of the same title, commenting directly or indirectly on the original. Many of these supplementary sections are highly critical, or even violently abusive, of the pieces of the same name to which they are attached: 'This is the work of a middle-class mind', he sneers; or 'The poem begins to rot after the third line, maybe after the second'. 'Claustrophobia!' another supplement exclaims, 'Bullshit! Air! Air! Give us air!'.[19] A beautiful lyric essay on 'How To Read Poetry' is no sooner over than it is sarcastically demolished. The effect is one of the most striking examples I know of 'double voicing'. The idea of an internal debate, carefully distanced by Crawford through the characters Hugh and Ion, is here dramatised on the page, as Leonard Cohen assails Leonard Cohen. The poems turn back on themselves in impassioned commentary. Earlier notebook drafts are called to bear witness against their later 'finished' state. The book becomes its own documentary.

From Cohen's statements, it appears that *Death of a Lady's Man*, as it was eventually published, is only part of a much larger body of manuscripts, to which Cohen has at various times given the titles *My Life in Art* or *The Woman Being Born*. These larger works have not appeared, and may never appear; they constitute parts of what is in effect one huge, continuing poem which, almost by definition, can never arrive at a final form. Such a life-long project is not uncommon in modern poetry – one thinks of Pound's *Cantos*, or Olson's *Maximus*, or MacDiarmid's *Haud Forrit* – or in Canadian poetry. Robert Kroetsch's *Field Notes* (1981-89) constitute such a project. Although Kroetsch has himself declared that the *Field Notes* are 'completed', they are so only in the sense that he has stopped adding to them. The work itself is so open-ended that any declared point of completion can only be arbitrary and provisional. Such poems challenge the very notion of a 'completed' work, one that can be neatly categorised and delimited. The longer the poem becomes, and the more it encompasses, then the harder it is to say where it could ever end.

The overwhelming example of the continuing, life-long poem in Canadian literature is bpNichol's *The Martyrology*. The first two Books were published in 1972, and Nichol continued to work on the poem until his death in 1988. On several occasions, he attempted to bring it to an end, but the text was developing its own momentum, and later writing declared itself part of *The Martyrology*. Many of these later sections turn back on the poem itself, and give a double voicing to its own history. Book 5 performs inventive deconstructions of passages in Book 2, while Book 9 recasts the characters of Book 1 as an opera libretto, accompanied by a full orchestral score. Eventually the poem stood as a monument to Nichol's writing life: vast, contradictory, and various, the strangest and most wonderful accomplishment of Canadian poetry.

It would be too simple to dismiss this kind of self-reflexiveness as indulgent linguistic game-playing, or as the gimmicks of a merely faddish 'postmodernism'. Rather, I believe that this double voicing, whether it takes the form of Roberts being haunted by Wordsworth, or Atwood imagining a resurrected Moodie, or Cohen berating Cohen, is a continuing presence in Canadian poetry. It reflects a profound instinct of our divided society, that nothing can ever be said only once. Single statement will never encompass Canada; only in double voicing can we begin to hear ourselves speak.

NOTES

1. This statement is based on practical experience. I have shown some Lampman poems to colleagues in English departments and had them unhesitatingly identified as Wordsworth; and vice versa.

2. Charles G.D. Roberts, *The Collected Poems of Sir Charles G.D. Roberts*, ed. Desmond Pacey. Wolfville, N.S.: The Wombat Press, 1985, 279-80.

3. I do not mean, necessarily, to suggest a conscious influence, or that Roberts in any way *intended* his poem to comment on Wordsworth's. I merely set the two passages alongside each other for the interest of what the juxtaposition reveals.

4. This perception – that the wilderness is hostile, and that the essential Canadian experience lies in the confrontation between a hostile wilderness and a wary, embattled, 'garrison' culture – became, in the 1960s, the central motif in an extended thematic reading of Canadian literature. The key texts are Northrop Frye's 'Conclusion' to *The Literary History of Canada* (1965), Doug Jones' *Butterfly on Rock* (1970), and Margaret Atwood's *Survival* (1972). It is worth noting that two of these three texts are by poets: thematic criticism, the devoted construction of meaning out of image patterns, is a highly subjective and creative form of criticism. A strong reaction against it was signalled by Frank Davey's essay 'Surviving the Paraphrase' (1976). – And one might also note that West Coast poets, living in the most climatically favoured region of Canada, have never quite bought in to the Ontario-centric view of Canadian nature as invariably hostile!

5. Earle Birney once wrote of Canada that 'It's by our lack of ghosts we're haunted'. With all due respect, I disagree. As this essay makes clear, I see ghosts everywhere. 'Haunting' seems to me a central image for Canadian culture.

6. Behind everything I have to say about 'double voicing' in English Canadian poetry runs another topic which I do not have the space to deal with here: the 'double voicing' of the whole of Canadian culture in the two languages of English and French. There has been very little direct contact between the poetic traditions in the two languages, but I think that the prevalence of (other forms of) double voicing is in itself evidence of the continuous unspoken awareness of the linguistic presence of The Other. (Canada is notorious for the 'double voicing' of our corn flakes boxes!) The French tradition haunts English Canadian poetry in much the same way as the English and American traditions do. The linguistic Other is the ghost of all language-oriented poetry in Canada, from 1963 on. The one area in which the Québecois presence is most strongly felt is in contemporary women's poetry, where the sense of feminist solidarity has often overcome the linguistic or national barrier. One thinks especially of the extreme importance of Nicole Brossard to many English-language poets, starting with Daphne Marlatt. And particular tribute should here be paid to the work of Lola Lemire Tostevin, which embodies within itself the linguistic double voicing of Canadian culture.

7. There were, of course, several other factors, which might be seen as equally, if not more, important. The 1960s saw a strong growth in Canadian nationalism, both positively (as a reaction to the Centennial celebrations of 1967) and negatively (as a revulsion from the America of the Vietnam era). Institutional support from new organisations like the Canada Council enabled small presses to survive financially, at the same time as technical advances like photo-offset printing reduced printing costs. By the end of the 60s, courses in 'Canadian literature' were becoming common in Canadian universities, providing both writers and readers with a more comprehensive view of the tradition. Organisations like the League of Canadian Poets sponsored poetry

readings all across the country. For all this activity, 1963 is as good a starting date as any.

8. Poems about shipwrecks form a flourishing sub-genre of Canadian literature, from E.J. Pratt's 'The Titanic' to Gordon Lightfoot's 'The Wreck of the Edmond Fitzgerald'. Margaret Atwood would doubtless link this to a national paranoia of disaster.

9. Rainer Maria Rilke, *Duino Elegies*, trans. J.B. Leishman and Stephen Spender. New York: Norton, 1939, 24-5.

10. George Bowering, *Kerrisdale Elegies*. Toronto: Coach House Press, 1984, 19.

11. And it is not coincidental how often Livesay's name occurs in any history of Canadian poetry. Students of the topic could do far worse than to begin a consideration of 20th century Canadian poetry with a careful examination of Livesay's poetry and career.

12. Dorothy Livesay, 'The Documentary Poem: A Canadian Genre', in *Contexts of Canadian Criticism*, ed. Eli Mandel. Chicago: University of Chicago Press, 1971.

13. Livesay's argument is much less convincing when she attempts to claim Isabella Valancy Crawford's 'Malcolm's Katie' (1884) as a 'documentary' poem. Crawford is a fascinating writer, who was much under-appreciated at the time of Livesay's talk, but she does not fit the definition of 'documentary' which Livesay was developing.

14. Ondaatje's was even more 'scandalous', in that its protagonist was American, not Canadian.

15. Margaret Atwood, *The Journals of Susanna Moodie*. Toronto: Oxford UP, 1970, 42.

16. Phyllis Webb, *The Vision Tree: Selected Poems*. Vancouver: Talonbooks, 1982, 154.

17. There may be more mundane reasons for this. Poets, publishers, and granting agencies all like the sound of a book-length project; it's easier to research, write, justify, and publicise.

18. The idea of 'double voicing' might also be applied to the interaction of words and music in the format of the song. I would point here to the number of excellent Canadian writers working in the genre of the popular song, especially in the 1970s: Cohen himself, and also Joni Mitchell, Neil Young, Bruce Cockburn, Robbie Robertson, Gordon Lightfoot. Another closely connected area is that of performance poetry, which has also flourished in Canada, in the work of bpNichol and the Four Horsemen, bill bissett, the Dub poets, Re:Sounding, etc. But to work out the implications of 'double voicing' for musical and vocal performance would take another essay.

19. Leonard Cohen, *Death of a Lady's Man*. Toronto: McClelland and Stewart, 1978, 25, 39, 129.

Behind the Scenes, or: What English-Canadian Plays Tell Us about Canada

Albert-Reiner Glaap

The nationalism of the seventies has given way to globalism; regionalism has gone out of fashion in favour of multiculturalism. We are in the nineties, and the frontiers of Canada are now considered to be *Fronteras Americanas*, which is the title of a play by Argentinean-Canadian actor/writer Guillermo Verdecchia, first produced at the *Tarragon Theatre*, Toronto, in 1992[1]. This play reminds Canadians that they are part of the Continent called America. What a difference compared to the sixties and seventies! 'When my family came to Canada, the designation for us was displaced persons, usually shortened to DPs and often alliteratively decorated with "dirty"', says *Tarragon's* Artistic Director Urjo Kareda, who is of Ukrainian descent. And he goes on to say: 'Other decades have produced their own formulations of national otherness: immigrants and foreigners, refugees and aliens, newcomers and new Canadians. Terminology apart, these people's journeys are all different and all the same'.[2] Canada is now considered to be only one of many possible worlds. American borders have become blurred by world-wide migration and free trade.

Other changes are also being dealt with in contemporary Canadian plays. The multiplicity of races, languages and cultures in present-day Canadian society is reflected in new theatrical themes and forms. The Cuban born playwright René Aloma compares Cuban and Canadian lifestyles in *A Little Something to Ease the Pain* (1980); and *Voiceless People* (1984) by the Italian-Canadian Marco Micone studies the problems of an Italian-Canadian family when confronted with the Francophone and Anglophone culture of Montreal. These are only two of numerous examples which indicate the interest that has developed over the past few years in the many facets of multiculturalism. Native drama has had an increasing influence on the Canadian theatre scene by giving more prominence to the interaction between the stage and the audience and – an aspect which especially applies to Native writers – to establishing links with elements of the orally transmitted literature.

50

Increasingly, English-Canadian drama has become a mirror of current issues. One of the important achievements, however, is that theatre and drama in Canada, since the early eighties, have not confined themselves to dealing with specifically Canadian issues. Canadian playwrights think of themselves primarily as playwrights in the sense that they write for the stage about any topic, be it Canadian or universal.

In this article, some of the most prominent issues thematized in contemporary Canadian drama will be illustrated with reference to eight English-Canadian plays which were written between 1980 and 1993 and which can help us to catch a glimpse of what goes into the making of contemporary Canadian drama.

1. Feeling out of context
Margaret Hollingsworth, *Ever Loving* (1980)[3]

Since the beginning of the 1970s Canadian playwrights have written about historically important events and ethnic themes, thereby trying to identify their plays as Canadian plays. But few of the many plays written in those days are about the immigrant experience. One of them is Margaret Hollingsworth's *Ever Loving*. The play is an account of the adjustment of three war brides to post World War II Canada. The female characters marry first generation Canadians, who have also been shaped by European consciousness. Essentially, the play is about dreams and how they are or are not realized. Hollingsworth has said in an interview: "The new country is the dream of the women, the war is the dream of the men, getting away from here, the country; ..."[4]

There are two dreams at different poles in each act which are then interchanged: the men come back home; the women, however, are still on an arduous voyage with no destination in mind. Wars change people fast; the men and women took chances that they would not have taken in peace time. The play flows along in short swift scenes and has a split focus. Two of the three war brides happen to meet on the train that brings them to their husbands in Canada, and the third meets the older two by chance in a supper-club twenty-five years later; their stories unfold separately.

Ever Loving is a play about immigration and the consequences which shape the lives of the different characters. The men and their girlfriends did not really know each other before they came to Canada, where the gulf between them is enormous. Behind their stories loom culture shock, disillusionment, even despair, which give them and other immigrants the feeling that they are out of context. Margaret Hollingsworth says that

> ... feeling out of context, out of place, motivates me and informs my work. Without it I wouldn't be writing anywhere. It's very important to me and yet at the same time it's unsettling; it's something I have to constantly keep exploring.[5]

In *Ever Loving* the European war brides from Scotland, England and Italy find themselves in different alien contexts, in Hamilton, Regina and Halifax respectively. Basically, it was the American myth together with wartime sentimentality that made them leave their native countries, and the audience gets to know how the brides try to adjust to post World War II Canada – with different results.

The plot covers thirty-five years in the lives of these couples. The Italian woman, Luce, was very rich when she still lived in Milan. She had always wanted to go to New York. Now she is married to Chuck, and finds herself in Halifax, despised by the local Neapolitans as a fascist. This couple is on the cutting edge of culture shock. Luce has gone the farthest from the European world; she ends up as an amateur talent in show business. Her relationship with Chuck fails.

Ruth comes from a village in Scotland; her family cannot boast wealth, but they are caring people. In Hamilton she finds out that her husband is a loser. They live in one room with their six children and can barely survive.

Diana's immigrant experience is similar, and yet different. She met a Ukrainian who kept talking about a promising political career. But when she arrives in Regina he turns out to be a farmer and not the man with a promising future. The two live in a shack with an outhouse. But Diana survives – a cool Englishwoman in the Alberta plains – married to a husband who is at least down-to-earth.

The three women are not driven by unbearable living conditions, but by their own aspirations. Canada is not so much a refuge, but a place of hope, which they think they know about through their husbands. It is the country of the men with whom they have fallen in love, in which – they hope – all their dreams will come true. It is not the threat of Europe that makes them go to Canada; it is the promise of Canada that makes them leave Europe.

Ever Loving is also a play on Canada as an English born playwright's land of residence. The main problem for immigrants from Britain seems to be that they are not regarded as an independent culture in Canada. Most of the other culture groups in Canada have their cultural centres and one day in the year on which they celebrate being who they are. British immigrants, however, are thought of as Canadians because they speak the same language. There seems to be no place to express being 'English'. Maybe this is also due to the English having dominated this country too long. Those who feel strong ties with Britain are most easily accepted in Canada.

52

2. Exploring communication barriers
Vittorio Rossi, *The Chain* (1989)[6]

Vittorio Rossi writes about life in the district of Ville Emard, in Montreal. After two one-act plays (*Little Blood Brother*, 1986, and *Backstreets*, 1987), *The Chain*, written in 1989, was his first full length-play. The title is a reference to the famous Italian 'catenaccio' in soccer, 'which is slang for "catena"' (54), i.e. 'chain'. The implication is that you build a wall, a defense, which – according to Enzo, one of the characters in the play – made Italy the champions of the 1982 World Soccer Championship Finals: 'Our whole game plan was based on defence. Score a goal. Then hold tight' (52).

In Rossi's play 'Chain Landscape Company' is the new name for 'Testa Landscaping' – named after the Testa family. We meet Tullio Testa, who is 55 years old, his wife and their two sons, Guiseppe (or Joe), who is 29, and Massimo, who is in his early twenties. There is also Tullio's sister, Anna Scuro, her 22-year-old daughter Rina and Enzo, her 17-year-old son. The action is steered by Zi (Uncle) Ubaldo, Tullio's brother, who is expected to come over from Italy for Rina's wedding. Tullio wants the fence to be painted before Zi Ubaldo arrives; Enzo is supposed to wear a brand new pair of pants just to greet him at the airport (40). This is astonishing, because we learn that Zi Ubaldo stole his brother Tullio's land; as Joe says: 'All this trouble for a man who stole Daddy's land' (33). There is a great deal of sibling rivalry going on between the two Tullio sons. Massimo was chosen by his father to take over from him as president of the company, and Joe envies his brother the education he has:

> Why don't you ever listen to me? You think you can take a few courses in university...what?...a degree?...and you can run a business. Daddy chose you because of a degree which you don't have yet (75).

Ubaldo remains an offstage character, even after he has arrived in Montreal. He has written a letter in which he tells Anna that he would be willing to offer all the money he took from his brother so that Tullio can save his company (89). Tullio does not want to take it: 'I will not be humiliated in this country by my own brother!' (90) Later on, when he has changed his mind, it is Joe who thinks that it is 'dead dead wrong' for his father to accept Zi Ubaldo's offer, because 'he took your home, Pa' (117). Tullio, however, does not care what is right or wrong any more. He decides to pick up Zi Ubaldo at the airport and wants them all to go to the wedding and be a family. But later Zi Ubaldo leaves the wedding. Joe has told him to his face that he is a crook because he stole the house that Joe was born in (143).

The play's climax, however, is the scene in which Massimo tells his father that it was he who 'fucked the company' and 'quit school', and also gives his reasons:

Because I hate you! I hate you! You make me hate you! I hate this whole fucking family [...] You and your talk of family. Are you serious? That is the biggest lie. There is no such thing as family. It's all lies! (156/57)

The worst thing, however, is that in this family nobody talks, nobody listens. Michael, Rina's fiancé, an outsider on the inside, sums it up like this:

In my family we do a lot of talking. We talk about feelings, but the expression of them – you know?...you get that wall. I come here... (Pause). Things are different. I know what I am dealing with here. Maybe that's not so bad. (164)

Finally, Massimo offers a way out: after all, he was the one who had the company incorporated. And he explains that if they declared themselves bankrupt, the two trucks and the company money would be taken from them. But they would not be bound to the contract any more. Another company could be set up then under someone else's name. 'Testa Landscaping' would not exist any more and could therefore not be sued. The play ends with Tullio saying that he will think about it.

The Chain tells the audience many things about the immigrant experience, which exerts great pressure on people to succeed in a career. Needless to say, an immigrant parent sees things in very practical terms. If you go to school, you learn and you end up with a diploma. Upon graduation you are expected to work. After all, that is the reason why the parents came to the country, to work. Why should it be different with a son?

Vittorio Rossi, the dramatist, was very explicit about all this in a personal communication he sent me. He, who is in his early thirties, has this to say:

There isn't a day that goes by where my mother or father won't remind me of what they experienced in Italy (before they immigrated to Canada in 1956) and at a much younger age. These pressures keep building throughout your teenage years, and the pressure can be enormous.

Rossi considers himself an 'Italian-Canadian', as he says,

who grew to appreciate his surroundings. My parents made their children very aware of their past. We as a family do not live with resentment. Rather we grow stronger and move on.[7]

It is the lure of another 'world' that makes the war brides in *Ever Loving* leave Europe. In Canada, however, they realize that they are out of context. The confrontation of three different women with three different Canadian 'worlds' is the pivotal point of the plot.

In *The Chain* the family is the main motor of life. What happens in the play is almost exclusively set in motion by an offstage character, who still lives in Italy.

3. Native people are like all people
Drew Hayden Taylor, *Someday* (1992)[8]

Drew Hayden Taylor was born in 1962 on the *Curve Lake Reserve,* or rather on *Curve Lake First Nations,* which is the politically correct term now. His father was white. He never knew him. His mother was Ojibway. Drew lived on the reserve with his mother and his mother's family, and later went to college in Toronto.

Someday is the play Drew likes best, because its impact is on a different emotional level than his other works, but also because it incorporates all the things he learned from practical experience. "I have never been trained in theatre. I never wanted to be a playwright. I was kidnapped by theatre," he said to me in an interview.[9] "I had to do a lot of my learning and searching on stage, and some of that went into the making of *Someday.*" When he started writing this play, he knew what he wanted to do and how he wanted to do it. *Someday* shows Drew Hayden Taylor's development as a playwright.

The story is not based on real people, but is nevertheless a true story. It has to do with the so-called 'Scoop-up', i.e. the policy by the Government to give kids away for adoption. *AIM* was the name of a programme in Saskatchewan (Adopt Indian Métis). In 1990 Drew had written a short story for *The Globe and Mail* which he was asked to rewrite as a play. He called the play *Someday.* His girlfriend at the time was an adoptee who had found her natural mother two years before she met Drew. The idea behind the Government policy that urged the taking away of Native children from Native families was to help Canadianize Natives; to stamp out Native culture. Adoption, in terms of what happened in Canada at that time, was something specific and *Someday* is a mirror of what was going on in regions all across Canada.

The play thematizes the sense of frustration which is still prevalent in many Native families. They believe that Native people have always been second-class citizens. Until 1960 they did not have the right to vote. "Now that we have our voice," Drew Hayden Taylor said in the interview, "we can talk about things that take our voice away." He thinks it is anger from two angles: from the family, who had the child ripped out, and from the child, who wanted to know why he or she was taken away. On another level, it is the anger of somebody else deciding that your culture is not viable; that your way of life is not viable. 'Trust us, we'll do better' is what those say who take the Natives' voice away, 'We know best, we'll do better – or suffer the consequences'. As the playwright himself says, the function of *Somehow* is to voice the emotions of Native people, their anger and their frustration. That is what he tries to draw attention to, opening the theatre-goers' eyes to what has been happening over the past 200 years. There are many different examples of why Native people are frustrated. Culture and language are extremely important to Native people. As Drew Hayden Taylor told me, according to a poll in a recent government survey only 3 of 53 Aboriginal languages will survive over the next 25 years: Ojibway, Cree and Inuit.

Native playwrights voice their anger in different ways. Tomson Highway's *The Rez Sisters*[10] is not all that angry on the surface, but underneath it is there – the sense of displacement, of distortedness. Highway tends to lean more to the surreal, whereas Taylor writes what is called 'kitchen-sink drama, reality-based'. He tells stories that happened to him, to his mother, to his family and about what affected these people. 'I want to show that Native people are – except for language and cultural differences – like all people. We cry and laugh and make toast. I want to educate the population at large saying to them: "These are Native people, they react this way. Can you see yourself in this?"'. Taylor believes that Native people are still very romanticized in some countries, but 'romanticism is only one step from racism'.

If there is anything Drew Hayden Taylor is fond of it is the fact that he has often been told that he is a very cross-cultural writer as opposed to those who are culture-specific. Indeed, non-Native people can understand what he is saying. And for that reason he is a very important spokesman of Native people in Canada.

4. The dual origin of a Native
Linda Griffiths, *Jessica* (1981)[11]

Jessica is a play which was written by a non-Native dramatist, and first performed in 1981 in Saskatoon and later, in 1986, staged in a revised version at the *Théâtre Passe Muraille* in Toronto. The play is based on *Halfbreed* (1973), an autobiographical novel by Maria Campbell[12], a Métis from northern Saskatchewan. Its subtitle is *A Theatrical Transformation*. Griffiths has 'transformed' the straightforward, first person narrative into a complex, allegorical play. But 'transformation' implies more than that. Jessica herself goes through a process of transformation from childhood – through rape, prostitution and drug addiction – to her work as a representative for Native interests. Griffiths dramatizes the conflict which has arisen out of the dual origins of a Métis: the Indian background and the culture of the Whites. Jessica has lost her identity in a world in which she is unable to cope. She looks for strength in the inheritance left her by her Métis ancestors.

The play works on three levels, each representing a different experience: on the spiritual level in the world of the gods, on the level of everyday realism, and on an intermediate level where Jessica finds her spiritual mentor in an old Métis woman who establishes contact with the gods and the ancestors. In the theatre the three levels are visually linked so that the characters can move from one level to the other. The whole action is presented as being continually in flux. Human and higher beings are transformed back and forth by the use of masks. *Jessica* is being transformed on the stage during this process into a single play at the centre of which a young Métis woman 'awakes' through the influence of her guiding spirits. She raises the question of whether there is still room in modern society for a primitive belief in the supernatural gods of the ancestors. Jessica discovers that one has to come to terms with oneself in order to survive but that the door to the supernatural world must also be kept slightly ajar if one is to gain strength to live on. By the end of the play she has learned to understand her own existence and her place in the world and the universe.

The autobiographical novel, *Halfbreed*, was by no means the only source that Linda Griffiths drew on. Maria Campbell recounted her own personal stories and revealed some significant details concerning her own life. Together the two women set off on a journey in a covered wagon in search of information. They visited Maria's family, learned about cultural ceremonies, traditions and legends. The impressions they gathered and the experiences they gained during the course of this journey, together with Maria Campbell's stories about her own life, eventually resulted in a patchwork carpet made up of incidents and memories, realistic reports and pure inspiration, fantasy stories and improvisations. The result was *Jessica*. In an interview I conducted with her, Linda Griffiths said

> Maria was the inspiring person. It was inspiring to see her do her work. I was trying to be a career actress in New York, but I was given *Jessica*. I knew I had to consider a less extreme acting career for myself so that I could follow what was my pattern.[13]

5. The juxtaposition of the familiar and the foreign
Dennis Foon, *New (Canadian) Kid* (1992)[14]

Dennis Foon is Canada's foremost playwright for young audiences. His plays have been performed around the world, winning numerous awards. *New Kid* (first produced in 1981 as *New Canadian Kid* and published in 1982) is part of a trilogy, *Invisible Kids* and *Skin* being the other two plays. *Invisible Kids* won Foon the *British Theatre Association* prize for best playwright for young people in 1986. In this play, Foon makes clever use of gibberish. He reverses the immigrant experience by having a young newcomer from 'Homeland', an imaginary country, speak English, while his schoolmates speak gibberish. Nick, the young boy, finds it difficult to cope with his fears about the new culture and language. His classmates taunt him because he is different, and the audience 'hears' the thoughts of the new Canadian, and is at the same time bombarded by a language it cannot understand. The play is very popular for its universal message of tolerance and appreciation for other cultures. In particular, it illustrates the problems and the sense of isolation of non-English-speaking immigrants in Canada. *New Kid* goes back to a workshop at *Lord Roberts School* in Vancouver. 'The children, most immigrants themselves, interviewed other New Canadians who spoke about their own experiences', Foon says in his introduction[15] to the play, 'the resulting transcripts were then edited by the children, and a script, *Immigrant Children Speak*, was developed. This script was then performed by the drama club in the school'. The idea of the Canadians speaking gibberish and the immigrants speaking English came from Jane Howard Baker, the director. It was Foon's hope 'that *New Kid* would give audiences a better understanding and identification with the problems of coming to a country for the first time'. For this reason, he did not choose a specific country, but – as he says – 'tried to focus on the situations I felt seemed to be shared by most immigrants' (7). The word-play used in the gibberish was partly modified as the play travelled from Canada to England, Denmark, Sweden, Hongkong, Singapore, Australia, New Zealand and the United States. In Denmark, for instance, 'the *gerseglob gipper* (=baseball bat) became *Badman-pin-e Robin* (=badminton racquet and birdie)' (8). The gibberish in the printed text can be used as a springboard for inventing a new language in each individual production.

Nick, according to Foon, should be dressed 'completely in shades of green, in contemporary store-bought clothing' (10). The reason for this is: 'The Homelanders should look alien to the Canadians – and to the audience, but their costumes should not be identifiable to any specific country' (10), Foon says. The Canadians should be dressed in other colours which may later become part of the design of Nick's costume when he feels more at home in Canada.

6. Canadians are part of the continent called America
Guillermo Verdecchia, *Fronteras Americanas (American Borders)* (1993)

Guillermo Verdecchia was born in Argentina, came to Canada at a young age, was raised there and saw Argentina again as an adult. In *Fronteras Americanas* he draws on his personal history and especially his own experiences with borders, clichés and stereotypes. The play treats of displacement both from one's surroundings and from oneself, of national otherness, of a person who is lost and looks for his place in the world. Its author retraces his steps and crosses the borders that have been so important in his life. He examines and parodies the Latino stereotypes which, he thinks, impede true perception. As to the term 'Latino', Verdecchia prefers it to 'Hispanic' or 'Chicano'.

> The term 'Latino' has its shortcomings, but seems to me more inclusive than the term 'Hispanic'. 'Hispanic' [...] is a term used in the U.S. for bureaucratic, demographic, ideological and commercial purposes. 'Chicano' refers to something else again. 'Chicano' identity, if I may be so bold, is based in the tension of the border. Neither Mexicans nor

U.S. Americans, 'Chicanos' synthesize to varying degrees Mexican culture and language – including its Indigenous roots – and Anglo-American culture and language.[16]

What are the Latino stereotypes? 'The Latins' are bullfighters, mad dictators, they dance to a special type of guitar music, they do the tango, they are 'real peasants'. In the Canadian production of the play Verdecchia himself is the performer in *Fronteras Americanas*. He begins by welcoming his audience, saying that he is lost and that he supposes that they are lost, too. He talks about borders, especially about the Mexico-U.S. border and asks: 'Where does the U.S. end and Canada begin?' 'A border', Verdecchia says, 'is more than just the division between two countries, it is also the division between two cultures and two memories'. He knows that it can be difficult to cross the border, but he 'will walk backwards so that it looks like I'm heading north'. (21) Soon he adopts an entirely new persona. Now he is Facundo Morales Segundo, whose nickname is Whiteload, also known as 'de Barrio Tiger'. Wearing bandito outfit he tells the audience that they have just crossed the border into Mexico:

Jou hab crossed de border. Why? What you lookin' for? Taco Bell nachos wif 'salsa sauce', cabrón? Forget it gringo. Dere's no pinche Taco Bell for thousands of miles. Here jou eat what I eat and I eat raw jalopeño peppers on dirty, burnt tortillas, wif some calopinto peppers to give it some flavour! (22)

After a while Verdecchia resumes and starts telling his life story. The play develops into a dialogue between the two stage personae, both represented by the same actor. Narrative passages and reflective comments are periodically interrupted by Whiteload, who is an inflated stereotype, the incarnation of a clichéd Latin gang member, and seems to have sprung from drug war movies and Speedy Gonzales caricatures. He is the pivot around which the play revolves; he does not merely represent but also debunks Latino stereotypes, he attacks clichés with clichés. An excerpt from the scene titled 'Dancing', in which he addresses the English-Canadian members in the audience, illustrates this:

Espeaking of music I haf to say dat I love de way you guys dance. I think you Saxons are some of de most interesting dancers on de planet. I lof to go down to the Bamboo; when my friend Ramiro is playing and just watch you guys because you are so free – like nothing gets in your way: not de beat, not de rhythm, nothing.
    What I especially like to watch is like a Saxon guy dancing wif a Latin woman. Like she is out dere and she's smiling and doing a little cu-bop step and she's having a good time and de Saxon guy is like trying really hard to keep up, you know he's making a big effort to move his hips independently of his legs and rib cage and he's flapping his arms like a flamenco dancer. (40)

The use of music and slides contributes to the effect that Verdecchia's play has on the audience: God Save the Queen, Navidad Negra, La Guacamaya,

59

Speedy Gonzales Meets Two Crows From Tacos; a slide of 'An Idiosyncratic History of America', a portrait of Christopher Columbus, passport photos, a photo of Rita Moreno. Quotations from Bolivar, Fuentes and Paz are projected onto a screen. Theatre is being deconstructed. References are made to historical facts and sociological data, and Whiteload is the witty commentator. *Fronteras Americanas* asks the audience to re-evaluate how they look at others and themselves. The play makes them laugh but also get angry. Towards the end, Whiteload calls upon the audience 'to throw out the metaphor of Latin America as North America's "backyard"', and he continues,

> because your backyard is now a border and the metaphor is now made flesh. Mira, I am in your backyard. I live next door, I live upstairs, I live across de street. It's me, your neighbour, your dance partner. (76)

And in the very short last scene ('Going Forward'), Verdecchia has found a way to define his place in the world:

> I am learning to live the border. I have called off the border patrol. I am a hyphenated person but I am not falling apart, I am putting together, I am building a house on the border. (77)

7. Subconscious fears in multi-ethnic neighbourhoods
Judith Thompson, *Lion in the Streets* (1992)[17]

"What links us in our neighbourhood, in our cities and in the world?" This is the question behind Judith Thompson's play *Lion in the Streets*. "I want to focus on an eighteen-year-old Portuguese girl, Isobel, who is based on a little girl in my neighbourhood, who is emotionally troubled, runs around the neighbourhood, screaming. Boys on bicycles circle her like vultures, try to provoke her, throw stones at her, or dirt, call her names. The isolation of this girl seemed to be a perfect kind of microcosm of what happens in a larger context,"[18] at least to Judith Thompson. The six people in the play relate to almost everything in the world. The gentrified upper middle-class people are linked to the paraplegic person living, with only occasional help, in the basement, and to the Portuguese family across the street. They are all part of the multi-ethnic neighbourhoods in the city of Toronto. "There is not much ghettoization any more, which is good. But people do not socialize. It is more a question of class boundaries than ethnic boundaries. The lawyer and the other characters are friendly across the fence, but it does not cross much further. There is a fear in the street. No matter how liberal-thinking people are, there is always separation." These were Thompson's own words in an interview which I conducted with her.

But what is it that links people all over the world? In *Lion in the Streets* we discover people of different class and backgrounds: a middle-class professional couple having a dinner-party. The wife comes running in, and the husband is there with his mistress, a telephone sex girl, a saleswoman. Then we see a day-care worker meeting her friend. And the waiter in the restaurant, a confession, a priest and so on.

Finally, there is the young girl who searches through the neighbourhood in a kind of Odyssey for the 'Lion in the Streets'. She is searching for her killer. She does not know him yet. She was killed by someone seventeen years before the play began. She tries to find succour, to find sanctuary in each of the scenes, and she does link with people in spiritual crises. She is like a little guardian angel. In the final scene she meets her murderer, who has come back to her grave-side. She has a big stick and is about to take revenge and kill him, but at the last minute she drops the stick and says: 'I love you'.

I asked Judith Thompson: "How could you write this? Wouldn't you kill him?" "I just wrote it down," she answered, "and I think I myself wouldn't kill him." "On second thoughts," she continued,

I don't believe in capital punishment, because I don't want to perpetuate the cycle of violence. Look at former Yugoslavia where violence is perpetuated for ever and ever and ever. Look at Germany where people are trying hard to forgive each other and themselves. Forgiving, not forgetting, I guess, is what we need. Speaking of murdering children: as a mother, I don't think I could contain myself, and I am not preaching, either. It simply happened to me!

Judith Thompson was brought up as a Catholic, but is now an agnostic. She has come to the recognition that the forgiveness of sin is preached but never practised in the Christian religion. The child in the play is seeing what is innocent in her killer before he was contaminated by the structures of society. We have to admit that people can murder children or each other everywhere in the world. "It is," as Judith Thompson said in the interview, "it is systemic." And she drew my attention to an event in Montreal, two years ago, when a man murdered fourteen women in the University of Concordia saying "Damned feminists! or something." People got into a big argument over this event. Some argued that he was simply an aberration, which – no doubt – he is, to a certain extent. Most feminists argued that he was nothing but a symptom of a misogynist society. Thompson's belief is that – to a greater or lesser extent – we all seem to condone violence: "It's systemic," she says, "that we can kill a child is contained within our whole society. We are all comparable."

As far as the 'lion' of the title is concerned, it is open to interpretation: there is the 'lion' in our blood vessels; the 'lion' in our streets. When the 'lion' is in the street, there is chaos. Fear of chaos is what links us. The 'lion' – according to Judith Thompson – conveys the idea that "something is going to happen, that the millennium is approaching." "All our deepest fears," the dramatist adds, summing up her play, "that's what links us."

In terms of structure, *Lion in the Streets* is a series of short scenes, of razor-sharp vignettes loosely linked by the device of making one character from each scene a protagonist in the next. These scenes amount to a mosaic of ordinary people trapped in an urban jungle from which there is no escape; a present-day inferno. Isobel flits through every scene like a ghost. She weaves her way through the lives of the people around her until she finds her killer. She points to what may destroy us all: fear, betrayal, hate, forgiveness and love. The scenes over which Isobel hovers, portray the various kinds of violence in our world. Not all of these scenes are plausible in a conventional sense, but they are not meant to be as easily accessible as all that.

8. A lesson to be learned by the living
Raymond Storey, *The Saints and Apostles* (1991)[19]

Angels in America (*Millennium Approaches* and *Perestroika*), two plays by Tony Kushner about AIDS, have been very successful in many countries and have contributed to raising public consciousness about society's current epidemic. The Canadian playwright Raymond Storey's *The Saints and Apostles* is also about AIDS, yet different. It is really a play about human relationships in a time when people are confronted with our contemporary health crisis almost every day. This play is not so much about the sufferers, those who are medically doomed, rather about all the others who seem to be getting tired of hearing about people who have no future on this earth. Storey does not attempt to solve any issues, there is no politics behind his play. 'As a theatre artist', the author says,

> I am woefully aware of the inadequacy of my tools to change the world. I am only a story-teller. All I can offer is to tell a story in as honest and as compelling a manner as I can. The themes that ribbon through my other work: the fear of intimacy, the desperate need to be loved, the quest for dignity, the absolute necessity of hope – are all present here.[20]

Daniel and Michael are the central characters in *The Saints and Apostles*. Daniel is HIV positive, but the story of the play is rather Michael's story. He gets involved with Daniel, whose father is a medical doctor oscillating between his professional obligation to cure his patients, try his best to save their lives, and the recognition that he has a son with something incurable. Michael has a girlfriend, Madelaine (or: Maddie), who has shared the room with him for a long time. She is divorced and loves her gay friend without the condition of sex. She is promiscuous and has no aspiration to marry him. Through her we sense what Storey's play is about.

The play starts with 'The First Testament of Michael', which is about how he and Daniel met. The same events are seen from the opposite side in the final scene which is titled 'The Gospel According to Daniel'. It must be stressed that what happens in between is not so much about those who are HIV Positive but rather about those around who long to be understood or even loved but all too often are reticent when being confronted with the medically doomed, who would need their understanding even more. Storey's message is that only those who go on living can learn. In this play, the sufferers are the 'Saints', they lose everything that they have considered to be valuable in their relationship with the person they love. The survivors, however, dwell too much on putting all the blame on 'them' and on warning each other not to disregard one's moral obligations. They keep talking about 'them' and 'us'. Storey himself, in the leaflet written for *Workshop West Theatre*, had this to say:

Like a lot of my generation, I had an indifferent religious training and like a lot of other thirty-somethings a growing awareness of my morality has been my principal inspiration for spiritual examination. And after having thought long and hard, I have come to accept that I probably do believe in God. But, I cannot believe that the force that created the universe is a narrow-minded avenger, preoccupied with our sex lives. No one is taught a lesson by dying. If a lesson is learned, it is learned by the living. Ennobling the sufferers does not excuse the waste; that still makes me angry. But by thinking of the sufferers as saints, it makes it easier for me to deal with my abiding shame – for not having been angry before.[21]

Raymond Storey, who had already written a play about the sour gas industry and its effect on human beings (*Something in the Wind* (1984)) felt the urge to write about AIDS when, in 1986, he came back to Toronto, where he was born. In those days he heard about quite a number of friends and acquaintances who shortly before had died of what, up to that point, had seemed to him just another of those American 'things'. His play was originally written for an 'AIDS hospice benefit' in Toronto – as a one-person show. But it was developed into a five-character play on the attitudes of modern people towards this epidemic. They need to be confronted which can often be detrimental to love. Their self-possession brings about preconceptions, and their reticence can, or even does, all too easily develop into indifference. If some people suffer and others survive, the survivors can, or even *should*, learn a lesson. "What would you do," Raymond Storey is reported to have asked, "how would you re-define your priorities, if the first person you ever really loved was the most dangerous person in the world for you?"

The eight plays discussed here reflect both specifically Canadian and general issues. What goes on in English-Canadian drama is much more by far than a 'navel gazing'. Needless to say, these plays tell us a great deal about Canadian culture with its special lifestyles and problems. But going 'behind the scenes' Canadian playwrights have increasingly come to realize how important it is for

Canadians to see their country as part of the American continent and define its role in the world of the 1990s.

NOTES

1. Verdecchia, Guillermo, *Fronteras Americanas (American Borders)*. Toronto: Coach House, 1993.
2. Kareda, Urjo, Foreword to *Fronteras Americanas*, 9.
3. Hollingsworth, Margaret, *Ever Loving*. Toronto: Playwrights Canada, 1981.
4. Glaap, Albert-Reiner, Interview with Margaret Hollingsworth. Toronto, 28th May 1984 [Typescript].
5. Wallace, Robert and Zimmerman, Cynthia, *The Work. Conversations with English-Canadian Playwrights*. Toronto: Coach House 1982, 93.
6. Rossi, Vittorio, *The Chain*. Montreal: Nu-Age, 1989.
7. Letter to the author of this article dated 24th March 1992.
8. Taylor, Drew Hayden, *Someday*. Saskatoon: Fifth House, 1993.
9. Glaap, Albert-Reiner, Interview with Drew Hayden Taylor. Toronto, 1993 [Typescript]. The quotations in this part of the article refer to the interview.
10. Highway, Tomson, *The Rez Sisters*. Saskatoon: Fifth House, 1988.
11. Griffiths, Linda, 'Jessica'. In Griffiths, Linda and Campbell, Maria, *The Book of Jessica. A Theatrical Transformation*. Toronto: Coach House, 1989, 113-175.
12. Campbell, Maria, *Halfbreed*. Halifax: Goodread Biographies, 1983.
13. Glaap, Albert-Reiner, Interview with Linda Griffiths. Toronto, 26th August 1988 [Typescript].
14. Foon, Dennis, 'New (Canadian) Kid', in: Foon, Dennis, *New Canadian Kid. Invisible Kids. 2 Plays*. Vancouver: Pulp Press, 1992, pp. 5-55.
15. Foon, *New Kid*, Introduction, 7. Further page references are given in the text.
16. Verdecchia, *Fronteras*, Endnotes, 79.
17. Thompson, Judith, *Lion in the Streets*. Toronto: Coach House, 1992.
18. Glaap, Albert-Reiner, Interview with Judith Thompson. Toronto, June 1993 [Typescript]. The quotations in this part of the article refer to the interview.
19. Storey, Raymond, *The Saints and Apostles*. Toronto: Playwrights Canada, 1991.
20. Raymond Storey, in a leaflet published by *Workshop West Theatre*, Edmonton, 1991.
21. Storey, Leaflet, 1991.

The Canadian Short Story in English: An Alternative Paradigm

Per Winther

Serious scholarly attention to the short story as a separate genre is a relatively short-lived phenomenon, even in countries that pride themselves on a viable short story tradition of long standing. In the U.S., for instance, the short story as a broadly addressed field of critical interest really only dates back to the 1960s. In the 1970s, and especially in the 1980s, this trickle grew into a steady stream of critical works, aligning comments on the short story more and more with general developments in literary theory.[1]

In Canada interest in the short story as a separate genre worthy of critical analysis *per se* has an even shorter history. W.H. New's book, *Dreams of Speech and Violence: The Art of the Short Story in Canada and New Zealand* (Toronto: University of Toronto Press, 1987; henceforth referred to as New), Michelle Gadpaille's *The Canadian Short Story* (Toronto: Oxford University Press, 1988; henceforth referred to as Gadpaille) and David Jackel's chapter on 'Short Fiction' in the fourth volume of the *Literary History of Canada*[2] are the only extensive discussions of the Canadian short story in English that I have been able to locate. There are of course a number of discussions of individual stories, as well as studies of the stories of individual writers, but usually these have a limited, often thematic, focus and are less concerned with the formal characteristics of genre developments.

Of the three critics I mentioned, New is most consistently concerned with form, emphasizing the importance of the sketch and the documentary impulse in the Canadian short story tradition. New's starting point is strongly cultural and the title of his book echoes what he sees as a consistent concern on the part of Canadian writers of short fiction, namely the need to discover a voice which is suited to dealing with the 'specifics of the local experience' (New, 21). Michelle Gadpaille does from time to time make use of categories like realist, modernist, narrative voice, open-ended versus closed, traditional versus experimental stories, but on the whole her study is an author by author survey which discusses these writers' individual characteristics and is less sharply focussed than William New on the formal developments of the genre. David Jackel is interested in the publication history and the reception of the Canadian short story, spending a large section of his article refuting John Metcalf's claim that the history of the Canadian short story really only started with the publication of Hugh Hood's *Flying a Red Kite* in 1962. However, in arguing for the existence of a viable short story tradition before 1960 Jackel does not significantly rewrite the history of the genre, since the earliest short-story writers of note that he finds worthy of mention are Morley Callaghan, Sinclair Ross, Raymond Knister, and Ethel Wilson.

I am convinced by New's argument that from the point of view of short story form what happened before 1920 may indeed provide a useful perspective for the analysis of Canadian genre developments at large. In the following I want to supplement his presentation by applying a paradigm used in the description and analysis of the American short story. The paradigm combines complementary formal categories developed by three different critics, John Gerlach, Valerie Shaw and Suzanne Ferguson.

In his book *Toward the End: Closure and Structure in the American Short Story* (University of Alabama Press, 1985) John Gerlach divides pre-twentieth century stories into two groups, characterized by direct and indirect form respectively. An example of direct form is the typical Edgar Allan Poe story. Here, Gerlach points out, we normally get 'an uninterrupted series of steps from the beginning to the end, without the intrusion of tangential episodes. The expectation of resolution is kept constantly before the reader, and the resolution itself is certain, even if the pace of the approach varies' (16-17). In the *indirect form* the reader readily senses that 'the storyteller is in no hurry to come to an end' (20-21). One knows one is heading for a conclusion of one kind or another, since all narrative must have one, but the ending is of less interest to us than the territory one travels across in order to get there.

In *The Short Story: A Critical Introduction* (London: Longman, 1983) Valery Shaw operates with a complementary set of terms. She distinguishes between 'artful' and 'artless' narration. By artful narration she understands the tradition that goes back to Poe and later Henry James, with their insistence upon the need for a tight structure if a story is to communicate effectively with the reader. Stories in the artless tradition have the appearance of paying little attention to structure. This is not to say that writers of artless stories, like Mark Twain and Bret Harte, are sloppier, artistically speaking, than artful writers like Poe and Henry James. An artless story may be just as carefully crafted as an artful one but the aesthetic objectives of the two differ. The artful story aims for compression and intensity of effect, whereas the artless tradition foregrounds the manner of telling, often seeking to create an impression of spontaneity.[3]

Gerlach sees a continuation of the direct form in twentieth-century stories characterized by *compressed form* (107-18), corresponding to Suzanne

Ferguson's concept of *elliptical plot*.[4] This is a technique of omission, aiming, among other things, at greater readership involvement. Bits and pieces of information are left out for the reader to fill in. Hemingway is of course the prime representative of artists favoring compressed form/elliptical plots.

In the twentieth century the artistic impulse behind indirect form, seeking vertical depth rather than horizontal action, gave rise to *imagist form*, as Gerlach calls it (94-107), corresponding to Suzanne Ferguson's concept of *metaphoric plot*. Sherwood Anderson and Katherine Anne Porter became the main advocates of this development. Rather than featuring linear plot these stories were structured around a central image or a cluster of images, often leading to a non-linear, fragmentary form, disjointed chronology and the like.

Direct and indirect form, artful and artless narration, compressed form/ elliptical plot, imagist form/metaphoric plot – how does this paradigm apply to the Canadian short story?

From the beginning Canadian short fiction was characterized by indirect form and artless narration. As William New has demonstrated fully, the dominant early form of short fiction in Canada was the sketch. Thomas McCulloch's *The Stepsure Letters*[5] from the early 1820s, and Thomas Chandler Haliburton's Sam Slick stories from the 1830s,[6] are satiric sketches, often taking the form of anecdote, but generally doing without the dramatic plot of the contemporary American tale. McCulloch, a Presbyterian Minister, conceived of Mephibosheth Stepsure for clearly didactic reasons; his protagonist preaches Protestant virtues by example, working hard, watching over his money, and he teaches his audience through quick portraits of less virtuous Canadians with very telling names like Parson Drone, Reverend Howl, Deacons Sharp and Scruple, as well as Misters Puff, Soakem, Tipple, M'Cackle and Trotabout. Haliburton fashions many of his sketches as dialogues between Sam Slick, a Yankee peddler travelling through Nova Scotia, and the Canadian narrator, referred to as 'the Squire'. Haliburton allows Slick to ridicule the slowness, in wit as well as in work, of Nova Scotians, while at the same time satirizing American self-glorification and cynicism through the talk and actions of Sam Slick. Haliburton in particular set an important example in foregrounding speech and the act of narration itself; much of the comedy involved in the sketches of *The Clockmaker* is owing to Sam Slick's expert handling of the vernacular, metaphor and anecdote. Artlessness, then, was part of the Canadian short fiction tradition from the beginning.

Even though the characters of McCulloch and Haliburton are invented and their sketches are fictional, their writing, New argues, is nevertheless heavily marked by a documentary impulse. Much of the freshness of Haliburton's fiction is due to his keen attention to sensory detail; both writers are clearly out to make a social comment, choosing the politics and everyday life of the Maritimes for their subject matter. Susanna Moodie's sketches in *Roughing It in the Bush* from 1852 are even more obviously documentary in that they report her own experiences as an immigrant wife in the Canadian backwoods. It might be argued that they do not belong in a survey of short fiction since they are not strictly fictional. But Susanna Moodie was also a writer of novels, and as New has shown, 'in her attempts at documentary she takes on the techniques of story-telling ... [assuming] the role of narrator and the guise of a persona' (33). *Roughing It in the Bush* contains, among other things, a series of character sketches where description is more important than event. Moodie's book has remained a central literary document, not least for Canada's many women writers, and the strong position that the book has held helped to further establish indirect form as the most important mode of Canadian narration before 1900.

The fact that the early sketch was so heavily informed by a documentary impulse in Canada gives rise to a comparison with the sketches by America's first professional writer, Washington Irving, whose *Sketch Book* appeared about the same time as McCulloch's *The Letters of Mephibosheth Stepsure*. The documentary impulse, if present at all, was far weaker south of the border. Washington Irving sought inspiration for his sketches from the European Romantic tradition, especially the German folk-tale. His most famous fictional creation, Rip Van Winkle, is a character out of North-European folklore transported to America. Even though he is placed in a historical context – he goes to sleep before the American Revolution and wakes up after – nevertheless, the documentary impulse is slight.

Why, then, the strength of the documentary impulse at a time when the ruling taste in the United States was the Romantic tale? One may perhaps speculate that it has something to do with a variation in historical tempo in relation to the formation of the two nation states. The U.S. also went through an initial documentary phase, but it came earlier. There was a strong documentary impulse behind much of Colonial literature and that of the Age of Reason. The early settlers had a sense of historical importance, and from day one set out to record the great national experiment in diaries, autobiographies and biographies, histories and essays. As one got into the nineteenth century, U.S.A. was no longer a colony, but a young and confident nation anxious to show the world that they could develop a culture that could match – even improve upon – the culture of Europe. With the American Renaissance, the U.S. became an important presence on the international literary scene, and the individualism and creative freedom of Romanticism matched the historical moment perfectly. Canada was to remain a colony for upwards of another century. Added to that was the very important fact of the country's size and ruggedness. Whereas in the U.S. the wilderness was something to conquer, a frontier holding immense promise, in Canada the absence of an expansionist ideology gave rise to what Northrop Frye has called 'a garrison mentality'.[7] Early Canadians also went into the wilderness, founding the economically important fur and lumber trades, but in Margaret Atwood's influential phrase, 'survival' rather than opportunity became the dominant concern.[8]

Nineteenth-century Canadian short fiction was certainly not completely controlled by indirect form. The Romantic tale had its practitioners, for instance Gilbert Parker, but whereas McCulloch, Haliburton and Moodie are still read with interest today – for reasons of cultural history, to be sure, but also because of the relatively modern character of their narrative strategies – Parker and other writers like him who wrote Romantic tales of adventure for the literary magazines (frequently American) are now largely forgotten.[9] But two other types of story marked by direct form deserve mention. The detective stories of Robert Barr helped to further perfect the form initiated by Poe and his tales of ratiocination.[10] The animal stories by Charles G.D. Roberts and Ernest Thompson Seton, where the animals were endowed with human psychology and motivation, became very popular, inside Canada and internationally. The stories of Roberts and Seton further illustrate the attraction of the documentary impulse. But they were traditionally plotted stories, featuring the struggles of animal and nature, and hence they lent little to the development of short fiction form.

As far as further development of form is concerned, one has to look elsewhere, to Duncan Campbell Scott and his collection of stories *In the Village of Viger* from 1896. With Scott's short fiction the genre takes a measured but important step in the direction of international developments in the short story form. I use the phrase 'measured step' because many of Scott's stories were characterized by a traditionally direct form, relying on adventure and melodrama, especially his stories set in the Canadian Northwest. Even in his Quebec stories, collected in *In the Village of Viger*, there are stories which rely rather heavily on plot; for instance three of them describe courtship and love ('The Wooing of Monsieur Cuerrier', 'No. 68 Rue Alfred de Musset', 'Josephine Labrosse'). But a central 'character' in the collection is the village of Viger itself. These are local color stories in the realist rather than the pastoral sense, describing, among other things, the loss of rural innocence. Scott published some of his earliest short fiction in *Scribner's Magazine*, which frequently published the stories of American local colorists.[11] One of these was Sarah Orne Jewett, a prominent practitioner of indirect form towards the end of the nineteenth century, not least in stories that focussed on internal, psychological response to outward event, as in, for instance, 'A White Heron'.[12] The two most frequently anthologized *Viger* stories are 'The Desjardins' and 'Paul Farlotte', and they, too, foreground mental response to outward event rather than allowing plot itself to be the main focal point of the stories. Hence these stories strive for the vertical depth so characteristic of indirect form, moving slowly and with twists towards the narrative endpoint.

Stephen Leacock, who started publishing his novels and sketches a decade or so after Scott brought out his Viger stories, is clearly a writer in the artless tradition of McCulloch and Haliburton in the sense that his stories so obviously foreground the act of narration itself. They are not so heavily infused with dialect as the sketches of Haliburton, but Leacock makes the first person narrator repeatedly address the reader through asides like 'I think I told you already', and 'Did I tell you ...', giving the stories a firm ring of orality. The predominant tone is that of apparently innocent hyperbole, the narrator claiming for politics and events in Mariposa a historical significance far greater than anything that might ever take place in Ottawa, Washington or London. The effect is one of total irony, leading the reader very quickly to question any statement the narrator makes. Leacock's main contribution to the tradition of short fiction in Canada is the modernization of unreliable narration. In the words of William New, 'After Leacock, it is hard to trust a Canadian narrator again' (New, 64).

New says further that even though Leacock 'mastered the art of tone', he invented no new forms (64). In one sense this is true; Leacock generally stayed within the conventions of the traditional sketch. But in those sketches where an element of plot enters, as in the frequently anthologized 'The Marine Excursion of the Knights of Pythias',[13] Leacock very skillfully manipulates the traditional narrative structure of direct form to further build the irony he is after. From the very beginning the story promises the high drama normally associated with sinking ships, foreshadowing suspense in a manner firmly established by romantic tales and formula story-telling. A main vehicle for the irony is the expert way in which Leacock avoids meeting the readership expectations that direct form normally builds. When in the end the *Mariposa Bell* sinks and sticks on the bottom in six feet of water, only to float back up once the passengers begin to leave the ship, this parodic closing of the story is totally incongruent with the flashy endings of the typical formula story. Another way in which Leacock very adeptly undermines readership expectations for ironic effect is by working the conventions of the sketch, or indirect form, *against* the conventions of direct form. For example, having promised suspenseful plot by pointing to the impending 'steamboat accident' (32) he immediately deflates this drama by going into lengthy and comical reports on the silly circumstances that kept a number of townspeople from going on the excursion in the first place. This kind of play with traditional narrative forms hardly makes Leacock a pioneer when it comes to new developments in short fiction form, but at least in some of his texts he anticipates, however modestly, the mixing of narrative conventions for artistic effect which we associate with postmodernist short fiction.

In the often quoted introduction to his short story anthology of 1928, Raymond Knister remarks about Scott's collection that it 'stands out ... as the most satisfyingly individual contribution to the Canadian short story'.[14] Knister was himself part of the movement that would modernize the Canadian short story in the 1920s, and his admiration for Scott is understandable in that his own stories are characterized by the same attention to human psychology as Scott's *Viger* stories. His topics are similar: isolated characters struggling with adjustments in relation to personal growth and the larger community. His attempts at newness show up in stories which are marked by plotlessness – slice-of-life stories which nevertheless only occasionally make full use of modernist forms. One of the stories in *The Selected Stories of Raymond Knister*,[15] 'Elaine', written in 1925, is an example of Knister's successful venture into compressed form, in Gerlach's terminology, or, as Suzanne Ferguson would call it, elliptical plot. The central plot, the marital infidelity of Elaine's mother, is revealed only gradually through snatches of conversation that Elaine picks up during a street car ride with her mother, forcing the reader to piece the story together as Elaine herself is learning it. The story thus makes full use of one of the central effects of compressed form: creating gaps in the narrative that the reader has to fill in, increasing readership involvement.

'Elaine', then, demonstrates Knister's involvement with modernist fictional techniques. Other stories in the collection, their minimal, slice-of-life plots notwithstanding, are more traditional, shown for instance in a predilection for a formal-sounding, abstract, and latinate diction (see Gadpaille, 20-21). Also some stories, such as the frequently anthologized 'Mist-Green Oats', are marred by intrusive comments by the omniscient narrator in a manner typical of the nineteenth rather than the twentieth century.

Morley Callaghan was, as William New has demonstrated fully, a speech oriented writer (see New, 71-78). Complaining in an interview with Margaret Laurence about the tendency on the part of Canadian writers to sound like the English, Callaghan described his own artistic efforts in terms which echo Sherwood Anderson, and at the same time show Callaghan to be very much in the slice-of-life tradition: 'I am writing after the manner of the modern because it seems to me to create union between the writer and the reader. The story must touch the imagination and must go on touching it. It does not end neatly because life itself does not. It is not decorated because human lives have, in the main, no ornament' (quoted by New, 68). Callaghan has frequently been likened to Hemingway, and in terms of the clipped language his narrators and characters employ, at least in some of his stories, like 'A Girl with Ambition', or 'Lunch Counter', the comparison is apt. But Callaghan seldom opts for compressed form to the extent that Hemingway does in many of his stories, for instance 'Cat in the Rain', and 'Hills Like White Elephants', where the reader has to fill in gaps in the narrative all the time.

Nor does Callaghan cultivate the imagist form that Sherwood Anderson developed in a story like 'Hands' and Katherine Anne Porter in 'The Flowering Judas' or 'The Fig Tree', stories where a central image rather than linear chronology governs the narrative structure. Callaghan's stories are undoubtedly modern in their emphasis on received rather than outward reality, focussing, in the manner of Duncan Campbell Scott and Raymond Knister, on psychological responses to events rather than the events themselves. But Callaghan's plots, rudimentary though they may often be, are usually linear. His short fiction brings to mind the *typical* Sherwood Anderson story, because, as John Gerlach has pointed out, only occasionally did Anderson manage to fully realize the artistic ambitions expressed in his credo, 'form, not plot' (Gerlach 98-99). Generally Anderson's stories have linear plots, like Callaghan's. And even though Callaghan at times may sound like Hemingway in terms of style, more frequently the intensity and wordiness of his internal monologues bring to mind those of Anderson. A story like 'Two Fishermen', for instance, might easily have found a place in a collection like *Winesburg, Ohio*, what with its small town setting, its exploration of the psychology of guilt and betrayal, even having a reporter as protagonist![16]

The titles of Sinclair Ross's most famous stories, 'The Lamp at Noon' and 'The Painted Door', would seem to suggest a movement in the direction of imagist form or metaphoric plots. In both stories the motifs suggested by the title do operate symbolically, in the one case reinforcing the threatening aspect of the sand storm on the prairie which necessitates the lighting of a lamp at noon, in the other case serving as a symbol of the wife's loneliness as she paints a door simply to have something to do while her husband is away during a snowstorm. However, in neither of these stories is the main symbol allowed to control the narrative structure of the text; both have story lines that move chronologically and inexorably through a stormy day and a night leading in both cases to the most forceful closure possible: death. These stories owe their undeniable force less to formal complexity than to a relentless psychological realism, carefully balancing the perspective so that moral judgment becomes difficult; in both stories husband and wife are equally much prisoners of their own psychology and the harsh facts of prairie living. Even in stories where Ross introduces a disjointed chronology, such as 'The Flowers that Killed Him', the structure seems less motivated by a modernist sense of fragmentariness than the need to build traditional suspense: the narrator knows all along that the man who sexually abused and killed his best friends is his own father, but he builds up to the revelation of this fact in the final line by jumping back and forth in time, that way providing the necessary 'explanation' for his father's actions as well as his own decision to kill the father to conceal the crime.

Sinclair Ross's *forte*, then, was traditional storytelling of the first order rather than formal experimentation. Ethel Wilson, who started publishing individual stories not long after Ross (in 1937, even though her stories were not collected until 1961), was clearly more audacious in trying out new short fiction forms. Reading *Mrs. Golightly and Other Stories* (1961; rpt. in the New Canadian Library Series by McClelland and Stewart, 1990) from cover to cover is rather like the experience of working through a collection of short stories by Eudora Welty, or Margaret Atwood: the stories vary greatly in voice, as well as narrative structure, to the point where one is almost tempted into believing that the stories are written by several rather than a single author. Here are traditionally structured, richly ironical, social satires like 'Mrs. Golightly and the First Convention' and 'God Help the Young Fishman'. Two stories are truly artless in orientation, emphasizing narrative voice every bit as much as Haliburton and Leacock. In particular, 'I Just Love Dogs' from 1937 is a masterpiece in unreliable narration, bringing to mind Eudora Welty's 'Why I Live at the P.O.' and 'Petrified Man', but the story 'Until Death Us Do Part' also offers a first person narrator who shifts attention *to* herself, and *away* from what she is trying to describe, both through the attitudes she reveals and in the way she voices her strong opinions about the world around her. Moreover, the collection contains three sketches, documenting further William New's point about the strength of the documentary impulse in Canadian short fiction; one of them, entitled 'On Nimpish Lake', is a brief fictional sketch, almost completely plotless, developing atmosphere and depicting conflicting personal attitudes to the Canadian wilderness in a manner which brings to mind Moodie's *Roughing It in the Bush*; the other two sketches ('The Corner of X and Y Streets' and '"To Keep the Memory of So Worthy a Friend"') are autobiographical, describing trips to London that Wilson and her husband made after World War II. There is also a prime example of the compressed form – the brief story entitled 'The Birds' – where interpretation involves constructing what Suzanne Ferguson calls a 'hypothetical plot' (17), that is, a fuller and more detailed story which can assist the reader in trying to make full sense of the narrator's agitated state of mind as well as the quick references in the text to the death of one of her sister's children. The meaning of the story is amplified by the central image, that of birds repeatedly dashing at the sister's window, meeting a painful death after having their mouths split and bodies broken. That image *is* a central motif in the story, as suggested by the title, but it doesn't quite dictate narrative structure in a way that invites the term imagist form.

The last story in the collection, 'The Window' – arguably Wilson's best short story altogether – is a superb demonstration of the rich artistic possibilities that imagist form may offer. The life of Mr. Willy, the story's protagonist, is marked by stasis, a life lived without aim. His inertia is nicely underscored by the absence of a linear plot. Throughout the story meaning is continuously built around the large window through which Willy is allowed to contemplate – from a distance – the life of Vancouver harbor, and the mountains opposite, which he now is too old to climb. Willy, who has escaped to British Columbia from his wife still living in England, cultivates his seclusion. During daytime the window enables him to look out, 'no people to spoil [the] fine view' (202). At night, however, the window turns into a mirror, revealing his loneliness even to himself. The window is also an emblem of the protagonist's human vulnerability, as it offers a burglar every opportunity to spy on the protagonist, awaiting the proper moment for his strike. Inside, in his living room, Mr. Willy is often lost in reflection over the wall that stands between him and belief in the meaning of creation. These, and other meanings connected with windows in general and that of Mr. Willy in particular, keep troubling both him and the reader in a manner typical of stories characterized by imagist form.

"Your work is long on style and short on story," Wilson's editor once told her, pressing her for stories with, in Wilson's own phrase, 'the Big Bow Wow' (Stouck, 'Afterword', 212). Refusing to comply, Wilson instead kept turning out stories in the modernist vein which now is standard in the contemporary short story, in Canada as well as in the U.S.. The year after *Mrs. Golightly and Other Stories* appeared, Hugh Hood published *Flying a Red Kite*, an event claimed by John Metcalf to mark 'the birth' of the Canadian short story.[17] The merits of that observation are obviously open to question, and I will return to this more fully towards the end of this essay. However, Metcalf was clearly right in noting that the 1960s witnessed a flowering of Canadian literary talent, not least in short fiction. One of the things that characterizes the short story scene during the last three decades is great formal variety – between writers, but also, as in Ethel Wilson's case, inside the short fiction by individual practitioners of the genre.

One undeniably important group is the one championed by John Metcalf in *Kicking Against the Pricks* (169) and whose stories and comments on writing he collected, along with some of his own, in *Making It New: Contemporary Canadian Stories* (1982). Taking no risks, he presented them in alphabetical order: Clark Blaise, Mavis Gallant, Hugh Hood, Norman Levine, Alice Munro, and Leon Rooke. These writers could be said, broadly, to move within the formal parameters of – to use David Jackel's highly apt term – modernist realism. Further names could be added to such a list: Margaret Laurence, Alistair McLeod, Audrey Thomas, W.D. Valgardson, some of Atwood's stories. In the concept of modernist realism should be included literary expressionism and impressionism; these movements brought increased attention to the subjective element, and important vehicles for these developments were the compressed and imagist form, which so dominated new developments in the American short story during the first decades of the century. These narrative forms are still very much alive indeed, in the U.S. as well as in Canada. Among the writers I just mentioned, we find both represented. Compressed form, with its preference for syntagmatically structured stories, but where important elements of the linear plot are left to inference, seems possibly to be the less frequently favored of the two. However, this mode is the one chosen for what George Bowering calls the mythic deconstructions of Sheila Watson and Audrey Thomas in 'Antigone' and 'Rapunzel', as well as Alice Munro's 'Walker Brothers Cowboy', and Clark Blaise's 'The Bridge'; these are all stories where the author's economy with narrative detail compels readers to fill in gaps, drives them, in keeping with modernist aesthetics, into what reception theorists refer to as active co-authoring of texts.

A way to create *conceptual* gaps is through imagist form. A clear-cut example of this is Atwood's 'The Sin-Eater' (Atwood and Weaver, 315-24) where the narrator forgoes linear chronology and instead structures the narrative around the central image of sin-eating, a practice stemming from old Welsh funeral customs, but here placed in the context of psychotherapy. The narrator's analyst introduces the notion to illustrate a therapeutical strategy, then goes off and dies, leaving his patient in emotional turmoil. The whole story is given narrative focus through the first person narrator's repeated examinations of the possible meanings of the motif in her own life. As is usual with indirect form, especially when the subject is emotional and intellectual confusion, the structure is paradigmatic rather than syntagmatic, developed according to a logic of association rather than causality.

A quite recent illustration of the fact that the tradition of imagist form is alive and well in Canada, is the title story of Leon Rooke's *Who Do You Love?* (Toronto: McClelland and Stewart, 1992). The story has a non-linear, associative structure built around a haunting refrain, that of the narrator's basically non-caring mother torturing him by forcing him again and again to choose between herself and the boy's father: "Who do you love most, him or me?" The story is told in retrospect by an adult narrator, who at his mother's death-bed relives those moments, recalling them non-chronologically in snatches, summoning up a childhood lived in squalor and deprivation.

A trend-setting modulation on the structure of imagist form takes place in a series of stories by Alice Munro. I am thinking of those stories of hers where plot, often quite minimal, is non-chronological, as in imagist form, and yet there is no easily recognizable central image; instead mood and atmosphere dictate the story's structure. 'The Peace of Utrecht' (in *Dance of the Happy Shades*, 1968) is such a story. The story is slow to declare the real issue: the two daughters' handling of guilt after the death of their severely handicapped mother. The narrator, the daughter who returns after many years, works her way slowly towards a facing of that issue, and the disrupted plot structure imitates the hesitant mental process she undergoes in facing up to her guilt.

The paradigm I have been examining would seem to lose its relevance in a discussion of post-modernist short fiction, at least that part of post-modernism which is in open rebellion against traditional approaches to narration, be it 'old' realism or modernist realism. Not necessarily so. Many of the so-called anti-stories in Canada, as well as in the U.S., in the 70s and the 80s wanted to focus upon what were considered the inadequacies, philosophical and otherwise, of traditional narrative forms. One of their strategies was to overtly frustrate, or else make fun of, readership expectations. This they would of course find difficult to do, unless the readers were reasonably conscious of how traditional narratives are structured. When for instance Matt Cohen, in

'The Empty Room',[18] offers us multiple versions of a short story with roughly the same opening sentence, 'She was wearing a khaki shirt, her hair bleached blond by the sun fell long and free past her shoulders', the point of his parody would be lost on readers insensitive to the conventions of the type of story he is parodying. Similarly, George Bowering presupposes familiarity with the aesthetic conventions of modernist direct form when he, in the short story entitled 'A Short Story' (ibid. 143-52), breaks up his narrative with sub-headings like 'Setting, Characters, Point of View, Plot' and so on. Therefore, even though the paradigm as such does not describe the manifestations of 'surfiction' as practiced by Cohen, Bowering, Dave Godfrey, and Ray Smith, it nevertheless may help readers to focus more sharply on where these writers deviate from established narrative norms.

Linda Hutcheon and others have shown that another important aspect of Canadian post-modernism is so-called overwriting of master narratives. Thus postmodernism is a vehicle for questioning received notions of history as well as traditional storytelling. I am thinking here of stories marked by a less overt experimentation than the one pursued by the surfictionists, as in Rudy Wiebe's frequently anthologized 'Where Is the Voice Coming From?'. The opening line of Wiebe's text, 'The problem is to make the story' (Atwood and Weaver, 270), has become a leitmotif in several recent short stories. It is remarkable that in the Fifth Series of Robert Weaver's *Canadian Short Stories* (Toronto: Oxford University Press, 1992) no less than three texts thematize this particular problem: Alice Munro's 'Menesetung', W.D. Valgardson's 'The Cave', and a second instance of short fiction overwriting received history by Rudy Wiebe, entitled 'A Night in Fort Pitt OR (IF YOU PREFER) The Only Perfect Communists in the World'. Even though all these texts adhere to a linear chronology, and thus share many features with traditionally syntagmatic narratives, the metafictional element, that is, the elaborations of the epistemological status of the stories, cause a lateral ideational movement which work in opposition to the forward thrust of linearity, much in the manner of stories characterized by indirect form.

This widespread fondness for a post-modernist deconstruction of historiography and traditional story-telling warrants two observations. For one thing the relative frequency of this type of narrative among recent short stories further attests to the prominence of the documentary impulse in Canadian short fiction which New has pointed to. Implicit in the motivation to look again at received versions of the nation's history is obviously a desire to come to terms with that history, to understand the present through a reinterpretation of the past.

My second observation I want to link to a major point implicit in what I have been saying earlier in this essay, which, by way of conclusion, I would like to make explicit. When John Metcalf used Hugh Hood's *Flying a Red Kite* as a yardstick for all Canadian short fiction, he was privileging a type of story belonging to what Frank Davey has aptly referred to as the Anglo-American, canonic, unified and autotelic tradition.[19] In terms of narrative form, the four stories by Wiebe, Valgardson and Munro just mentioned work with a different set of codes; even though Munro in most stories *is* what one would call a canonical writer (in the modernist rather than the Poe sense of the word), this particular story by her represents, it seems to me, a departure from the narrative forms she normally favors. It could be argued that a narrative platform for the four stories under discussion here was prepared for already in the nineteenth century; all four texts are definitely characterized by indirect form. In all four there are elements of the sketch as well as the personal essay, once more bringing to mind the example of Susanna Moodie, even though, admittedly, her agenda was a different one.

Which brings me to my conclusion. The Canadian short story tradition has had a separate focus and a rhythm all its own. Direct form, for instance, never took on the canonical authority that it did in the United States. Paradoxically, this situation seems to have prepared Canadian short fiction particularly well for the formal flexibility which more than anything else characterizes the contemporary short story and which makes the Canadian short story such a particularly healthy genre, nationally as well as internationally.

NOTES

1. For a bibliographical survey of recent work in short story theory, see Susan Lohafer and Jo Ellyn Clarey (eds.), *Short Story Theory at a Crossroad.* Baton Rouge: Louisiana State University Press, 1989, 329-36.
2. In W.H. New (ed.), *Literary History of Canada: Canadian Literature in English.* Toronto: University of Toronto Press, 1990, 46-72.
3. Shaw develops and illustrates these categories in Chapters 3 and 4 of her study.
4. Suzanne C. Ferguson, 'Defining the Short Story: Impressionism and Form', *Modern Fiction Studies* 28, Spring 1982, 13-24.
5. McCullogh published these serially in *Acadian Recorder* in 1921-21, then collected them in *The Letters of Mephibosheth Stepsure* (Halifax, 1862). The stories were republished as *The Stepsure Letters*, edited by Northrop Frye as part of The New Canadian Library Series in 1960.
6. Collected as *The Clockmaker.* First series, Halifax, 1836; second and third series, London, 1838, 1840.
7. See *The Bush Garden.* Toronto: Anansi, 1971, passim.
8. In *Survival.* Toronto: Anansi, 1972, passim. Linda Hutcheon, among others, has pointed out that this pattern has persisted into the postmodernist period. Whereas a typical feature of American postmodernism is the deconstruction of national myths and identity, this tendency is nearly absent in the writings of Canadian postmodernists. The reason for this, argues Hutcheon, is that Canadian culture has yet to arrive at a 'deconstructable' sense of national identity (*The Canadian Postmodern: A Study of Contemporary English-Canadian Fiction.* Toronto: Oxford University Press, 1988, 6).
9. See New, 42-45.

10. 'Barr was one of the creators of the detective story, and his story, "The Absent-minded Coterie," is still frequently anthologized and regarded widely as one of the three or four best detective stories ever written' (David Arnason, 'The Historical Development of the Canadian Short Story', *Recherches Anglaises et Americaines* 16, 1983, 162).

11. See James Doyle, 'Duncan Campbell Scott and American Literature', in: K.P. Stich, ed., *The Duncan Campbell Scott Symposium*. Ottawa: The University of Ottawa Press, 1980, 104.

12. For a discussion of Jewett's use of indirect form, see Gerlach, 66-69.

13. First published in *The Sunshine Sketches of a Little Town* (1912); rpt. in Margaret Atwood and Robert Weaver, *The Oxford Book of Canadian Short Stories*. Toronto: Oxford University Press, 1988, 29-44.

14. Raymond Knister (ed.), 'Introduction', *Canadian Short Stories*, 1928; quoted by New in *Dreams*, 55, and Gadpaille, 18.

15. Michael Gnarowski, ed., *The Selected Stories of Raymond Knister*. Ottawa: University of Ottawa Press, 1972.

16. For a full discussion on the stylistic similarities in the stories of Sherwood Anderson and those of Morley Callaghan, see New, 71-77.

17. John Metcalf, *Kicking Against the Pricks*. Downsview, Ontario: ECW Press, 1982, 149.

18. In George Bowering (ed.), *Fiction of Contemporary Canada*. Toronto: The Coach House Press, 1980, 155-60.

19. Frank Davey, 'Genre Subversion and the Canadian Short Story', *Recherches Anglaises et Americaines* 20, 1987, 10.

Contemporary Native Literature in Canada and 'The Voice of the Mother'

Hartmut Lutz

When we talk about Contemporary Native Literature in Canada, we should remember that the literature of First Nations people, written down in English or French, or any Native language, is a new mode of expression. Originally, and to this day, First Nations people transmit/ted their history, their myths, fables, philosophy and verbal art forms by word of mouth, passing it on from generation to generation with an accuracy and tenacity that is both admirable and astounding for us who are used to almost exclusively literate (or electronic) forms of information transmission. Through the oral tradition, First Nations people learned who they are, where their ancestors came from, who all other beings around them are, how to behave, what to do and what not to do. In short: the oral tradition, encompassing both the sacred and the profane, lies at the heart of the cultural identity of Native nations.

It is a very vulnerable existence, however, because, as Basil Johnston, the Anishinabe (Ojibway) scholar and writer said, the oral tradition is removed only 'one generation from extinction' (Johnston 1990). If only one generation in the chain of cultural transmission breaks down or is removed from the process by cultural alienation such as enforced acculturation or other forms of ethnocide, the whole chain breaks apart and the oral tradition may be lost forever. When we think of the banning of Native languages in residential schools, the separation of children from their parents, the destruction of Native traditions by the missionary onslaught, the economic uprooting of Native communities, and the removal of many from their ancestral territories, we may begin to understand and lament the irreparable losses in lives and lifestyles most Native cultures have suffered. No wonder that Native people fought hard to preserve as much as they could, often by taking underground their rituals and ceremonies, or by hiding children from school agents. So, despite the onslaught, much has survived, and today Native writers are the rich inheritors of a vibrant tradition from which they can draw.

Out of originally twelve linguistic stocks in Canada, as diverse as Finno-Ugrian and Indo-European, branching out in over fifty different languages, today only three larger Native languages stand a chance of surviving also as literate languages, either in the Roman alphabet or in syllabics. These are Inuktitut, Cree and Ojibway, the latter two belonging to the same Algonquin stock. While other languages are also surviving in smaller communities, English, and to a far lesser extent French, has become the predominant linguistic means of international relations among First Nations peoples and in their dealings with the non-Native world. Accordingly, today the oral tradition is carried on among Indians, Inuit and Métis people in various forms, in tribal languages, Inuktitut or Mitchif, or, increasingly, in English. Moreover, English has also become the *lingua franca* of contemporary Native literary expression.

In July 1992 the first 'Festival of North American Native Writers' at the University of Oklahoma brought together over two hundred Native storytellers, poets, prose fiction writers, dramatists, performers, scholars and critics from Canada, the United States, the Pacific and Latin America, to celebrate the flowering of Native literatures today. Commemorating, or rather critiquing, Columbus' mistaken voyage to India, the festival was entitled 'Returning the Gift', i.e. a thanksgiving for the gift of literacy, despite all the other negative effects of conquest and colonization. The generosity and gentleness of this title humbles all Europeans, both here in Europe and in the European diaspora throughout the world.

1. The Sixties and Seventies

Before 1960 in Canada there was very little written literature by Native authors. The lone example of Emily Pauline Johnson's (Tekahionwake) publications in the early 20th century stresses the absence of printed texts by Native authors rather than fills the void. While Native people continued their Oral Tradition throughout the century that lies between treaty making and the present, there are next to no books by Native authors until the late Sixties, when Canadian Natives were made citizens of Canada and received the right to vote. Even then, texts stemming from the oral tradition were usually collected, translated and often heavily edited by non-Native missionaries, anthropologists and hobbyists. Moreover, they tended to represent Native 'tales' from the igloo, the smokehouse or the campfire as 'quaint' or 'exotic', fit for ethnological inquiry perhaps, but not for serious literary study. Carl F. Klinck's *Literary History of Canada* (vol. III, 1965ff) lists a few Native texts under 'Children's Literature.'

There were several attempts, however, in the late Sixties to overcome the colonial domination of Native authors by non-Native collectors and editors. Among these, George Clutesi's achievements deserve the greatest admiration.

In 1967 he published *Son of Raven, Son of Deer: Fables of the Tse-Shaht People*, and two years later his celebrated *Potlatch* came out (Clutesi 1967; 1969). The first is a collection of tales from the oral tradition of his Nootka nation, the second book gives an 'eyewitness-account' of the elaborate ceremony that lies at the heart of West Coast Native cultures. He gives the account 'with trepidation' and 'lingering fear', because when he attended the potlatch, it was still banned under the Indian Act, like other Native religious ceremonies. Harold Cardinal's *The Unjust Society* (1969) caught the spirit of political change in a powerful attack on dominant society beyond 'the buckskin curtain'. But in general, the Sixties were not inducive to literary production, because for First Nations people they were 'bread and butter years', as Howard Adams explained retrospectively in an interview in 1991, stating that 'you cannot talk culture or literature when you are hungry' (Adams 'Interview', 137).

In the Seventies Native authors began writing down their own (his)stories and expressing their views on Canadian society. Seminal books were Harold Cardinal's aforementioned *The Unjust Society* (1969), Maria Campbell's *Halfbreed* (1973), Howard Adams' *Prison of Grass* (1975) and Lee Maracle's *Bobbi Lee: Indian Rebel* (1975). Until recently these texts were dismissed, however, as 'protest literature' (*Oxford Companion to Canadian Literature*, 1983), not really considered part of Canadian 'Literature' as defined by English Departments and literary scholars in mainstream. However, this attitude is beginning to change dramatically, due to the quality and proliferation of Native texts on the market. Such a proliferation, as in all post-colonial literatures, will pave the way for the development of new art forms and modes of expression, or, as Northrop Frye put it with regards to 'Can Lit': 'Such a quantitative increase eventually makes for a qualitative change:...'(Frye 1976:318).

2. The Flowering of Native Literature in the Eighties and Nineties

In the 1980s Native women in Canada began writing themselves into Canadian letters. Beatrice Culleton's *In Search of April Raintree* (1984), Jeannette Armstrong's *Slash* (1985), Ruby Slipperjack's *Honour the Sun* (1987), and Joan Crate's *Breathing Water* (1990) are first novels by a new generation of authors addressing the lives of Métis and Indian people in Canada today. Lee Maracle's *I Am Woman* (1988) went beyond the format of the novel, combining West Coast Big House oratory with poetry, memoir, and political essay in a book on oppression and liberation which presents 'theory and philosophy... through story and poetry' (Maracle 1979:171). Two years later, her as-told-to autobiography, *Bobbi Lee: Indian Rebel*, originally published in 1975, came out in a new edition by Women's Press, prefaced by a powerful essay reflecting the colonial structure which the then current Oka standoff exposed. In 1991 her collection of stories, *Sojourner's Truth*, harked back to the storytelling she experienced as a child, and in 1992 her second novel, *Sundogs*, gave a Native perspective of the hot Canadian summer of 1990, when Elijah Harper brought down Meech Lake, and First Nations all over the continent rose in support of the Mohawk struggle at Oka.

Lenore Keeshig-Tobias, co-founder of the Toronto based Committee to Re-Establish the *Trickster*, began editing her magazine *Trickster* in 1988, in which she published works by new and established Native writers. At the same time Native women are also engaged in publishing anthologies, often in cross-cultural coalitions with non-Native women. Books such as *Telling It: Women and Language Across Cultures* (Maracle et.al. 1990), *Writing the Circle* (Perrault/Vance et al. 1990), *Living the Changes* (Turner 1990) and *Sounding Differences* (Williamson 1993) bear witness to the involvement of authors like Jeannette Armstrong, Lee Maracle, and Emma LaRocque in literary/political alliances even with Euro-Canadian writers/editors. Often, such multi-ethnic cooperation across the boundaries of class and race is very painful, evoking feelings of guilt and shame on the non-Native side, and anger and frustration on the other. Maria Campbell's and Linda Griffith's *Book of Jessica* (Campbell/Griffiths 1989) demonstrates such a process in great and painstaking detail. It led to the Métis author's resolution, 'I'll never do it again!' (Campbell 1991:57). The conflict about 'appropriation' (Lutz 1990; Lutz 1993) looms large in all Native writing, and after centuries of colonial dispossession and oppression, Native people have learned to grow suspicious of outside 'help' or interest.

In this context, anthologies collected, edited and published entirely by Native people themselves are vitally important, and Native presses (Pemmican, Theytus) address this need. Theytus Books and the first International School of Native Writing at the Okanagan nation's En'Owkin Center in Penticton, B.C., directed by Jeannette Armstrong, have produced several such anthologies, *Seventh Generation*, a collection of poetry (Hodgson 1989), and since 1990 their annual *Gatherings: A Journal of First North American Peoples*, containing writings by both students and more established Native authors. Similarly, Pemmican Press published *Our Bit of Truth* (Grant 1990), a collection of texts by Canadian First Nations authors which the non-Native editor used successfully in her Native Literature classes at Brandon University. Other anthologies coming out of non-Native academia are: since 1985, *Whetstone Magazine*, published by the University of Lethbridge English Department, and in 1990 the University of British Columbia celebrated its 75th anniversary with a double issue of Canadian Literature dedicated to Native authors in Canada, which also came out as a separate book (New 1990). The most comprehensive and most representative *Anthology of Canadian Native Literature in English* is a Native/non-Native collaboration (Moses/Goldie 1992).

Increased scholarly attention also reflects the growth of Native writing. In 1990, Oxford University Press published the first book length survey, *Native*

Literature in Canada by Penny Petrone, who had also edited earlier anthologies of Native literature: *First People, First Voices* (1983), and *Northern Voices* (1988). My own collection of *Conversations With* [eighteen] *Canadian Native Authors* came out under the title *Contemporary Challenges* in 1991, and in 1992 we published in the Osnabrück OBEMA-series an anthology of Indian and Métis short stories and poems under the title *Four Feathers*. Julia Emberley's and Janice Williamson's studies (both 1993) bear witness to the fact that non-Native feminist scholars are critically coming to terms with earlier (appropriatory) attention given Native women writers by outsiders.

Next to the Cree dramatist Tomson Highway, the university professor Tom King, himself a Cherokee-Greek-German from California, has acquired international recognition as the most successful Native promoter and writer of First Nations Literature in Canada. In 1987 Thomas King guest-edited a special 'Native' volume for *Canadian Fiction Magazine*, which he later collected into the first anthology of Native short stories *All My Relations* (1990). His first novel, *Medicine River*, came out in hardback in the spring of 1990, and went into a Penguin paperback edition the same year. He is currently working on another anthology and in 1993 he published a second novel, *Green Grass, Running Water*, which takes Canadian First Nations Literature into the intertextual sophistication and structural intricacies of postmodernism.

Other authors also had breakthroughs in very recent years. Jordan Wheeler's first monograph, *Brothers in Arms*, containing three novellas, established his name among Native authors in Canada in 1989. Several poets, female and male, came out with their own books in the same period: Bruce Chester's *Paper Radio* (1986), *Rita Joe's Song of Eskasoni* (1988), Beth Cuthand's *Horsedance to Emerald Mountain* (1987) and *Voices in the Waterfall* (1989), Joan Crate's *Pale as Real Ladies*, Annharte's *Being on the Moon*, Wayne Keon's *Sweetgrass II*, Daniel David Moses' *The White Line* (all in 1990), Connie Fife's *Beneath the Naked Sun* (1992). This busy period in Native Literature production witnessed both the emergence of new writers and the continuance of older more established ones. Posthumously, Pauline Johnson's *Moccasin Maker* was re-edited by A. LaVonne Brown Ruoff in 1987, Basil Johnston moved from rendering the oral tradition to writing a personal and collective memoir of his generation in *Indian Schooldays* (1988), Rita Joe republished her first book of poetry privately, and Howard Adams' classic *Prison of Grass* came out in a revised and updated edition in 1990.

3. Native Drama and New Forms and Media

In the performing arts, Canada has for years been represented internationally by Native actors and playwrights. The two Oscar nominations Canadian actors have received in the last twenty-five years both went to Native actors: Chief Dan George in *Little Big Man* (1971) and Graham Greene in *Dances with Wolves* (1991). Micmac-Métis singer Willie Dunn's record *Willie Dunn* came out in the early seventies and was re-released in Germany several years later; singers/actresses Buffy Sainte-Marie and Alanis Obomsawin enjoy a stable international reputation. Songs from Kashtin, a Native two-man band from the Maritimes, even made it into the European charts. There are hundreds of tape recordings of both modern pop, pow-wow and traditional music available at Indian traders and Native Culture centers in Canada. Native people are using non-literary forms of preserving and disseminating Native verbal art to a much larger degree, it seems, than we do in Europe. Native authors network and cooperate on putting on tape to traditional or modern music texts from poetry, politics and prose fiction, so as to reach the young. One of the producers and editors of such projects, the poet Greg Young Ing, explained:

> Music is something that is more entertaining than straight reading, and something that you can listen to at leisure while you are carving, or cooking, or whatever. It is also something that young people listen to a lot. A lot of people probably will not be so likely to pick up a book and read, as they would be to put on some music. When music is added to poetry, it also enhances the experience of the word, and it adds another dimension to it. (Young-Ing 1991:117)

During readings and story telling sessions, Native authors from Canada often accompany their literature by using the drum, by acting out stories and even by singing. The 'performance' character, the multi-medial creative and exuberantly active approach of Native writers was a prominent Canadian contribution to the 'Returning the Gift Festival' in Oklahoma in the summer of 1992.

In no other field have Native authors from Canada been so successful internationally as in the performing arts. Native drama has repeatedly been chosen to represent Canadian culture abroad: George Kenny's *October Stranger* (Monaco 1978), Tomson Highway's *The Rez Sisters* (Edinburgh 1988) and Evan Adams' *Dreams of Sheep* (Sydney, Australia, 1990). It is, above all, in the field of drama that Native writers have found recognition, starting with Tomson Highway's *Rez Sisters* tour of Canada in the fall of 1987 and followed by an abundance of new plays by other playwrights, including, most prominently, Daniel David Moses, Drew Hayden Taylor (both 1990), Beatrice Culleton (1992/93), Greg Daniels and Eugene Stickland (1990), and actresses/playwrights Shirley Cheechoo (1993), Margo Kane (1989/92) and Monique Mojica (1991). Besides, there are numerous Native people, Métis, Indian and Inuit, working in film and video, both as script writers, performers, directors, producers or as journalists.

4. 'Voice of the Mother'

If literature indeed provides 'the major avenue for exploring (the ethnic individual's) ... relationship to family heritage, ethnic community, ethnic mythology and ... society' (Staub 1990:65), then Canadian Native authors offer their readers views of a reality far more complex than that which a European linear, causal mode of perception may usually grasp. Native authors in Canada have access to cultural traditions which enabled their ancestors to survive under extreme conditions in ways that not only enhanced the lives of all members of their respective societies, but that enabled their co-existence in mutual respect with all their relations, whether they were rocks, plants, four-legged, winged, finned or scaled. This dimension of Native writing cannot be expounded extensively, nor even comprehensively, in a short written paper – if ever at all in English. Instead, a short quote from poet and playwright Daniel David Moses may suffice here. When asked for his reasons for becoming involved in editing the *Anthology of Canadian Native Literature in English*, he explained to his co-editor Terry Goldie:

> ... I think the ideas presented by Native people are particularly important. I think Native people have a sense of a larger responsibility to the planet, whether we come at it just from the idea that Native traditions honour the environment as a mother, or whether we come at it from the idea that we're looked at as people who should have those ideas and therefore we're allowed to have them. (Moses/Goldie 1992:xii)

And referring to the relationship between Native literature and the mainstream and the dangers of absorption and appropriation or tokenization and ghettoiza-tion he said: 'My image of that mainstream is that it is pretty wide but it's spiritually shallow. I don't think we are worried about being "subsumed". If we become part of that mainstream we're going to be the deep currents' (Moses/Goldie 1992:xiv). This statement by a Native poet and dramatist is the proud assertion of the inherent value of the Native Voice, which carries, as lit-erary scholar and critic Arnold Krupat put it, 'an ecosystemic, nonanthropocen-tric perspective on the world that we may at last be coming to see .... as being centrally rather than marginally important to human survival' (Krupat 1989:55).

In Canada the ties of modern Native Literature to the Oral Tradition seem far stronger than in the United States. Native literatures and languages, in turn, are tied to the land (as Maria Campbell, Ruby Slipperjack, Tomson Highway and others stress in their interviews). But how can Western literary criticism accommodate this relationship? How will critical theory deal with a statement like Maria Campbell's comment that the English language in Canada has 'lost the Mother' (Campbell 1991:49ff)?

Unless such a comment is brushed aside as 'non-academic' in a gesture of colonial arrogance and/or academic provincialism, it posits a serious challenge to contemporary academia. It would require an amount of cross-cultural learning on the side of non-Natives, which could seriously question (and thereby 'impede') the progress of literary-theory-development in mainstream academia, where, as Black critic Barbara Christian and Chicana critic and writer Gloria Anzaldúa stress repeatedly, literary scholarship and literary scholars have removed themselves further and further from the literary texts and the voice, the intentions, the social conditions and the history of its authors – particularly, of authors of Color. Such criticism, I feel, is very pertinent to what we are doing, and I think it behooves us to stop to listen and think, before developing further sophisticated theories along the lines of Western traditions of philosophy.

At a Canadian Studies conference at Aarhus in 1992, Lenore Keeshig-Tobias, the Anishnabe storyteller, writer, critic and cultural activist from Ontario, took up the definition of Native Literature as being the Voice of the Mother, and she explained in a much more down to 'earth' and concrete fashion: since mothers give birth to children and raise them, since most children hear the voices of their mothers first, singing to them, talking to them, telling them stories and teaching them, the voice of the mother encodes the first and most important exposure of a Native child to the oral tradition. Thus, in Native literature, 'the Voice of the Mother' carries the earliest and most often heard expression of Native traditions passed for generations from the grandmothers to the mothers, daughters and granddaughters. That this is so, has to do with traditional gender roles and modes of child rearing as well as with the importance of women as carriers of cultures and bearers of life.

Of the many contemporary First Nations authors in Canada who hear and express in their writings the Voice of the Mother, the Okanagan teacher, writer and activist Jeannette Armstrong stands out as the internationally most widely travelled representative of that Voice. In her writing she brings together the strands of various collective traditions while rooting her literature and all her educational and political work in general in her Okanagan culture, finding in the geographically and culturally specific tribal tradition the answers to questions that are global and universal.

Leaving aside Beatrice Culleton's fictionalized Métis-autobiography *In Search of April Raintree*, the first First Nations novel in Canada is Jeannette Armstrong's *Slash* published in 1985. The novel goes beyond the personal and individual and portrays a collective Native history of the last twenty-five years in North America, giving an account of the American Indian Movement and related activities in Canada through the eyes of a male protagonist. Thomas Kelasket drifts from one event to the next, more as an observer than an activist, a hanger-on rather than a leader. Through his manifold experiences, both in the political movement and on skid row, Thomas Kelasket finally comes to realize that he must live his Native culture if he is to preserve it, and he goes back to the Okanagan Valley he comes from. So, like many other

Native novels, the story describes a circle that moves from a tribal or traditional identity through separation, alienation and conflict towards a return and a re-achievement of tribal identity through taking part again in ceremonial life (Lutz 1989). The novel has met with considerable critical acclaim from both Native and non-Native readers and critics (Currie, Emberley, Fee, Petrone). As one of very few Native historical novels[1], it has become a standard text for courses in Native Literature in Canada. Without discussing the novel *per se*, it is illuminating to contextualize it, having the Voice of the Mother in mind.

First of all, Jeannette Armstrong's *Slash* stands within – and continues – a personal family tradition as well as an Okanagan tribal or national tradition: Jeannette Armstrong's great aunt was one of the very first Native woman to publish a novel at all: Hum-Ishu-Ma (Mourning Dove, 1888-1936)'s *Cogewea: The Half-Blood* came out in Boston in 1927. So, Armstrong is related by blood to an earlier literary woman, but since Humishuma lived on the U.S. side of Okanagan territory, and since her book was published in the U.S.A., as were her other works, it was received as U.S. Native Literature, and was republished as such in 1981 in the University of Nebraska's successful 'Bison Books' series. Armstrong herself said about this connection 'I was intrigued because she was my relative, my blood relative. And I was intrigued by her thinking', but in the same interview she also stressed that with *Slash* she 'never set out to set precedent or to be the first Native woman novelist' (Armstrong 1991c, 14, 13). Besides following that personal family tradition, the novel is firmly set in the tribal traditions of the Okanagan nation's culture.

Secondly, the book stands within a new women's tradition of Native (novel) writing in Canada. Along with other Native novelists like Beatrice Culleton, Lee Maracle, Ruby Slipperjack, and Joan Crate, Jeannette Armstrong has started and/or continued a female tradition in Native letters in Canada, which can also be perceived in other fields, such as poetry and short fiction, where the presence of women authors is much stronger than that of men (exceptions: Johnston, King, Highway and Moses).

Native women have broken the silence and speak up for life. This process is summed up in the words with which Christine Welsh concludes her essay in *Canadian Literature*, 'Voices of the Grandmothers: Reclaiming a Métis Heritage':

Native women will be rendered historically voiceless no longer. We are engaged in creating a new history, our history, using our own voices and experiences. And as we raise our voices – as we write, sing, teach, make films – we do so with the certainty that we are speaking not for ourselves but for those who came before us whom history has made mute. We have a responsibility to our children and our people to ensure that the voices of our grandmothers are no longer silent.

And so the voices of our grandmothers are alive today, for they speak through me. (Welsh 1991:24)

Thirdly, there is the general context of Canadian mainstream literature, which is shaped by women authors to such a remarkable degree. It would be misleading, however, to see the novel as part of the larger 'feminist' tradition in English literatures, and in Canadian letters in particular. Relationships between the white Women's Movement, even between poststructuralist feminist critics, and Native women authors are often strained and marred by cultural misunderstandings. There are accusations of cultural imperialism and racism from Native women against white feminists, while from white feminist circles Jeannette Armstrong had the question thrown at her why in *Slash* she used a male character.

> That question has been thrown at me, and I say, 'Well, I don't talk about it in this way!' I can talk about it in this way that it is a very feminist book, and it really works with, and talks about, female thinking and the empowerment of people through love and compassion, and spirituality. And whether you want to call it female power, that's beside the point, but that's currently what it's being called. I think it's human at its best.
>
> And its not dependent on sex, men and women. But currently women, womankind, I guess, has been promoting that thinking, and so it's being called 'feminist thought.' And I disagree! I think it's fundamental to our thought as humans, and the real humanity in us!
>
> I like to say that when I am asked that question. (Armstrong 1991c:18)[2]

Fourthly: Rather than seeing Armstrong and other Native women writers as part of the general feminist movement or as part of the specific Canadian national tradition, which is predominantly white and middle class, it seems more 'appropriate' to see their works in the context of Third World Women Writers or Women of Color Writers worldwide, be they Chicana, Black, Asian, Indian, Maori or Métis. While Alice Walker, Toni Morrison, Paula Gunn Allen, Gloria Anzaldúa, Ana Castillo, Maxine Hong Kingston or Marlene Nourbese Philip are among the most prominent ones, there are literally thousands of others. In their sphere the global village has arrived. There are multiple coalitions and personal alliances spanning continents between Black women writers from the Caribbean, the USA, Europe and Canada, and Chicanas, Maori women, Asian American and Asian Canadian writers, and Native women. Within these networks, lesbian women of Color are particularly active and prominent.[3] Often, women writers of Color insist on their cultural, ethnic, economic and political difference from white feminists. Alice Walker coined the term 'womanist' for a 'humanist' attitude distinctly more colored and colorful than white feminism: 'Womanist is to feminist as purple is to lavender.' (Walker 1983:xii).

In the context of literature and literary criticism, women of Color often express their indignation at the Eurocentrism of critical theory, and particularly of the fact that literary criticism today seems to be moving further and further away from literary texts, from authors and contexts, and seems to be growing more and more self-referential: 'Critics are no longer concerned with literature, but with other critics' texts, for the critic yearning for attention has displaced the writer and has conceived of himself as the center' (Christian 1990:335). Barbara Christian, a Black critic from the Caribbean in an essay fittingly and ironically entitled 'The Race for Theory' even states:

> For I feel that the new emphasis on literary critical theory is as hegemonic as the world which it attacks. I see the language it creates as one which mystifies rather than clarifies our condition, making it possible for a few people who know that particular language to control the critical scene – that language surfaced, interestingly enough, just when the literature of people of color, of black women, of Latin Americans, of Africans began to move to 'the center.' (Christian 1990:338)[4]

Similarly, other women writers of Color, most prominently Chicanas and Blacks, argue for the development of new critical theories which will accommodate their specific views of reality, which in the case of Latin American literature has been called 'magic realism', but which in traditional Native viewpoints would be perceived, I think, as just that: reality, albeit in a wider sense than the eye can see.[5]

A dissatisfaction with the literary establishment is also apparent in the works of Women of Color writing in Canada. But it is more than just a literary dispute, it addresses the issue of hegemony and the lack of equity and respect between the mainstream and authors belonging to marginalized ethnic groups. When asked in an interview 'What do you see as the future for Canadian writers who are not white?', Dionne Brand, a Black Torontonian from the Caribbean, responded:

> I think that we are probably the new wave of Canadian writing. Twenty years ago there was a national wave of Canadian writing which set itself up against American writing and the deluge of American culture in Canada. We are the new wave of Canadian writing. We will write about the internal contradictions. (Brand 1990:277)

Obviously, Brand foresees for Canada a development similar to that in the United States, where Women of Color are the most innovative and successful authors – this is true also for Native American authors like Leslie Silko, Paula Gunn Allen or Louise Erdrich. Undoubtedly, on the Canadian side, Jeannette Armstrong's works would have to be seen in this context.

5. Survival

Native women, Chicana, Métis or Indian, are particularly conscious of the legacy of endurance and stamina they have inherited from their grandmothers. The words of Nimipu-Chicana, or Nez Percé-Texan-American, author and critic Inés Hernandez echo the words of Canadian Métis Christine Welsh when she stresses the strength of First Nations women for survival:

I see in all of the Indian women, especially the old ladies, the toughest, strictest ones, I see in my mother, that Indian womanness – humility and dignity and pride – the ability to hold out, until forever if they have to, in silent strength and continuance until their conditions are met. (Hernandez 1992:164)

The strength to hold out, to outlast, to endure and to survive and thrive in the end is a deep conviction of many women of Color – and of First Nations women in particular. It is based on cyclical rather than linear concepts of time, and it is collective rather than individual, always thinking in terms of past and future generations.

Jeannette Armstrong in her novel, in her essays and speeches, and in her poetry again and again addresses issues of global survival. In the poem 'ROCKS' (Armstrong 1991a) she thematizes the enduring strength and lasting power of rocks as the oldest beings on earth, as messengers from the past that convey a sense of geological dimensions in history measured in millennia, outlasting human existence by far. Armstrong's metaphor juxtaposes images of violence and destruction with images of prayer and ritual. The bearstone in the center pit of the sweat lodge, the red smooth familiar shape of the sacred pipe in which the poetic voice lifts tobacco in prayer, and the stone circle on the mountain top, which opens to the east from where all new life comes, speak of renewal and hope; while the disintegration of stones in acid rain, bedrock blasted for roads, ore smelted into jewelry and weapons, and the 'tiny grain' of uranium, waiting to 'flower into (the) blazing white' of a nuclear blast present images of global death. Rocks, the old ones, called 'grandfathers' (tunkashila, Lakota) in the sweat ceremony, reveal the past, as do the Thunder eggs or the moment frozen inside agate. Contained in each rock is also the future, and while the rock may be thrown in anger through police barricades at Chateauguay to hit one of the Natives, the Earth People, Mother Earth herself may also release a rock slide hitting policemen in B.C. who are clearing a human blockade of Natives protecting their graves on Liliwat land. Mother Earth, most Natives say, is no longer tolerating her destruction in silence but is starting to hit back in earthquakes, rock slides, floods, and volcanic eruptions, and regardless of whether these catastrophes are man made or the warnings of Earth as a living entity, it is up to humans to halt the destruction.

Armstrong's poem shows that a tribal and specific vision is neither quaint nor provincial, but transcends national and continental boundaries addressing global issues. Her metaphors extend from the sacred prayer on top of the mountain to Hiroshima and Chernobyl. The tribal is also the universal, and everything is connected in a holy and holistic manner. The 'I' in this poem is a collective one, transcending time and gender, but aware of historical memory, which Hernandez and others call 'racial memory.' It is fitting therefore, that Armstrong dedicated her collection of poetry, *Breath Tracks*, to her grandmothers:

In memory of those Okanagan Grandmothers whose blood and words live inside me

Humishumi	Mourning Dove
Skumxenelks	Christine Joseph
Silxielks	Mary Katherine Louie
Sahapxenelks	Margaret Stelkia

(Armstrong 1991a:5)

and she concludes the volume with poems that tie in Indian women with Mother Earth. In 'Indian Woman' she overcomes the stereotyping as 'squaw' and celebrates her role as giver of life, ending with the verses 'I am sacred trust/ I am Indian woman'. This fifth but last poem is followed by a poem dedicated to Mourning Dove, her blood and literary ancestor, and another poem 'For Tracey', her daughter, who is already an activist and a published poet. Finally, in the last two poems, she addresses the survival and continual change of earth in 'Earth Renewal Song' and in 'Untitled', which ends 'and the land changes again'. Thus women, survival, and earth are tied together in a circle that encompasses all life, and that promotes continuity and 'the empowerment of people through love, and compassion, and spirituality' (Armstrong 1991c:18). In her engagement for global survival from a First Nations perspective, Jeannette Armstrong acts out of a concern which we might perceive as deeply humanist and which seems to be a direct extension of the Native (oral) Tradition.

> ... Native people's words, and their thinking, and their process, and their system, their philosophy, world view or whatever, need to be understood, and looked at, and assimilated by other people. That's so important, and so critical, and so necessary, because we all deserve – we all deserve – the happiness, and the joy, and the cleanness, and the purity. We all deserve that! (Armstrong 1991c:32)

REFERENCES

Adams, Howard, *Prison of Grass: Canada from the Native Point of View*. Toronto: General Publishing, 1975, repr. 1977f. Rev. ed. Saskatoon: Fifth House, 1990.

Adams, Howard, 'Howard Adams (Interview)', in: Hartmut Lutz (ed.), *Contemporary Challenges: Conversations With Canadian Native Authors*. Saskatoon: Fifth House, 1991; 135-154.

Annharte (Marie Baker), *Being on the Moon*. Winlaw, B.C.: Polestar Book Publishers, 1990.

Armstrong, Jeannette, *Enwhiskeetkwa: Walk in Water*. Penticton: Okanagan Tribal Council, 1989.

Armstrong, Jeannette, *Neekna and Chemai*. Illustrations: Kenneth Lee Edwards. Penticton: Theytus, 1984.

Armstrong, Jeannette, *Slash*. Penticton, B.C.: Theytus Books, 1985.

Armstrong, Jeannette, 'Words', in: Lee, S., L. Maracle, D. Marlatt, and B. Warland (eds.), *Telling It: Women and Language Across Cultures*. Vancouver: Press Gang Publishers, 1990; 23-29.

Armstrong, Jeannette, *Breath Tracks*. Stratford/Vancouver: Williams-Wallace/Theytus, 1991a.

Armstrong, Jeannette with Douglas Cardinal, *The Native Creative Process: A Collaborative Discourse*, with photographs by Greg Young-Ing. Penticton: Theytus, 1991b.

Armstrong, Jeannette, 'Jeannette Armstrong (Interview)', in: Hartmut Lutz (ed.), *Contemporary Challenges: Conversations With Canadian Native Authors*. Saskatoon: Fifth House, 1991c; 13-32.

Brand, Dionne, 'Interview by Dagmar Novak', in: Linda Hutcheon and Marion Richmond (eds.), *Other Solitudes: Canadian Multicultural Fictions*. Toronto: Oxford University Press, 1990; 271-277.

Campbell, Maria, *Half-Breed*. Toronto: McClelland & Stewart, 1973; repr.: Goodread Biographies, Halifax: Formac Publishing, 1983.

Campbell, Maria, *People of the Buffalo: How the Plains Indians Lived*, Ill. by Douglas Tait and Shannon Twofeathers. Vancouver: J.J. Douglas Ltd., 1976.

Campbell, Maria, *Riel's People: How the Métis Lived*, Ill. by David Maclagan. Vancouver/Toronto: Douglas & McIntyre, 1978; 1st paperback 1983.

Campbell, Maria, *Achimoona*. Saskatoon: Fifth House, 1985.

Campbell, Maria, 'Maria Campbell (Interview)', in: Hartmut Lutz (ed.), *Contemporary Challenges: Conversations With Canadian Native Authors*. Saskatoon: Fifth House, 1991; 41-65.

Campbell, Maria and Linda Griffiths, *The Book of Jessica: A Theatrical Transformation*. Toronto: The Coach House Press, 1989.

Canadian Women Studies/les cahiers de la femme. Native Women-Issue, 10/2 and 3 Summer/Fall 1989.

Cardinal, Harold, *The Unjust Society: The Tragedy of Canada's Indians*. Edmonton: Hurtig, 1969.

Cardinal, Harold, *The Rebirth of Canada's Indians*. Edmonton: Hurtig, 1977.

Cheechoo, Shirley, *Path With No Moccasins*. West Bay, Ont.: author, 1993.

Christian, Barbara, 'The Race for Theory', in: Gloria Anzaldúa (ed), *Making Face, Making Soul*/Haciendo Caras: Creative and Critical Perspectives by Women of Color. San Francisco: Aunt Lute Foundation, 1990; 335-345.

Clutesi, George, *Son of Raven, Son of Deer. Fables of the Tse-shaht People*. Sidney, B.C.: Gray's Publishing, 1967.

Clutesi, George, *Potlatch*. Sidney, B.C.: Gray's Publishing, 1969 (repr. 1973).

Crate, Joan, *Pale as Real Ladies: Poems for Emily Pauline Johnson*. Idlerton, Ont.: Brick Books, 1989.

Crate, Joan, *Breathing Water*. Edmonton: NeWest Publishers, 1989.

Culleton, Beatrice, *In Search of April Raintree*. Winnipeg: Pemmican Publications, 1983. 6th repr. 1987.

Crate, Joan, *April Raintree*. Winnipeg: Pemmican Publications, 1984. 3rd repr. 1987.

Crate, Joan, *Spirit of the White Bison*, ill. by Robert Kakaygeesick, Jr. Winnipeg: Pemmican Publications, 1985. repr, 1987.

Crate, Joan, *The Night of the Trickster* (unpublished play, 1992/93).

Currie, Noel Elizabeth, 'Jeannette Armstrong and the Colonial Legacy', in: W.H. New (ed.), *Native Writers and Canadian Literature*. Vancouver: UBC Press, 1990; 138-152.

Cuthand, Beth, *Horse Dance to Emerald Mountain*. Vancouver: Lazara Publications, 1987.

Cuthand, Beth, *Voices in the Waterfall*. Vancouver: Lazara Press, 1989.

Daniels, Greg and Eugene Stickland, *The Third House from the Corner*. Regina: Laughing Dog Productions (xerox), 1990.

Emberley, Julia V, *Thresholds of Difference: Feminist Critique, Native Women's Writings, Postcolonial Theory*. Toronto, Buffalo, London: University of Toronto Press, 1993.

Fee, Margery, 'Upsetting Fake Ideas: Jeannette Armstrong's "Slash" and Beatrice Culleton's "April Raintree"', in: W.H. New (ed.), *Native Writers and Canadian Literature*. Vancouver: UBC Press, 1990; 138-152.

Fife, Connie, *Beneath the Naked Sun*. Toronto: Sister Vision Press, 1992.

Frye, Northrop, 'Conclusion', in: Carl F. Klinck (ed.), *Literary History of Canada: Canadian Literature in English*, 2nd. ed., vol. III. Toronto: U. of Toronto, 1976; 318-332.

Gatherings: The En'Owkin Journal of First North American Peoples, ed. En'Owkin Center/Theytus Books, Penticton, B.C. published annually, 1990ff.

Grant, Agnes (ed.), *Our Bit of Truth*. Winnipeg: Pemmican, 1990.

Heath, Caroline, (ed.), *The Land Called Morning: Three Plays*. Saskatoon: Fifth House, 1986.

Hernandez, Inés, *Con Razon Corazon*. San Antonio, Texas: M&A Editions, 1987.

Hernandez, Inés, 'An Open Letter to Chicanas: On the Power and Politics of Origin', in: Ray Gonzalez (ed.), *Out With-/With-Out Discovery: A Native Response to Columbus*. Seattle: Broken Moon Press, 1992, 153-166.

Highway, Tomson, *The Rez Sisters: A Play in Two Acts*. Saskatoon: Fifth House, 1988.

Highway, Tomson, *Dry Lips Oughta Move to Kapuskasing*. Saskatoon: Fifth House, 1989.

Highway, Tomson, 'Tomson Highway (Interview)', in: Hartmut Lutz (ed.), *Contemporary Challenges: Conversations With Canadian Native Authors*. Saskatoon: Fifth House, 1991; 89-95.

Hodgson, Heather (ed.), *Seventh Generation: Contemporary Native Writing*. Penticton: Theytus Books, 1989.

Hutcheon, Linda and Marion Richmond (eds.), *Other Solitudes: Canadian Multicultural Fictions*. Toronto: Oxford University Press, 1990.

Johnson, Emily Pauline/Tekahionwake, *Canadian Born*. Toronto: George N. Morang & Co., 1903.

Johnson, Emily Pauline/Tekahionwake, *Legends of Vancouver*. Vancouver: Vancouver Daily Province, 1911; repr. Toronto: McClelland & Stewart, 1983.

Johnson, Emily Pauline/Tekahionwake, *Flint and Feather: The Complete Poems of E. Pauline Johnson*. Toronto: Hodder & Stoughton, 1911; repr. Markham, Ontario: Paper Jacks Ltd., 1972; 3rd 1981.

Johnson, Emily Pauline/Tekahionwake, *The Moccasin Maker*; Introduction, Annotation and Bibliography by A. LaVonne Brown Rouff. Tucson: University of Arizona Press, 1987.

Johnston, Basil, 'One Generation from Extinction', in: W.H. New (ed.), *Native Writers and Canadian Writing*. Vancouver: UBC Press, 1990; 10-15.

Kane, Margo, 'Moonlodge' (one-woman play), in: Daniel David Moses and Terry Goldie (eds.), *An Anthology of Canadian Native Literature in English*. Toronto: Oxford University Press, 1992, 278-291.

Kenny, George, *Indians Don't Cry*. s.l.: Chimo Publishing, 1977.

Kenny, George in collaboration with Lacroix, Denis, *October Stranger*. Toronto: Clunio, 1978.

Keon, Wayne, *Sweetgrass II*. Stratford, Ont.: The Mercury Press, 1990.

King, Thomas (guest ed.), *Canadian Fiction Magazine* (special issue on Native writing), 60, 1987.

King, Thomas, *Medicine River*. Markham, Ont.: Penguin Books-Canada, 1990.

King, Thomas (ed.), *All My Relations: An Anthology of Contemporary Canadian Native Fiction*. Toronto: McClelland & Stewart, 1990.

King, Thomas, *Green Grass, Running Water*. Toronto: Harper Collins Publishers, 1993.

Krupat, Arnold, *The Voice in the Margin: Native American Literature and the Canon*. Berkeley: University of California Press, 1989.

LaRocque, Emma, *Defeathering the Indian*. Agincourt, Canada: The Book Society of Canada Ltd., 1975, 1983.

Lutz, Hartmut, 'The Circle as Philosophical and Structural Concept in Native American Fiction Today', in: Laura Coltelli (ed.), *Native American Literatures*. Pisa: Servizio Editoriala Universitario, 1989, 85-100.

Lutz, Hartmut, 'Cultural Appropriation as a Process of Displacing Peoples and History', *Canadian Journal of Native Studies* 10/2, 1990, 167-182.

Lutz, Hartmut, *Contemporary Challenges: Conversations With Canadian Native Authors*. Saskatoon: Fifth House, 1991.

Lutz, Hartmut and students (eds.), *Four Feathers: Poems and Stories by Canadian Native Authors/ Vier Federn: Gedichte und Geschichten kanadischer Indianer/innen und Métis*, O.B.E.M.A. (Osnabrück Bilingual Editions of Minority Authors), No. 7. Osnabrück: VC-Verlagscooperative, 1992.

Lutz, Hartmut, 'Robbed Graves, Whiteshamans, and Stolen Stories: (Re-)Appropriations of Native Cultures', in: Sigrid Markmann (ed.), *Cultures in Contact*. Hamburg: Kovac, 1993, 245-258.

Maracle, Lee, *I am Woman*. North Vancouver: Write-on Press Publishers Ltd., 1988

Maracle, Lee, 'Moving Over', *Trivia: A Journal of Ideas*, No. 14, Spring 1989, 9-12.

Maracle, Lee, *Sojourners' Truth and Other Stories*. Vancouver: Press Gang, 1991.

Maracle, Lee, *Bobbi Lee: Indian Rebel*. Toronto: The Women's Press, 1990 [orig.: s.l.: LSM Information Center, 1975].

Maracle, Lee, 'Lee Maracle (Interview)', in: Hartmut Lutz (ed.), *Contemporary Challenges: Conversations With Canadian Native Authors*. Saskatoon: Fifth House, 1991; 169-179.

Maracle, Lee, *Sundogs*. Penticton: Theytus, 1992.

Maracle, Lee, *Ravensong: A Novel*. Vancouver: Press Gang Publishers, 1993.

Maracle, Lee, Daphne Marlatt, Betsy Warland & Sky Lee, *Telling It: Women and Language Across Culture*. Vancouver: Press Gang Publishers, 1990.

Meili, Dianne, *Those Who Know: Profiles of Alberta's Native Elders*. Edmonton: NeWest Press, 1991.

Mojica, Monique, *Princess Pocahontas and the Blue Spots*. Toronto: Women's Press, 1991.

Moses, Daniel David, *Delicate Bodies*. Vancouver: Blewointmentpress, 1980.

Moses, Daniel David, *The White Line: Poems*. Saskatoon: Fifth House, 1990.

Moses, Daniel David, *Coyote City: A Play in Two Acts*. Stratford, Ont.: Williams-Wallace Publications, 1990.

Moses, Daniel David, *Almighty Voice and His Wife. A Play*.

Moses, Daniel David and Terry Goldie (eds.), *An Anthology of Canadian Native Literature in English*. Toronto: Oxford University Press, 1992.

New, W.H. (ed.), *Native Writers and Canadian Writing*. Vancouver: UBC Press, 1990 (reprint of Canadian Literature, Native Issue, no. 124/5; without book review section).

Pelletier, Wilfred & Ted Poole, *No Foreign Land: The Biography of a North American Indian*. Toronto: McClelland & Stewart, 1973.

Perrault, Jeanne & Sylvia Vance (eds.), *Native Women of Western Canada: Writing the Circle: An Anthology*. Edmonton: NeWest, 1990.

Petrone, Penny, (ed.), *First People, First Voices*. Toronto, Buffalo, London: University of Toronto Press, 1983.

Petrone, Penny, *Northern Voices: Inuit Writing in English*. Toronto: University of Toronto Press, 1988.

Poelzer, Dolores T. and Poelzer, Irene A, *In Our Own Words: Northern Saskatchewan Métis Women Speak Out*. Saskatoon, Sask.: Lindenblatt & Hamonic, 1986.

Robinson, Harry (as told to Wendy Wickwire), *Write it on Your Heart: The Epic World of an Okanagan Storyteller*. Vancouver: Talon Books/Theytus, 1989.

Silman, Janet (ed.), *Enough is Enough: Aboriginal Women Speak Out*. Toronto: The Women's Press, 1987.

Slipperjack, Ruby, *Honour the Sun*. Winnipeg: Pemmican Publications, 1987.

Slipperjack, Ruby, 'A Spirit of Wings', in: Lynne Sharman (curator) (ed.), *Flight Pattern Uninterrupted* (catalogue for exhibition of art by Alice Crawley, A. Whitlock and Michael Belmore, with a written work by Ruby Slipperjack). Thunder Bay, Ont.: Definitely Superior, Nov. 11, 1989, s. pp.

Slipperjack, Ruby, 'Ruby Slipperjack (Interview)', in: Hartmut Lutz (ed.), *Contemporary Challenges: Conversations With Canadian Native Authors*. Saskatoon: Fifth House, 1991; 203-215.

Slipperjack, Ruby, *Silent Words*. Saskatoon: Fifth House, 1992.

Staub, Michael, 'Contradictory Memories, Conflicting Identities: The Autobiographical Writing of Kingston and Rodriguez', in: Wolfgang Karrer and Hartmut Lutz (eds.), *Minority Literatures in North America: Contemporary Perspectives*. Frankfurt am Main: Peter Lang, 1990; 65-76.

Taylor, Drew Hayden, *'Toronto at Dreamer's Rock' and 'Education is Our Right'. Two One-Act Plays*. Saskatoon: Fifth House, 1990.

Taylor, Drew Hayden, *The Bootlegger Blues*. Saskatoon: Fifth House, 1991.

Trickster. The Magazine to Re-Establish The Trickster: New Native Writing, ed. Lenore Keeshig-Tobias, 1/1, Fall 1988, and 1/2, Spring 1989.

Turner, Joan (ed.), *Living the Changes*. Winnipeg: University of Manitoba Press, 1990.

Tyman, James, *Inside Out: An Autobiography by a Native Canadian*. Saskatoon: Fifth House, 1989.

Walker, Alice, *In Search of Our Mothers' Gardens: Womanist Prose*. London: The Women's Press, 1983.

Welsh, Christine, 'Voices of the Grandmothers: Reclaiming a Métis Heritage', *Canadian Literature* 131, Winter 1991, 15-24.

Wheeler, Jordan, *Brothers in Arms: Three Novellas*. Winnipeg: Pemmican Publications, 1989.

Whetstone Magazine, Dept. of English, University of Lethbridge, Alberta (Special Native issues Spring '85, Spring '87 and Fall '88).

Williamson, Janice, *Sounding Differences: Conversations With Seventeen Canadian Women Writers*. Toronto, Buffalo, London: University of Toronto Press, 1993.

Willis, Jane, *Geniesh: An Indian Girlhood*. Toronto: New Press, 1973.

Wolfe, Alexander, *Earth Elder Stories: The Pinayzitt Path*. Saskatoon, Sask.: Fifth House, 1988.

Young-Ing, Greg, 'Greg Young-Ing (Interview)', in: Hartmut Lutz (ed.), *Contemporary Challenges: Conversations With Canadian Native Authors*. Saskatoon: Fifth House, 1991; 117-120.

NOTES

1. In the USA there are Dallas Chief Eagle's *Winter Count* (1967) and James Welch's Fools Crow (1986), both dealing with the second half of the nineteenth century, i.e. the Plains 'Wars.' In Canada most recently Lee Maracle's *Sun Dogs* (1992) could come under the label 'historical novel', since it portrays in detail through the perception of a young Native female protagonist what went on in Native Canada before and during the Oka standoff of 1990.

2. Without wanting to start a discussion here about the maleness of the term 'humanism' in our Western tradition and the possible inappropriateness to use it as representative of all of (wo)mankind, *alla människor*, let me just conclude this by cautioning anybody who might feel inclined to subsume Native women writers under the very admirable and very widespread Canadian tradition of women writing and feminist Canadian literature. Such subsumation would be 'patriarchial' at best, even a term like 'our native people(s)' (Hutcheon 1990, 8, 9) used by a well-meaning white feminist and cultural critic like Linda Hutcheon is objectionable.

3. The late Audre Lorde was perhaps the most prominent figure in this debate, but other Black women writers like the Caribbean Gloria Joseph or the German Marion Kraft network internationally with Maori authors Powhiri Rika Heke and Cathie Dunsford, who in turn visit white womanists as well as Native and Chicana writers like Gloria Anzaldúa, Cherrie Morraga, Emma Perez, Chrystos, Paula Gunn Allen, Beth Brant – as always, the borderlines are transient, and many white (wo)men are included in a network, which is open and encompassing rather than exclusively lesbian or even female only.

4. Critical theory, Christian claims, excludes the political aspect inherent and central to the writings of People of Color, forming a new vertical boundary along the lines of color:

   > ... the literature of blacks, women of South America and Africa, etc., as overtly 'political' literature was being pre-empted by a new Western concept which proclaimed that reality does not exist, that everything is relative and that every text is silent about something – which indeed it must necessarily be. (*ibid:*340)

5. I think that as Western critics we have a hard time to acknowledge and respect other cultures' perceptions of reality. In particular, we often tend to underestimate the importance of the ceremonial, the 'supernatural' and spiritual aspects of Native art and existence. It is illuminating, however, to follow Danish scholar Bo Schöler who suggested an approach to Native literature on at least four levels: a physical, a psychological, a social and a spiritual level (in: *Engelsk Meddelelser*; Temanummer Nr. 32 'To Live and to Notice It: An Introduction to Native American Studies in Denmark' (Sept. 1985): 42f). Schöler writes about a poem by Joy Harjo: 'Digtet har karakter af en bøn. Bønnen er livet, jorden – og digtet. Denne grænseoverskridende dimension er indiansk litteraturs begyndelse og slutning; det kraftcenter der sikrer de indianske folks og kulturers overlevelse' (74).

From Violent Duality to Multi-Culturalism: Margaret Atwood's Post-Colonial Cultural and Sexual Politics

Charlotte Beyer

This article explores the intersection of post-colonial cultural and sexual politics in Margaret Atwood's writing. I focus on the shift in Atwood's writing in thinking about difference, away from an earlier 'colonial' fiction which was concerned with the problems of defining a specifically Canadian identity and of writing in a colonized space to a 'post-colonial' fiction which emphasizes the provisional nature of all cultures and identities. The article also explores the construction of place as a site for negotiating identity in Atwood's writing, and looks at Atwood's use of the Canadian wilderness, and more recently the metropolis, as literary discourse.

Recent critical work on post-colonial literary discourses is useful in bringing out important aspects of Atwood's writing which have previously been overlooked. In their recent book on Canadian and Australian post-colonial literatures, the critics Diana Brydon and Helen Tiffin focus on the production of certain textual traces as a result of British imperialism and post-colonial resistance. They argue that 'post-colonial writers write "decolonizing fictions", texts that write back against imperial fictions and texts that incorporate alternative ways of seeing and living in the world'.[1]

The question of post-colonial Canadian identity has attracted much attention from post-modernist and post-colonial theorists. The political implications of defining 'difference', in the context of the Canadian post-colonial struggle to come to terms with its complex colonial heritage, has been noted by Laura Mulvey, who argues that:

> The question of Canadian post-colonial identity is political in the most direct sense of the word, and it brings the political together with the cultural and ideological issues immediately and inevitably. For the Canada delineated by multi-nationals, international finance, U.S. economic and political imperialism, national identity is a point of resistance,

defining the border fortifications against exterior colonial penetration. Here nationalism can perform the political function familiar in Third World countries.[2]

Mulvey's comment reflects on the function of nationalism in Canada, using terms which clarify the importance of a work like Atwood's *Survival: A Thematic Guide to Canadian Literature*.[3]

Post-colonial writing is preoccupied with naming the historical circumstances of colonial experience, and identifying discursive practices and thematic concerns which reflect and resist the wide-ranging cultural and psychological consequences of that experience. The critics Adam and Tiffin observe, in attempting to define the post-colonial:

> Post-colonialism might be characterized as having two archives. The first archive here constructs it as writing... from countries or regions which were formerly colonies of Europe. The second archive of post-colonialism is intimately related to the first, though not co-extensive with it. Here the post-colonial is conceived of as a set of discursive practices, prominent among which is resistance to colonialism, colonialist ideologies, and their contemporary forms and subjectificatory legacies. The nature and function of this resistance form a central problematic of the discourse.[4]

In Atwood's writing, resistance to oppressive ideologies and their past and present forms is signalled by her use of discursive and thematic strategies which expose the politics of language and metaphor.

Atwood emerged as an important figure in the Canadian nationalist movement in the 1970s. In the following I shall discuss the implications of Atwood's critical book from 1972, *Survival. Survival* played an important role in helping to place Canadian literature in an international context, and in raising the complex issues of post-colonialism as valid questions for literary and cultural critique. With *Survival*, Atwood was among the first to discuss the problems of constructing a post-colonial Canadian identity, and looked at literary representations of the colonial culture and its self-denigrating attitudes. By suggesting strategies for resisting and changing a situation of cultural stagnation, Atwood put the question of cultural and national identity as survival strategy onto the agenda.

In *Survival* Atwood names the sense of self-denigration and survival as key sentiments in Canadian cultural expression for much of the nineteenth and twentieth centuries. She defines them as reflections of 'the colonial state of mind'. In an interview with Mary Ellis Gibson, Atwood discusses the effects of this sense of cultural ex-centricity on cultural production in Canada, arguing that:

> Literatures of colonies are disregarded, both by the people outside and inside the colony, because part of the colonial state of mind is to think that the mother country or the dominant culture has the real goodies and that anything that you yourself might produce is either an inferior imitation or out of the question.[5]

Atwood's observations also serve as a critique of the marginalized position of women's writing vis-a-vis the dominant masculinist culture. Commenting on the intersection of post-colonialism and feminism, the critics Helen Tiffin and Diana Brydon argue that:

> Feminist studies of unacknowledged gender bias in literary criticism have opened the way for questioning of the ideological assumptions implicit in all writing from the perspective of an analysis of power relationships – reminding us to ask: who is doing what to whom and to what effect? (Brydon and Tiffin, 73)

Survival is concerned with defining the 'field markings' culturally and historically specific to late nineteenth and twentieth century Anglo- and French-Canadian literatures. Atwood demonstrates the effects on cultural production of the physical and psychological scarring and regional divisions resulting from the realities of a colonial economy, and proclaims the need for development of strategies which can resist the stranglehold of the imported imperial cultures.

Although criticized when it initially appeared, *Survival* remains a significant work in the context of post-colonial critical theory. The critic Colin Nicholson also comments on this function of *Survival*, arguing that:

> Looking back, what has become evident is that ... *Survival* establishes parameters, in substance if not in terminology, for much of the recent theorizing of post-colonial representations of literary subjectivity, whether Indian, African, Caribbean or Australian.... Generally concerned to challenge what Roland Barthes might have termed the 'myths' inscribed in literature and literary criticism emanating from imperial centres, a wide spectrum of work that was to be carried out in the 1970s and 1980s relates in one way or another to Atwood's formulations.[6]

Atwood's most important contribution in *Survival* is the clarification of a set of cultural attributes and discursive predispositions encoded in Canadian writing, and the key notion in Atwood's vision of change, the *'basic victim positions'*:

Position One: To deny the fact that you are a victim.

Position Two: To acknowledge that you are a victim, but to explain this as an act of fate, the Will of God, the dictates of Biology (in the case of women, for instance), the necessity decreed by History, or Economics, or the Unconscious, or any other large general powerful idea.

Position Three: To acknowledge that you are a victim but to refuse to accept the assumption that the role is inevitable.

Position Four: To be a creative non-victim. (*Survival*, 38-39)

This personalized representation of different responses to cultural domination also provides a useful paradigm for feminist consciousness and resistance. However, Atwood does not explicitly employ feminist concepts, such as consciousness-raising, which insist on the interrelation between the personal and the political, and provide a strategic starting-point for using collective action as a response to patriarchal domination.

Survival engages with historical change, and examines the politics of narrative and poetic production within a formerly colonized society. Highlighting the communicative function of writing, the rhetoric of *Survival* must be seen in its specific context, designed to meet particular needs in an audience which is not specifically academic. Furthermore, Atwood's preoccupation with place as a site for the construction of identity in *Survival* and later works is based on a *regional* understanding of a situated national and gendered sense of self, not on the concept of a universalizing centre.

As a post-colonial writer Atwood attempts to write from within her own sense of place, and to interpret its particular cadences and rhythms for her own community instead of mimicking the 'foreign' accents of English literature. Another aspect of interpreting the rhythms and cadences of place is reflected in a shift in Atwood's more recent work, in her imaging of 'place' and of wilderness as a literary discourse.

The tension between the direct personal address and expository style of *Survival* and Atwood's fiction and poetry highlights the complexity of articulating identity and location in *language*. The intersection of imperial and post-colonial languages in Canadian literature lends the question of identity a degree of ambivalence. The articulation of difference in language raises particular problems for Canadian writers who speak the same languages as their historical colonizers, but attempt to assert their specifically Canadian voices. Language becomes a political, cultural, and literary concern. As suggested by the narrator of *Surfacing*:[7] 'language is everything you do' (129). Commenting on the problem of language for post-colonial writers, the critics Brydon and Tiffin argue that: 'The postcolonial literatures in English appear to use the same language, yet use it very differently. They seem at once familiar and strange, neither English nor completely foreign' (Brydon and Tiffin, 22).

From a feminist perspective, the problem of using language is further complicated by the fact that women must negotiate a language which is masculinist and Eurocentric in structure and outlook. Language plays a part in the construction of the white, middle-class, Anglo-Saxon, European male as the norm, and the positioning of the feminine and postcolonial as the 'other'. There is no uncontaminated alternative space existing outside imperialist discourse from which the post-colonial may speak. However, as the critic William New observes, commenting on the potentially subversive functions of language: 'The challenge is to use the existing language, even if it is the voice of a dominant 'other' – and yet speak through it: to disrupt... the codes and forms of the dominant language in order to reclaim speech for itself.'[8]

Expressing herself in a language which she shares with the former colonizers of Canada Atwood uses discursive strategies which help challenge and displace the hierarchical symbolic order which positions the post-colonial woman as a marginalized Other. In her writing, Atwood investigates possible strategies for thinking about difference which are not submitted to the law of otherness which constructs the self by dehumanizing the other.

Colonialism is instrumental in inscribing a sense of doubleness as the mark of a colonial consciousness, by its paradoxical move to enforce cultural sameness, at the same time as it produces differentiations between colonizer and colonized. The reality of Canadian culture becomes a marginal or unreal construct, whereas the fictions promoted by for example colonial literature are perceived as the 'real' Canadian referent.

This double focus, which Atwood has termed a 'violent duality', is central to the representation of Canadian identity and femininity in much of Atwood's early work. 'Violent duality' also serves as a trope for the complex and ambiguous positioning of the white settler-invader woman, who is *both* colonizer *and* colonized. In the 'Afterword' to the poetry collection *Journals of Susanna Moodie* (1970) Atwood suggests that:

> We are all immigrants to this place even if we were born here: the country is too big for anyone to inhabit completely, and in the parts unknown to us we move in fear, exiles and invaders. This country is something that must be chosen... and if we do choose it we are still choosing a *violent duality*. (*Journals of Susanna Moodie*, 'Afterword', 62; my emphasis)

Journals of Susanna Moodie is held together by a single coherently assumed persona. By conjoining her own poetic voice and sensibility with the evoked words and imagined experiences of the historical woman Susanna Moodie, Atwood explores the process of British settlement in Canada, and the experience of coming to terms with the wild otherness of the Canadian natural environment.

Using this strategy, Atwood achieves a *double* focus on Canadian history and feminine identity in *Journals of Susanna Moodie*. The poems are constructed around the tension created between Atwood's twentieth-century interpretation of the colonial past, and the nineteenth-century response to contemporary developments in Canada articulated by the persona Moodie. Atwood foregrounds the sense of 'cultural schizophrenia' in *Journals of Susanna Moodie* by her use of visual images in the eight collages in black and white which accompany the poems.

Atwood highlights the performative functions of the text in the process of cultural decolonization, subverting the imperial fictions of Britain and invoking the counter-cultures of post-colonial hybridity. The poem 'The Immigrants' in

Journals of Susanna Moodie portrays Susanna Moodie's observations of immigrants arriving in Canada in the nineteenth century. The poem registers not only their sense of displacement, but also Moodie's own ambivalent feelings towards cultural difference. In many ways she still sees herself as a British person living in a foreign country.

Moodie's Euro-Anglocentric assumptions are at the centre of her continued perception of herself as being at the centre of cultural production. Using the image of immigrants sidelined from the mainstream, Atwood illustrates the marginalization of cultural difference:

> They are allowed to inherit
> the sidewalks involved as palmlines,
> ...
> only to be told they are too poor
> to keep it up, or someone
> has noticed and wants to kill them; or the towns
> pass laws which declare them obsolete.   (*Journals of Susanna Moodie*, 32)

Journals of Susanna Moodie depicts the internal conflict between Moodie's identification with Britain and its norms, and the changes in perception caused by the confrontation with Canada. There can be no return to 'home', the notion of the centre giving way to a sense of being displaced in both worlds:

> and if they go back, the towns
> in time have crumbled, their tongues
> stumble among awkward teeth, their ears
> are filled with the sound of breaking glass.
> I wish I could forget them
> and so forget myself.   (*Journals of Susanna Moodie*, 33)

A different order, emerging from a sense of place, and reflecting the coming together of multiple differences, not an 'imported' order from the old world, has to be constructed:

> the old countries recede, become
> perfect, thumbnail castles preserved
> like gallstones in a glass bottle, the
> towns dwindle upon the hillsides
> in a light paperweight-clear.
> ...
> they think they will make an order
> like the old one, sow miniature orchards,
> carve children and flocks out of wood
> but always they are too poor, the sky
> is flat, the green fruit shrivels
> in the prairie sun   (*Journals of Susanna Moodie*, 32-33)

In *Surfacing* Atwood questions whether a dominated person can 'surface' from relations of oppression into freedom on her own. Upon her return to the wilderness of northern Quebec, the narrator of *Surfacing* makes a poignant comment, observing to herself 'Now we're on my home ground, foreign territory' (*Surfacing*, 11). The paradoxical identification of the feminine subject with a position which is both 'home ground' and 'foreign territory' presents the starting-point for the exploration in *Surfacing* of feminine and post-colonial experiences of cultural, physical, and spiritual dislocation. The novel describes a young woman's attempt to construct and articulate a sense of herself as a Canadian and a woman which will *empower* her.

By aligning the narrator's personal crisis with that of post-colonial Canada, Atwood problematizes the concepts of a unified integrated subject and a monolithic national identity. Atwood locates the problem in the Western construction of identity and its concepts of cultural 'authenticity'. The novel vacillates between a scepticism towards the concept of an 'authentic' Canadian identity uncontaminated by Eurocentric values, and a utopian desire for a sense of national and gendered identity arising out of an organic connection with the land and its indigenous peoples. However, the pervading sense of complicity and guilt in the novel points to the problematic positioning of the white settler-invader woman and her identification with the colonized native Other.

The identification of woman with the *wilderness* in *Surfacing* has been seen by feminist critics as a problematic and essentialist construction of femininity. Certainly, the novel echoes the influences of early 1970s radical and cultural feminisms, in its identification of femininity with nature, the irrational and the semiotic. However, it can be argued that the validation in *Surfacing* of this side of the binary opposition is a necessary step in the process of deconstructing that opposition.

The novel raises important questions for feminists about the provisional and strategic use of essentialism in particular historical, cultural, and political contexts. Atwood's use of the wilderness as a trope for an authentic femininity is an attempt to positively assert a Canadian female difference, which inscribes itself in a specifically Canadian literary preoccupation with the wild otherness of nature. As the critic Rita Felski points out in her reading of *Surfacing*:

> Gender is not the only relevant issue here; the critique of social values is also influenced by quite specific national and cultural contexts. In the Canadian novel, for example, the nature-culture opposition serves to demarcate national as well as gender boundaries and can also be read as the celebration of a distinctive cultural identity in the face of the homogenizing and imperialistic tendencies of an American culture ... the preoccupation with wilderness [is] a distinctive theme in recent Canadian women's writing which grows out of a long-standing fascination with the representation of landscape in the Canadian literary tradition.[10]

The narrator's experiences in northern Quebec serve the function of establishing a sense of a personal *place*, from which to speak and write. The merging themes of feminine difference, Canadian national identity, and the body in *Surfacing* illustrate the positioning of the narrator, who writes from a 'foreign territory' of the Other, while at the same time occupying the 'home ground' of the self.

The female protagonist of *Surfacing* is able to narrate her experience by inscribing the difference which arises out of her particular context, as a woman, as a body, as a Canadian. *Surfacing* explores the problems of establishing and retrieving those spiritual and cultural values which can survive and resist the negative and oppressive legacies of patriarchy and colonialism. The imaginative reconstruction of a different relation with body and place in *Surfacing* is a strategy for survival.

The title of Atwood's poetry collection *True Stories*[11] (1982) emphasizes the possibility of a plurality of stories and competing discourses which challenge a universal, monolithic version of reality. Her use of the word *stories* implies that truth differs, depending on the subject's position:

The true story lies
among the other stories,

a mess of colours, like jumbled clothing
thrown off or away,

like hearts on marble, like syllables, like
butchers' discards.

The true story is vicious
and multiple and untrue

after all. Why do you
need it? Don't ever

ask for the true story.   (*True Stories*, 11)

This shift echoes recent developments in feminist and post-colonial criticisms suggesting useful strategies for distinguishing the textual politics of marginal voices. The critic Linda Hutcheon comments on the influence of postmodernist thought in scrutinizing constructions of identity, arguing that 'The postmodernist urge to trouble, to question, to make both problematic and provisional any ... desire for order or truth through the powers of the human imagination.'[12] Although foregrounding multiplicity in identity and as a narrative strategy, Atwood's writing, and the political commitments which it reflects, implicitly distances itself from the 'word games' and refutation of the referent which characterize some post-structuralist and post-modernist writing, and which can be seen as limiting or damaging to the postcolonial project of self-determination.

Atwood's more recent works depict a plurality of Canadian differences, exploring the provisional nature of gendered and national identities. These fictions exceed the conception of difference in terms of the cultural schizophrenia reflected in the binary opposition inscribed in the trope 'violent duality'. The short story 'Wilderness Tips'[13] (1991) and the novel *The Robber Bride*[14] (1993) mark a shift away from the desire for homogeneity in *Surfacing*, towards an exploration of cultural diversity and celebration of multiple differences within Canada. Atwood examines stereotypical representations of immigrants in Anglo-Canadian culture, problems of assimilation and linguistic alienation, and the necessity for a constant revision and renegotiation of the meanings of cultural heritage and traditions.

In 'Wilderness Tips' Atwood deconstructs the notion of 'wilderness', revealing it to be a white colonial fantasy. The story also problematizes contemporary shifts in Canadian social attitudes, registering disruptions on the personal and public levels. In this narrative set in contemporary Canada, wilderness is under threat from urban development and environmental disaster, and features mainly as a fictional construction, a colonial romance about a pioneering past and a cultural mythology.

The name of the week-end cottage in the story, Wacousta Lodge, refers to a nineteenth-century British colonial romance. In 'Wilderness Tips', however, this intertextual reference has a rather ironic twist. Wacousta Lodge is now the setting for acting out fantasies of week-end pioneering and has been taken over by George, one of the protagonists, a Hungarian former refugee and now a successful businessman. While the story's portrayal of the predatory George is questionable in terms of 'political correctness', the following passage conveys a sense of anxiety about the historical and contemporary visibility of immigrants in Canadian society:

> Yesterday, [Roland] drove up from the centre of the city, past the warehouses and factories and shining glass towers, which have gone up, it seems, overnight; past the subdivisions he could swear weren't there last year, last month. Acres of treelessness, of new townhouses with little pointed roofs – like tents, like an invasion. The tents of the Goths and the Vandals. The tents of the Huns and the Magyars. The tents of George. ('Wilderness Tips', *Wilderness Tips*, 211)

The above passage also illustrates that Roland the Canadian brother feels alienated and displaced, much like the Hungarian immigrant George. 'Wilderness Tips' looks at the problems of accommodating cultural diversity into narratives about nationhood; at the different meanings of 'wilderness', urban or rural, in a multi-cultural context; and at the problematic weight of a complex colonial heritage, represented in the story by the trope of the great-grandfather's library.

The story also carries a certain irony, in Atwood's self-reflexive references to and revisions of the strategies for personal and cultural renewal suggested in her own post-colonial text, *Surfacing*. Towards the end of *Surfacing*, the narrator submerges herself in the lake, an act which signifies her quest for personal coherence and healing. When Portia slides into the lake at the end of 'Wilderness Tips', having just discovered that her husband George is cheating on her with her sister and that her whole life is based on a lie, the lake does not bring healing or personal transformation.

Portia's vision at the end of the landscape sliding into the lake leads us to revise the meaning of the story's title, and of wilderness as a universal trope for Canadian identity and femininity:

> She wades into the lake, slipping into the water ... There's a bell, ringing faintly from the distant house.... The bell rings again, and Portia knows that something bad is about to happen.... She looks at the shore, at the water line, where the lake ends. It's no longer horizontal, it seems to be on a slant, as if there's been a slippage in the bedrock.... She thinks of a boat – a huge boat, a passenger liner – tilting, descending, with the lights still on, the music still playing, the people talking on and on, still not aware of the disaster that has already overcome them. She sees herself running naked through the ballroom ... screaming at them, 'Don't you see? It's coming apart, everything's coming apart, you're sinking. You're finished, you're over, you're dead!' She would be invisible, of course. No one would hear her. And nothing has happened, really, that hasn't happened before.'
> ('Wilderness Tips', *Wilderness Tips*, 221)

The story posits a post-colonial cultural crisis scenario, and by constructing a sliding, shifting perspective, Atwood suggests instead a re-visioning of place as a space for negotiation of national and gendered identities.[15] The displacement of the wilderness trope in Atwood's recent novels *Cat's Eye*[16] and *The Robber Bride*, which are both set in Toronto, (the metropolis) has interesting implications in this regard. Representations of the city, of course, allow for different constructions of place and identity, as mosaics of diversity. *T h e Journals of Susanna Moodie* and *Surfacing* are preoccupied with the traditional and highly symbolic representation of the wilderness as a trope for Canada which is associated with femininity, whereas urban modernity is associated with masculinity. In *The Robber Bride* the primitive wilderness myth has been displaced by the urban landscape and the historical and cultural changes reflected in this environment. The city inscribes other, different stories of confrontation, pioneering and survival, as illustrated by the family histories of the four female protagonists in *The Robber Bride*. The novel explores issues of cultural pluralism through the concern with *origins*, and with conflicts and resolutions.

The representation of the city in *The Robber Bride* reflects how the import of European imperial styles, blending them into a post-modernist mix of architectural styles where 'anything goes', results in a cityscape where nothing is 'authentic' or indigenous to the culture. The marketing of previously seedy and poverty-ridden areas as trendy and exotic represents a superficial erasure of class and cultural differences. In the economy of the novel, the Island

106

functions as a liminal space where the boundaries between nature/city, life/death are being blurred.

The *topography* of the city plays an important symbolic role, exploring pockets of wilderness in the city as tropes for excessive femininity in man-made/patriarchal cultural structures. The topography of the city also functions as an imaginary map for the entire novel which inscribes the histories of the four women and their relationships, an otherwise untold story:

> [Tony] spreads out a street map, a map of downtown Toronto. Here is the Toxique, here is Queen Street, here is Roz's renovated office building; here are the ferry docks, and the flat Island where Charis's house still stands. Over here is the Arnold Garden Hotel, which is now a big clay-sided hole in the ground, a site of future development, because failing hotels go cheap and someone cut a good deal. Here is McClung Hall, and, to the north, Tony's own house, with West in it, upstairs in bed,... with the cellar in it, with the sand-table in it, with the map on it, with the city in it, with the house in it, with the cellar in it, with the map in it. Maps, thinks Tony, contain the ground that contains them. Somewhere in this infinitely receding headspace, Zenia continues to exist. Tony needs the map for the same reason she always uses maps: they help her to see, to visualize the topology, to remember. What she is remembering is Zenia. (*The Robber Bride*, 464)

The character Zenia is revealed to be as much a construction by the other characters and the reader, a fiction in which feminine excess and power otherwise censured can be imagined and narrated, which acts as a vehicle for narration itself.

In *The Robber Bride* Atwood's perceptions of personal fragmentation are explored in all the characters. This strategy exposes the bourgeois individualist discourse that denies the complex and contradictory nature of subjectivity and posits a coherent and autonomous subject. In the libidinal economy of Atwood's gothic text, the unleashing of feminine desire and fury undermines the dominant Western myths of gender and identity. That excess also challenges the stereotypical representations of female characters in popular fiction such as Gothics and the detective genre.

Atwood's complex treatment of fairy-tale discourse in *The Robber Bride* is the most radical and postmodernist element of the novel. Atwood illustrates that women are not passive consumers of colonial, patriarchal ideology as inscribed in fairy-tale discourse, but can actively and creatively subvert language and form to foreground issues of feminine desire and power.

This paper has explored developments in Atwood's articulation of post-colonial cultural and sexual politics. This has involved looking at the discursive strategies used by Atwood, in exploring colonial myths and contemporary reappraisals and revisions of constructions of national identity. The construction of a sliding, shifting perspective, using the mosaic as a trope for Canadian national identity, allows for a re-visioning of place as a space for negotiation of national and gendered identities.

NOTES

1. Diana Brydon and Helen Tiffin, *Decolonizing Fictions*. West Yorkshire: Dangaroo Press, 1993, 11. Further references are given in the text.
2. Mulvey, 'Magnificent Obsession', *Parachute* 42, 1986, 6-12. Cited in Linda Hutcheon, 'Circling the Downspout of Empire', in Adam and Tiffin (eds.) 1991 (see note 3), 179.
3. Margaret Atwood, *Survival: A Thematic Guide to Canadian Literature*. Anansi, Toronto, 1972. Page references are given in the text and relate to this edition.
4. Ian Adam and Helen Tiffin (eds.), *Past the Last Post: Theorizing Post-Colonialism and Post-Modernism*. University of Calgary Press, Calgary, 1991, vii.
5. Mary Ellis Gibson, 'Thinking About the Technique of Skiing When You're Halfway Down the Hill', in Earl G. Ingersoll (ed.), *Conversations*. London: Virago, 1992, 34.
6. Colin Nicholson (ed), *Margaret Atwood: Writing and Subjectivity*. London: Macmillan Press, 1994. Introduction, 5.
7. Margaret Atwood (1972), *Surfacing*. London: Virago, 1979. Page references are given in the text and relate to this edition.
8. William New, *Dreams of Speech and Violence*. Toronto: University of Toronto Press, 1987, x. Cited in Linda Hutcheon, 'Circling the Downspout of Empire', in Adam and Tiffin (eds.) 1991, 177.
9. Margaret Atwood, *Journals of Susanna Moodie*. Toronto: Oxford University Press, 1970. Page references are given in the text and relate to this edition.
10. Rita Felski, *Beyond Feminist Aesthetics*. Hutchinson Radius, 1989, 149. The reference in the excerpt is to the article by Sherill Grace, 'Quest for the Peaceable Kingdom: Urban/Rural Codes in Ray, Lawrence and Atwood', in: Susan Merrill Squier (ed), *Women Writers and the City*. Knoxville: University of Tennessee Press, 1984.
11. Margaret Atwood, *True Stories*. London: Jonathan Cape, 1982. Page references are given in the text and relate to this edition.
12. Linda Hutcheon, *The Canadian Postmodern: A Study of Contemporary English-Canadian Fiction*. Toronto: Oxford University Press, 1988, 2. Cited in Janice Kulyk Keefer, 'Hope Against Hopelessness: Margaret Atwood's *Life Before Man*', Nicholson (ed.), 1994, 162.
13. Margaret Atwood, 'Wilderness Tips', in Atwood, *Wilderness Tips*. London: Bloomsbury, 1991. Page references are given in the text and relate to this edition.
14. Margaret Atwood, *The Robber Bride*. London: Bloomsbury, 1993. Page references are given in the text and relate to this edition.
15. This point was made by Coral Ann Howells, to whom I am indebted, in her presidential address at the British Association for Canadian Studies, 1994, *Margaret Atwood's Canadian Signature: From Surfacing and Survival to Wilderness Tips*.
16. Margaret Atwood (1988), *Cat's Eye*. London: Bloomsbury, 1989.

A Bird in the House of Metafiction: Fantasizing Narratological Power in Margaret Laurence's Manawaka Stories

Brian Johnson

Traditionally, Margaret Laurence's critics have been reluctant to see the function of writing in *A Bird in the House* in anything other than liberal humanist terms. As Jon Kertzer suggests, 'through the perspective of art [Vanessa MacLeod] seeks a *moral* focus – a way of seeing that is also a way of accepting and forgiving' (24). Such a moral focus in the short stories is also closely tied to the sentimental since sentimentalism is itself 'connected loosely to a version of liberal humanism: valuing the individual, intrinsic value, emotion or pathos, the endorsement of niceness and cooperation and the family farm' (Clark 12). Hence, for Vanessa, as for Laurence, the writing act seems to be a means of what Kertzer calls 'figurative embracing' (28): a redemptive process that retrospectively and sympathetically connects the older, wiser writing subject with the ghosts of her ancestral past.

Significantly, however, this redemptive function of art in Laurence's novel is often marked by a strong anxiety about the authority of the bifurcated narrator and her relation to postmodernism's preoccupation with metafiction – a form of writing that 'self-consciously and systematically draws attention to its status as an artefact in order to pose questions about the relationship between fiction and reality' (Waugh 2). According to Kent Thompson, an early reviewer of the book, such troubling questions about artifice must not even be considered since, he assures us, 'By her *complete control of the method*, Margaret Laurence has avoided the usual dangers of this method – the danger of betraying the child's perspective by imposing judgements and thereby rewriting history and the danger of betraying the present by nostalgia – and has accomplished the virtues inherent in the method. That is, the adult narrator learns from what the child experienced and failed to understand' (152; my emphasis). The defensiveness of such critical gestures is just as evident in Jon Kertzer's more recent study, in which he argues that 'Vanessa discovers that

109

remembrance, confession, and personal identity all depend on story-telling', not because 'reality' is itself a problematic term, but rather, 'because understanding always falters behind experience' (24). Ultimately, however, the apology for art as a simple humanist reflector of deferred truth and the corresponding defense of realism that must accompany it are based on a respect for Laurence's own staunch adherence to the realist position that 'Fiction relates to life in a very real way' (quoted in Easingwood 20), even though Laurence herself admits that the 'narrative device' of dividing the narrator into two voices 'was a tricky one, and I can not even now personally judge how well it succeeds' ('Time' 158).

If the stubborn critical resistance to metafictional questions about form precludes any treatment of authority in the novel, Thompson's language at least provides a small window of opportunity through which such a discussion might be pursued. Because Thompson bases his argument that the narrator learns through 'the process of re-valuing Vanessa's judgements' on an appeal to Laurence's mastery of narrative form, the moral success of Vanessa's confession too must be predicated on a virtuoso performance of authorial control. As autobiographer, Vanessa herself becomes profoundly implicated in the same kind of rigid textual control that Thompson attributes only to Laurence – thereby occasioning a serious rupture between the ostensibly humanist ethic of the stories and the very form of their telling. In other words, the narrator's desire 'to forge an over-arching vision, which is sympathetic, creative, and humane' (Kertzer 34), seems to be at odds with a narrative mode that emphasizes the 'over-arching' authority of its own narrator.

Although Thompson is quick to diffuse 'the dangers' of Vanessa's retrospective narrator, and his notions of authorial 'control' are vague, their implications are elaborated and laid out more concretely by Peter Easingwood in a recent essay, 'Semi-autobiographical Fiction and Revisionary Realism in *A Bird in the House*' (1991). Easingwood raises the problem posed by Laurence's commitment to a realist tradition which 'appears to grant a higher priority to the content of a novel than to its form' (19) for the postmodern critic who scorns the notion 'that fiction can conceal the art by which it is produced ... as an outrageous imposition on the reader' (19-20). Easingwood's treatment of this contradiction in Laurence's work is deeply apologetic. He argues that, despite its conventional form, Vanessa's narrative at least puts into question the traditional social order and 'the sources of authority which dictate it' (21), inscribing a kind of 'revisionary realism' that is 'deeply opposed to a form of realism that would take for granted the conditions it describes' (29). This sounds remarkably similar to what Nancy K. Miller in a feminist context describes as 'italicization': the novel's inscription of 'the demand of the heroine for something else ... the extravagant wish for a story that would turn out differently' (352). Although Easingwood attempts to rescue Laurence's unfashionable adherence to realism by focussing on its subversive 'italicizing' elements, his essay too is ultimately silent on the question of the work's troublingly authoritative narrative form. If, as he insists, Vanessa's autobiography is engaged in questioning the sources of authority which dominate her childhood, Vanessa herself is exempt from any such scrutiny. Her own writerly authority remains, in the comforting fashion of the Victorian novelist's, undisputed (and indisputable) throughout the book.

Significantly, Laurence's commitment to realism in *A Bird in the House* extends beyond Easingwood's evocation of mimesis to accommodate realism's formal structure as well. The doubling of the narrative voice which speaks 'as though from two points in time, simultaneously' (Laurence 'Time' 159), artificially recreates the conditions of realist fiction whereby '[t]he conflict of languages and voices is apparently resolved ... through their subordination to the dominant voice of the omnipotent, godlike author' (Waugh 6). As David Williams argues, 'the narrative form of the stories, apart from their theme, suggest[s] the double perspective of historical autobiography, much like Augustine dividing himself into a wandering protagonist and a converted, far-seeing narrator ... The narrative technique, in other words, is reassuringly authoritative' ('Response'). Realist assumptions of transparent narrative and the authoritative tone it connotes are particularly problematic for a *Künstlerroman* like Laurence's in which the female artist ostensibly seeks to achieve a sympathetic understanding with her past by writing about it, even as her narrative voice constantly reinscribes her own omniscient and aesthetically distanced authority in its project 'to discipline the frightening disorder of the past, to assess its meaning and to redeem its faults' (Kertzer 32). Writing as a realist, therefore, Laurence leaves her work open to a serious contradiction since the artist novel typically 'opposes the heroic writer to a world still blinded by the false "transparency" of language' (Williams, *Confessional* 11). What, we might ask, are the consequences for a *Künstlerroman* in which the artist herself seems to partake of a similar blindness, what some might call 'an outdated and naive conception of her business as a novelist' (Easingwood 20)?

If the grammar of realist form insistently raises questions about power and authority that seem to qualify Vanessa's 'humanism', and Easingwood's apologia ultimately fails to account for the formal questions it raises, Nancy K. Miller suggests ways in which fantasies of power have always been a central, but hidden concern of women's fiction. In 'Emphasis Added' (1985), Miller bases her semiotic study of the plots of women's fiction on a feminist re-reading of Freud's 'The Relation of the Poet to Daydreaming' (1908), in which Freud posits a difference between male and female plots in fiction which he accounts for by arguing that the daydreams or 'phantasies' from which those fictions originate are gender-distinct. In the course of her argument, Miller exposes the claim that, contrary to ego-driven male fantasies, the plots of female fiction are characterized exclusively by a recourse to Romance, revealing Freud's affinity for socially-constructed patriarchal maxim that sets up 'a grammar of motives ... prescribing ... what wives, not to say women, should or should not do' (340). According to Freud's economy, women's 'erotic wishes dominate the[ir] phantasies *almost entirely*, for their ambition is *generally comprised* in their erotic longings' (quoted in Miller 346; her emphasis). Conversely, Miller argues that '[t]he repressed content [of women's fiction] ... would be not erotic impulses, but an impulse to power: a fantasy of power that would revise the social grammar in which women are never defined as subjects' (349). As Miller goes on to explain:

> The daydreams or fictions of women writers would then, like those of men, say, 'Nothing can happen to me!' But, the modalities of that invulnerability would be marked in an essentially different way. I am talking, of course, about the power of the weak. The inscription of this power is not always easy to decipher because ... 'the most essential form of accommodation for the weak is to conceal what power they do have'. (348-49)

The similarities between Miller's conception of women's fiction and the power dynamics inherent in Vanessa's own pretense to 'realism' are striking and they make Miller's argument particularly suggestive as a model for reading *A Bird in the House* as a text deeply implicated in the power fantasies of its narrator. As I will argue, Vanessa's storytelling is profoundly concerned with the hidden 'modalities of invulnerability', and it is precisely this masking of authority in a cloak of humanism that, as Easingwood says, 'leaves the critic uneasy' (19). When viewed from this perspective, realism may be the perfect narrative mode for the narrator who wishes to conceal the extent of her desire for authority and who wishes to exert that authority without fear of being challenged.

Thus, adapting Miller's revision of Freud to the female *Künstlerroman*, we might consider ways in which Vanessa's active re-membering of her past participates to a large degree in an 'ambitious wish' (Freud quoted in Miller 346) for *narratological* power. To do so, however, entails not simply exposing the hidden mediations of the adult Vanessa's narrative technique, which, as I have already suggested, is highly authoritarian, but also a recognition that such a need for writerly authority has informed her fiction from the beginning. It is surely striking that virtually all of the humanist readings of *A Bird in the House* ignore the careful attention given by the narrator to processes of artistic creation within the body of the work itself in the form of Vanessa's juvenile fictions. Here again, I turn to Kertzer for a representative (and typically dismissive) summary: 'She [Vanessa] composes several improbable, historical sagas (as Laurence herself did while a girl), but they are childish fantasies which we never take seriously except as signs of a lively imagination and an undeveloped talent' (34). As I will argue, however, Vanessa's 'childish fantasies' are absolutely central to an understanding of the apparent rupture between form and content in the work insofar as they reveal at every point a fierce desire for narratological power that is never really relinquished in the adult narrator's deployment of her own more sophisticated, but no less authoritarian, narrative. My approach to Laurence's collection of stories, then, is informed by a critical re-reading of Thompson's humanist, evolutionary dictum that 'the adult narrator learns from what the child experienced and failed to understand'.

From the very first story in the collection, Vanessa's storytelling seems to arise out of a response to the sources of patriarchal authority in Manawaka of the 1930s which 'mistrusts too much self-assertion by women and provides few opportunities for work, power, or freedom', channelling such female energies instead 'toward marriage or positions of support and service' (Kertzer 36). In the Brick House where women's discourse is strictly regulated by a maxim of silence that keeps them from offering any real challenge to Grandfather Connor's authority and reduces Aunt Edna's 'indomitability' to small verbal rebellions, 'whispered angrily' (33), Vanessa's Romantic fictions articulate a form of silent, hidden rebellion that is deeply rooted in a fantasy of power. Her story that begins: '*Sick to death in the freezing log cabin, with only the beautiful halfbreed lady* (no, *woman*) *to look after him, Old Jebb suddenly clutched his throat* – and so on' (23): for example, inscribes an imaginary reversal of her grandfather's domestic power that dominates her childhood in 'the Brick House' (11). 'Old Jebb' is, for a change, clearly at the mercy of a female figure who derives her power from her potential withholding of beneficence. Similar inscriptions of female power can be found in Vanessa's mythologizing of Piquette into 'a daughter of the forest, a kind of junior prophetess of the wilds, who might impart to me, if I took the right approach, some of the secrets which she undoubtedly knew – where the whippoorwill made her nest, how the coyote reared her young or whatever it was that it said in Hiawatha' (112), or her imaginative rendering of the 'beautiful and terrible' 'barbaric queen' (66).

It is certainly tempting to see stories like these as instances of a crude sort of proto-feminism in which the writing of women into positions of power traditionally denied to them by the patriarchal structure of Manawaka life may articulate an intuitive critique of that structure which is at some level socially motivated. As Helen M. Buss argues, 'Psychologically, Vanessa must invent a version of womanhood that is not as powerless as her two maternal figures, her mother and her aunt. On a cultural level, the split our society makes between the feminine as beautiful and the feminine as strong must be healed by the interruption of this figure in the imagination of the creative girl, in order to create the archetypal wholeness that the feminine world-view seeks.... Outside her writing, Vanessa finds no such manifestations; she searches her family circle in vain for the qualities of womanhood that rise unbidden in her fictional creations' (*Mother and Daughter* 56-7).

However, the young Vanessa's running authorial commentary and the circumstances surrounding the production of her fictions suggest that something very different from 'cultural' concerns motivates their composition. That is, her writing's fascination with female power has less to do with an incipient feminist social consciousness than it does with Vanessa's own desire for autonomous control, particularly since the women around her seem, typically and simply, to 'adapt, and hide their true selves to meet the demands of the patriarchy' (Buss, *Mother and Daughter* 57). In fact, by her own admission, Vanessa's childhood vision was never communal but always narcissistic: 'I still needed the conviction that no one except myself ever suffered anything' (19); 'I loved to talk about myself' (29). A critic like Buss, who sees in the stories in *A Bird in the House* an 'aware[ness] of a strong feminine world existing seemingly only to support and nurture its patriarchal masters, but engaged in a continual, *though perhaps largely unconscious*, subversion of that world ('Autobiographical' 155; my emphasis), can only do so with radical qualification. If Vanessa partakes in this 'subversion' as a young girl, any recognition of her social critique must be tempered with the comparable recognition that any gesture toward a larger social concern in her storytelling is always undercut by a reflection of the author's gaze back onto herself. In 'The Sound of Singing', for example, Vanessa's confession, 'I rarely listened in Sunday School, finding it more entertaining to compose in my head stories of spectacular heroism in which I figured as the central character, so I never knew what the text had been' (14), suggests ways in which the story of the female artist grows out of a rejection of the very scriptural authority that underwrites Manawaka's patriarchal social structure. The subversive implications of this detail, insofar as they speak to a desire to 'revise the social grammar' (Miller 348), are immediately undercut, however, by Vanessa's inwardly turned fantasy of personal power – her recurrent need to be 'the central character' in her own fictions.

A similar story of narratological power unfolds in 'The Mask of the Bear' where Vanessa turns once again to those patriarchal texts, appropriates them, and begins the process of their rewriting:

I thought about the story I was setting down in a five-cent scribbler at nights in my room. I was much occupied by the themes of love and death, although my experience of both had so far been gained principally from the Bible, which I read in the same way that I read Eaton's Catalogue or the collected works of Rudyard Kipling – because I had to read something, and the family's finances in the thirties did not permit the purchase of enough volumes of *Doctor Doolittle* or the *Oz* books to keep me going.

For the love scenes, I gained useful material from The Song of Solomon. *Let him kiss me with the kisses of his mouth, for thy love is better than wine*, or *By night on my bed I sought him whom my soul loveth; I sought him but I found him not*. My interpretation was somewhat vague, and I was not helped to any appreciable extent by the explanatory bits in small print at the beginning of each chapter – *The Church's love unto Christ. The Church's fight and victory in temptation*, et cetera.... To me, the woman in The Song was some barbaric queen, beautiful and terrible, and I could imagine her, wearing a long robe of leopard skin and one or two heavy gold bracelets, pacing an alabaster courtyard and keening her unrequited love. (65-66)

For a critic like Giovanna Capone, this story of how an exotic heroine is separated from her Sphinx-carving lover by a 'cruel pharaoh' (66) functions as little more than a set-up for the real-life reversal that follows when 'the image of passion, the reality of love, true pain, Aunt Edna's sacrifice to solitude' (Capone 167), lay bare the ineptness of Vanessa's romantic vision: 'I thought of my aunt, her sturdy laughter, the way she tore into the house-work, her hands and feet which she always disparagingly joked about, believing them to be clumsy. I thought of the story in the scribbler at home. I wanted to get home quickly, so I could destroy it' (78). Clara Thomas goes only slightly further by suggesting that Vanessa's storytelling records 'not only a process of emotional maturing ... but also Vanessa's growing awareness of appropriate and inappropriate modes of fiction, of the insufficiencies of the high romantic mode for the actual presentation of life's losses and agonies' (103). The maturing writer learns to give up romantic fantasy for 'real' life. However, to regard the story merely as a functional device through which Vanessa can chart her acquisition of 'life experience' or the sophistication of her writing technique is to ignore the power dynamic encoded in the writing process itself.

On one level, the narrative about the barbaric queen who is appropriated from both the biblical text and another classic of patriarchal narrative – Conrad's *Heart of Darkness* – seems to reflect Miller's notion of 'emphasis: an italicized version of what passes for neutral or standard face. Spoken or written, italics are a modality of intensity and stress; a way of marking what has always already been said, of making a common text one's own' (343). While a writerly act of this nature, like the first example of composing stories in church, does encode a discourse of difference by its maternal italicization of scripture, the motives for the production of the story itself point to ways in which the author's self-absorption and will to absolute power supersede the intuitive social critique. That is, the emphasis of the passage describing the events of 'The Silver Sphinx' is not on the themes of love and death, as Vanessa insists, or even, as I have suggested, on an imaginary assertion of matriarchal power. Rather, the narrative focus of this passage shifts away from the details of plot to settle on the power inherent in the writing act itself, suggesting ways in which the content of the story is actually peripheral to the writerly authority it engenders. In this case, the story's unwritten ending affords Vanessa an opportunity to exert her own kind of narratological power:

Should I have her die while he was away? Or would it be better if he perished out in the desert? Which of them did I like the least? With the characters whom I liked best, things always turned out right in the end. (66)

Thus, for the young Vanessa, writing is not simply 'frivolous' or 'escapist' (Kertzer 53); it also articulates her desire for near magus-like power that is not so different from the biblical authority she ostensibly transforms, even as it furnishes an outlet for the expression of that power by transforming the author into the god of her fictional world.

Vanessa's interest in narrative, then, seems to be informed by the same kinds of power fantasies that are operative in the doll-making sequence from 'The Sound of Singing' in which Vanessa discovers that

> It had become, somehow, overwhelmingly important for me to finish it. I did not even play with dolls very much, but this one was the beginning of a collection that I had planned. I could visualize them, each dressed elaborately in the costume of some historical period or some distant country, ladies in hoop skirts, gents in black top hats, Highlanders in kilts, hula girls with necklaces of paper flowers. But this one did not look at all as I imagined she would. Her wooden face, on which I had already pencilled eyes and a mouth, grinned stupidly at me, and I leered viciously back. *You'll be beautiful whether you like it or not,* I told her. (22)

Here again, the focus of the activity is explicitly directed away from product towards the process of making itself, since Vanessa has no interest in playing with the dolls, only in creating them. In her doll-world, Vanessa's is the voice that names, that dictates order: *'You'll be beautiful whether you like it or not'*. Significantly, the imperative, commanding *'you'* of the first story is picked up again in 'The Mask of the Bear' where it is similarly revealed as a syntactical reflex of power:

> Whenever I went into Simlow's Ladies' Wear with my mother, and made grotesque faces at myself in the long mirror while she tried on dresses, Millie Christopherson who worked there would croon a phrase which made me break into snickering until my mother, who was death on bad manners, tapped anxiously at my shoulders with her slender, nervous hands. *It's you,* Mrs. MacLeod, Millie would say feelingly, *no kidding it's absolutely you.* I appropriated the phrase for my grandfather's winter coat. *It's you,* I would simper nastily at him, although never, of course, aloud. (63)

In this case, Vanessa's appropriation of the saleswoman's discourse allows her to freeze Grandfather Connor as an aesthetic image and define him as 'The Great Bear' (63) – the literal embodiment of the coat that he wears – just as she defined her dolls in 'The Sound of Singing'. *'It's you'* works like a finger poised on the shutter of Vanessa's apparently all-seeing camera.

Doll-making in this early story anticipates the functional value that writing holds for Vanessa in 'The Mask of the Bear' where the author is figured in terms of divine power, not only because of her godlike relation to her fictional creations, but also because her own authority is metaphorically allied in other ways with patriarchal structures. Vanessa's description of her mother as 'slight and fine-boned, with long-fingered hands like those on my Chinese princess doll' (18) links her construction of the dolls with the patriarchy's analogous construction of women as dolls. Furthermore, Vanessa's 'vicious' assertion of that power sounds distinctly like the Old Testament God that Vanessa invokes who is '[d]istant, indestructible, totally indifferent' (138). Consequently, Vanessa's 'ambitious wish' manifests itself as a desire for power of the arbitrary masculine sort represented by Grandfather Connor, the Church, and God; Miller's communal and very positive vision of female power is seriously undermined by the ruthlessness of Vanessa's juvenile fictions.

This possibility that Vanessa's quest for power, at least as a girl, is no more than a reversal of the male-female binary in which the tyrant king is simply replaced by a comparable figure of female power rather than an attempt to collapse the hierarchical structure of power altogether, seriously problematizes feminist readings of the stories like Judith Lowder Newton's that want to see ways in which 'the portrayal of women's sphere can upset our preconceptions about power, because even though the sphere limits women's ability to act, it redefines power as capability, creative energy, and talent rather than as masculine force', thereby promoting 'a growth of consciousness that is potentially revolutionary' (quoted in Kertzer 63-4). In fact, Vanessa herself tells a very different story. As she says in 'The Half Husky' upon the discovery that Harvey Shinwell has finally given her an opportunity for revenge by stealing her telescope: 'I felt like shouting some Highland war-cry, or perhaps whistling *The MacLeod's Praise*. Or quoting some embattled line from Holy Writ. Vengeance is mine, *saith the Lord*' (155; my emphasis). Vanessa here is not simply 'quoting scripture', but rather exposing a desire to write herself into a position of divine authority that is dangerously at odds with the ostensibly humanist project of her later writing. In fact, the appearance of this tendency to figure herself as God or as a moral authority in a story that ends with so profound a rejection of humanism in the dramatic moment – when Vanessa rejects Harvey's aunt on the street – emphatically suggests the incompatibility of absolute authority with the humanist ethic. If the adult Vanessa's narrative presents itself as the actualization of what Newton sees as a move to redefine power in feminist, or even humanist terms, her juvenile fictions suggest that she has a very long road ahead.

Related to Vanessa's narrative narcissism and her desire for god-like authority are Vanessa's attempts to escape her oppressive origins by recreating herself through fiction. As she says of the biblical passages she memorizes to recite at the Brick House, 'My lines were generally of a warlike nature for I did not favor the meek stories and *I had no use at all for the begats*' (14; my emphasis). In fact, Vanessa's rejection of 'the begats' typifies her denial of origins in her own writing as well as her resistance to Aunt Edna's belief that she takes after Grandfather Connor throughout the book. For Vanessa, the escape from bloodlines is closely tied to the possibility that the self can be created anew through language. This impulse for self-begetting narrative is not only apparent in Vanessa's obsessive inscription of herself as the 'central character' in all of her stories, it is also thematized in an early section of her pioneer epic, 'The Pillars of the Nation':

> I was planning in my head a story in which an infant was baptised by Total Immersion and swept away by the river which happened to be flooding. (Why would it be flooding? Well, probably the spring ice was just melting. Would they do baptisms at that time of year? The water would be awfully cold. Obviously some details needed to be worked out here.) The child was dressed in a christening robe of white lace, and the last the mother saw of her was a scrap of white being swirled away towards the Deep Hole near the Wachakwa bend, where there were blood-suckers. (24-5)

Within the context of Vanessa's desire for independence, her narrative erasure of the infant girl just prior to the ritual naming that will define her as part of a spiritual and social community, emphatically points to the author's similar desire for the power to erase her own ancestral past and begin again, self-authored.

If the young Vanessa is already implicated in metafictional issues of self-creation, her juvenile fictions invite us to compare her obvious falsification of reality to the apparently legitimate version presented by the adult narrator. Although the voice of the adult narrator that shapes the stories – by 'choos[ing] which parts of the personal past, the family past and the ancestral past have to be revealed in order for the present to be realized and the future to happen' (Laurence, 'Time' 160) – constantly assures us that she has abandoned the need for an authoritarian discourse, her reconstruction of the past suggests the persistence of that concern. The implicit commentary on her new writerly motives inherent in the past tense construction in phrases like 'I still [then] needed the conviction that no one except myself ever suffered anything', or 'I could not [then] bear to be laughed at' (34), records an affirmation that the adult narrator has grown to accept an awareness of others and the value of self-mockery; just as implicitly, however, her narrative form seriously challenges those assumptions.

Perhaps the most suggestive example of this challenge occurs in 'To Set Our House in Order' where the thematic focus is shaped by Vanessa's growing apprehension of the suffocating and debilitating nature of order as it is embodied in Grandmother MacLeod's maxim which, significantly, she inherited from the patriarchy:

> 'God loves Order,' Grandmother MacLeod replied with emphasis. 'You remember that, Vanessa. God loves Order – he wants each one of us to set our house in order. I've never forgotten those words of my father's.' (49)

In fact, 'To Set Our House in Order' records the process of Vanessa's unlearning of this maxim and rejection of its dehumanizing effects until the contemplation of a world that is dangerous, unfair and chaotic, in which 'the accidents that might easily happen to a person – or, of course, might not happen, might happen to somebody else' (60), gives way to her articulation of a new maxim in the final lines of the story:

> I could not really comprehend these things, but I sensed their strangeness, their disarray. I felt that whatever God might love in this world, it was certainly not order. (61)

As Miller says, 'A heroine without a maxim, like a rebel without a cause, is destined to be misunderstood' (340) in the narratives of the patriarchy. The feminist rebel with a cause might well reject 'the maxims of the sociolect' (345); but in this instance, Vanessa's rewriting of the maxim places her in the position of the 'God [who] loves Order' who has just been revealed as an imposter. The impulse, in other words, to 'demaximize' the maxim only maximizes the authority of the iconoclast.

Kertzer and others have typically read these lines as watermarks in Vanessa's 'moral development', suggesting ways in which 'she learns to appreciate how people suffer and then go on living with their pain', or how, '[b]ecause she shares their grief, she enlarges her conscience as well as her consciousness' (50). Only Michael Darling has pointed out the narrator's contradictory resistance to her own intuitive maxim in her orderly composition of the remembrance itself. Arguing for the ultimate triumph of artistic order over the messiness of everyday affairs, Darling returns us to the problem of Vanessa's 'metafiction' since the memoir's achievement of 'some kind of unity out of the apparent disorder of her past' (quoted in Kertzer, 50) is at odds with Vanessa's supposedly humanist recognition that someone other than herself 'ever suffered anything'.

Kertzer's elaborate response to this textual aporia is revealing because he too finds that the only way to accommodate the fact that 'Laurence ... never breaks down the precision of her narrative as other modern writers do, to mimic the disruption that she presents' (51) is to fall back into arguments that value narrative authority and the monumental order it instills. As he says,

> The unwavering gaze of the narrator nimbly sorts out the details and only apparently recalls things at random. Each detail contributes to the significance of the whole and neatly converges at the end in a muted finale. The second last paragraph reassembles images and symbols (the dead sister and uncle, the volumes of Greek, the iced cake, the pictures in the house), so that the disarray that Vanessa discovers in her family does not *taint* Laurence's style. (51; my emphasis)

The 'disarray' whose recognition only a page previous had been so central to Vanessa's 'moral development' is figured here as a threat that might 'taint' Laurence's narrative. Ironically, Kertzer finds himself caught in the same contradictions as Vanessa since he too can only justify the stories' narrative form by rejecting their thematic conclusions. Also significant, however, is the fact that Kertzer attempts to avoid the contradiction altogether by positing a distinction between Vanessa and Laurence that would allow the adult Vanessa to retain her position as narrator in a thematic capacity, but whose traditional style must ultimately be ascribed to (and excused by) Laurence. As Kertzer's two-step makes clear, without this radical concession on the part of the reader, the narrative remains hopelessly fractured.

Although I have already discussed at some length the problem posed by this bifurcation of narrative selves with respect to the stories' replication of realist omniscience, David Williams suggests other ways in which Vanessa's construction of story resists a simple humanist reading:

> One of the troubling things for me about the stories in *A Bird in the House* is the arbitrary nature of their resolutions. The retrospective narrator drags in the mask of a bear to remember that there was once a human being behind Grandfather Connor's mask. She discovers long after her father's death an unlikely photograph in his desk to help her understand the depth of his feeling about the Remembrance Day Parade. She summons up Ovid in 'Horses of the Night' to put into new perspective Chris's fascination with imaginary horses. The narrative technique, in other words, is reassuringly authoritative. The converted narrator, like Augustine, sees everything from an unmoving still-point above time. Does this not suggest that Laurence meant what she said – that in *The Stone Angel* and *A Bird in the House* she discovered 'a good deal of the matriarch' in herself? ('Response')

Thus, Thomas's concern that the stories finally become 'somewhat oppressive' due to 'the restrictions of their circumference and the sameness of their final effect' (105) might be seen in terms of the narrator's desire for a humanist connection that is falsified, or at least undercut, by her inability to give up her own authority. In 'The Mask of the Bear', for example, if Vanessa's failure to forgive her grandfather for his betrayal of Grandmother Connor is redeemed by her retrospective humanizing of him, redemption is predicated on a refusal to accept anything but her own 'converted' sentimental vision of reality that sees masks as 'equivocal symbols because they reveal the truth by attempting to hide it' (Kertzer 52). In other words, Vanessa finds herself ultimately unable to embrace the contradictions of Grandfather Connor's personality, so, instead, she sublimates the details of the realist narrative into the totemic symbol of the bear mask at the end of the story in order to effectively discard what doesn't fit:

> It was a weird mask. The features were ugly and yet powerful. The mouth was turned down in an expression of sullen rage. The eyes were empty caverns, revealing nothing. Yet as I looked, they seemed to draw my own eyes towards them, until I imagined I could see somewhere within that darkness a look which I knew, a lurking bewilderment. I remembered then that in the days before it became a museum piece, the mask had concealed a man. (88)

By turning her attention finally to the mask as illusion, Vanessa authoritatively inscribes a sentimental identification with her grandfather at the cost of the

Bear himself. In short, she appropriates his memory and rewrites it in order to accommodate the demands of her own 'humanist' vision.

As we have seen, such acts of appropriation and circumscription are hardly new to Vanessa. By simply displacing the bear coat with the mask of the bear, she attempts to name – and in naming, fix – Grandfather Connor as she did in the story's opening pages: 'It's you', she insists. Although her metaphors have shifted, their authoritative power is comfortably sustained. 'The Mask of the Bear', in other words, is not progressive in Thompson's sense – that the narrator 'has been learning throughout the book by the very process of re-valuating [the young] Vanessa's judgements' (153) – but circular, in its valorization of authority in Vanessa's fictions. Along similar lines, Vanessa's reduction of the man to an aesthetic symbol uncovers a gap in the story's flow that is symptomatic of her thirst for control. Although Vanessa suggests that her appropriation of the bear coat to define her grandfather may be a crucial strategy for her own empowerment, the apparently arbitrary substitution of *her own* symbol at the end of the story reveals yet another level of one-upmanship operative in her narrative. Stripping Grandfather Connor of his bear coat, Vanessa demonstrates the full potency of her narratological power that can, 'through a *final* metamorphosis, transform the bear back into a man' (Kertzer 50; my emphasis).

The acts of 'literal or figurative embracing' (28) that Kertzer finds in all of Laurence's fiction, however, are also troubling because they are always retrospective and always fictionalized. Vanessa's emotional connections with her father, with Piquette, with Chris, and with Grandfather Connor are all established outside the dramatic moment – in a narrative consolation of form – after a failure of compassion in her own life. Thus, for Vanessa, it would seem, forgiveness can only be accomplished '[m]any years later, when Manawaka was far away from me, in miles and in time' (86); 'Once when I was on a holiday from college' (143); or 'Twenty years later [when] I went back to Manawaka again' (190). Still more disturbing is the fact that not one of Vanessa's moments of redemption takes place with a living person – with the sole exception of Chris, who, as a patient in a mental hospital, is sufficiently absent to remain unthreatening, and even this 'gentl[e]' and 'ruthless' embrace is confined to the solipsism of the imagination. To what extent, then, does the absence of the real person become a necessary condition of Vanessa's retrospective forgiveness? In other words, are there ways in which Vanessa's humanism is predicated on an authority that is itself underwritten by a paradigm of absence?

Returning to Vanessa's juvenile fictions, there is ample evidence to suggest that narratological power is only effective in the absence of an intervening reality. As a young writer, Vanessa consistently cuts short her narratives at the point where story and real life intersect and the ineffectuality of her writerly power to contain, alter, or escape from that reality is painfully exposed. Her desire to destroy her manuscript of the barbaric queen when confronted by the reality of Aunt Edna's suffering is but one example of the interrupted story. Vanessa's unfinished epic, '*The Pillars of the Nation*', presents itself as yet another instance of a story whose power is interrupted by the intrusion of a reality that Vanessa would prefer to avoid:

> That had been my epic of pioneer life. I had proceeded to the point in the story where the husband, coming back to the cabin one evening, discovered to his surprise that he was going to become a father. The way he ascertained this interesting fact was that he found his wife constructing a birch-bark cradle. Then came the discovery that Grandfather Connor had been a pioneer, and the story had lost its interest for me. If pioneers were like *that*, I had thought, my pen would be better employed elsewhere. (68)

The interruption of narrative by reality is once again the focus of Vanessa's last and most comprehensively resonant juvenile fiction which can be read as a metonymy for her own desperation to escape Manawaka. The similarities of Marie's 'unpromising life' and her imprisonment in 'the grey stone inn' to Vanessa's own circumstances in the Brick House transparently point to a movement toward uniting narratological power with real power. Thus, the question on which the plot turns, 'How to get Marie out of her unpromising life at the inn and onto the ship that would carry her to France' (163), takes on a very personal, if not practical significance for the author. After rejecting as improbable the possibility that Marie might marry either Radisson or Groseilliers, Vanessa finds herself and her story at a loss:

> I lay on the seat of the MacLaughlin-Buick feeling disenchantment begin to set in. Marie would not get out of the grey stone inn. She would stay there all her life. The only thing that would happen to her was that she would get older. Probably the voyagers weren't even Radisson or Groseilliers at all. Or if they were, they wouldn't give her a second glance. I felt I could not bear it. I no longer wanted to finish the story. What was the use, if she couldn't get out except by ruses which clearly wouldn't happen in real life? (165)

Finally, the intervention of the real, which impedes the merger of life and narrative, brings about the end of writing by exposing the futility of its fantasies. As Easingwood notes, 'None of Vanessa's many childhood stories and daydreams ... allows her for a moment to triumph over a given reality' (25). According to Vanessa's childhood experiences with writing, then, narratological power seems to be illusory and ultimately unfulfilling. However, for the older Vanessa who stands outside of narrative time, the circumstances of writing are significantly different. If we consider that the collected stories of *A Bird in the House* are the only finished narratives in a work characterized by interrupted stories, the success of Vanessa's humanism must ultimately hinge on whether, in the writing of the book itself, Vanessa overcomes her predilection for blurring the boundaries between narratological and social power that inhibits her earlier tellings, or whether she merely evades the problem altogether by writing about the past from a position of incontestable authority. As the sole survivor of her story, she risks the danger of having it all her own way, of guaranteeing her own authority by leaving no one who can contest it.

Although narrativity clearly fails to present an effective means of power when confronted by presence, the conclusions of Vanessa's *Künstlerroman* suggest the founding of a different kind of power – one that entails the possibility that the artist can appropriate the past as a means of retrospectively asserting her own authority. In the final pages of the last story, 'Jericho's Brick Battlements', Vanessa seems to achieve the humanist goal of her narrative by figuratively internalizing a connection with her grandfather when she proclaims, 'I had feared and fought the old man, yet he proclaimed himself in my veins' (191). However, the circumstances informing this ostensible embrace resist so simple a reading. The exorcism of her grandfather's story that had previously oppressed her own creativity, for example, occurs 'suddenly' at her grandfather's funeral when 'the minister's recounting of these familiar facts struck me as though I had never heard any of it before' (188). Following the funeral, Vanessa initially finds herself unable to forgive – 'I could not cry. I wanted to, but could not' (189) – but as she moves outside to her grandfather's MacLaughlin-Buick, she finds that the vehicle itself 'had altered' (189):

> I wondered what the car might have meant to him, to the boy who walked the hundred miles from Winnipeg to Manawaka with hardly a cent in his pockets. The memory of a memory returned to me now. I remembered myself remembering driving in it with him, in the ancient days when he seemed as large and admirable as God. (190)

As Kertzer suggests, this passage is central not only to Vanessa's artistic development but also to her acceptance of her grandfather as a human being, because it records her attainment of 'the aesthetic detachment of the mature artist' that enables 'the sympathetic but critical perspective that Vanessa needs to cultivate if she is to be a writer' (84). There is, however, something disturbing in the fact that, for all her yearning for connection, Vanessa's narrative cannot begin until the people she wishes to embrace are dead. Even the tentative identification with her grandfather in 'Mask of the Bear' which occurs early in the collection doesn't happen chronologically until years later, after Grandfather Connor's death, just as his humanizing in the last story is bound up in the proceedings of the funeral itself – at the moment of his most radical absence.

If the death of her subject becomes the necessary condition for an 'autobiographical fiction' that purports to establish a living link with the past, one is inclined to question the critic who claims that Vanessa 'has finally accepted the past, represented at its most domineering by her grandfather' (Kertzer 80) in those oft-quoted lines of the last story. Hasn't she rather reached a point where writing permits her to possess and own that past, to aesthetically reshape it, that exists only in absentia – as a memory of a memory? As David Williams insists, 'The acknowledgement that "he proclaimed himself in my veins" does not do away with her need for authority' ('Response'). Thus, Vanessa's affirmation, 'he proclaimed himself in my veins', seems disarmingly like a sentimental non sequitur – the necessary, but mechanical conclusion of a 'humanist' work that has until this point been extremely critical and even punitive in its treatment of Grandfather Connor. For a work that tries to articulate 'the pain and bewilderment of one's own knowledge of other people' (Laurence, 'Time' 159), the conclusions of its stories, particularly the last one, reveal the pervasiveness of Vanessa's opposing desire for aesthetic closure that is clearly not possible in life. Ultimately, Vanessa's humanist conclusion is painfully ironic since the authoritarian blood of her grandfather does indeed proclaim itself in her veins, but even more strongly in the hidden body of her carefully controlled metafiction.

If the authoritative form of the stories in *A Bird in the House* represents the hidden actualization of Vanessa's frustrated pursuit of narratological power in her juvenile fictions, perhaps the critical befuddlement over the rupture between the competing discourses of authority and humanism needs to be redressed. Miller's discussion of silence and plausibility in women's fiction is helpful here since, we remember, '[t]he inscription of [women's] power is not always easy to decipher, because ... "the most essential form of accommodation for the weak is to conceal what power they do have"'. 'Moreover', she writes, 'when these modalities of difference are perceived, they are generally called *implausibilities*' (349; my emphasis). Miller's formulation of 'implausible narrative', based on Genette's recognition that '[t]he relationship between a plausible narrative and the system of plausibility to which it subjects itself is ... essentially mute: the conventions of genre function like a system of natural forces and constraints which the narrative obeys as if without noticing them, and *a fortiori* without naming them' (quoted in Miller, 343), points to ways in which the critic's objection to the 'implausibility' of Laurence's metafictional realism is based on Laurence's construction of a narrative whose form encodes the authority of silence by its refusal 'to trouble, to question, to make both problematic and provisional any ... desire for order or truth through the powers of the human imagination' (Hutcheon quoted in Williams, 'Confessional' 31).

Thus, rather than refocussing our attention on the ostensible discrepancies between form and content in the work, Miller's account of implausible narrative – such that 'the refusal of the demands of one economy may mask the inscription of another ... [that] ... may seem silent, or unarticulated in/as *authorial commentary (discourse)*, without being absent' (344) – draws the work together into an ironic consistency even as it admits the possibility that Laurence herself, through her adherence to realist modes of fiction, participates in an unconscious assertion of narratological power. To reconsider at every level the role of writing in *A Bird in the House* as a modality of power is ultimately to repudiate – at least in part – the argument that Vanessa's fiction, to say nothing of Laurence's, is hopelessly fractured. Rather, tracing the development of writing in the novel forces us to ask radical new questions about the origins, practice, and consequences of narratological power in Laurence's fiction.

REFERENCES

Buss, Helen M, 'Margaret Laurence and the Autobiographical Impulse', in: Kristjana Gunnars (ed.), *Crossing the River: Essays in Honour of Margaret Laurence*. Winnipeg: Turnstone Press, 1988, 147-68.

Buss, Helen M, *Mother and Daughter Relationships in the Manawaka Works of Margaret Laurence*. Victoria: English Literary Studies, 1985.

Capone, Giovanna, '*A Bird in the House*: Margaret Laurence on Order and the Artist', in: Robert Kroetsch and Reingard M. Nischik (eds.), *Gaining Ground: European Critics on Canadian Literature*. Edmonton: NeWest Press, 1988, 161-70.

Clark, Suzanne, *Sentimental Modernism: Women Writers and the Revolution of the Word*. Bloomington, Indianapolis: Indiana University Press, 1991.

Easingwood, Peter, 'Semi-autobiographical Fiction and Revisionary Realism in *A Bird in the House*', in: Carol A. Howells and Lynette Hunter (eds.), *Narrative Strategies in Canadian Literature*. Philadelphia: Open UP, 1991, 19-29.

Kertzer, Jon, *'That House in Manawaka': Margaret Laurence's A Bird in the House*. Toronto: ECW Press, 1992.

Laurence, Margaret, *A Bird in the House*, 1970. Toronto: McClelland & Stewart, 1994.

Laurence, Margaret, 'Time and the Narrative Voice', in: W.H. New (ed.), *Margaret Laurence*. Toronto: McGraw-Hill Ryerson, 1977, 156-60.

Miller, Nancy K, 'Emphasis Added: Plots and Plausibilities in Women's Fiction', in: Elaine Showalter (ed.), *The New Feminist Criticism: Essays on Women, Literature, and Theory*. New York: Pantheon, 1985, 339-60.

Thomas, Clara, *The Manawaka World of Margaret Laurence*. Toronto: McClelland & Stewart, 1988.

Thompson, Kent, 'Review of *A Bird in The House*', In W.H. New (ed.), *Margaret Laurence*. Toronto: McGraw-Hill Ryerson, 1977, 152-55.

Waugh, Patricia, *Metafiction: The Theory and Practice of Self-Conscious Fiction*. London, New York: Routledge, 1990.

Williams, David, *Confessional Fictions: A Portrait of the Artist in the Canadian Novel*. Toronto, Buffalo, London: University of Toronto Press, 1991.

Williams, David, *Response*, paper presented to Kanadistik/Canadian Studies: Perspectives on Canadian Writing, University of Manitoba, September 23-25, 1987.

Re-imagining a Stone Angel: The Absent Autobiographer of *The Stone Diaries*

David Williams

In an interview with Joan Thomas, Carol Shields sketches the avant-garde character of her fictional autobiography of Daisy Goodwill Flett as told in *The Stone Diaries* (1993): 'There's a sort of postmodern box-within-the-box, within-the-box. I mean, I'm writing the novel, and I'm writing her life, and I'm writing her knowledge of her life – so that's one. But it's also her looking at her life, so I think she has to be in first person sometimes to comment from outside. But the really tricky part was to write about a woman thinking her autobiography in which she is virtually absent' (Thomas 58-9).

The idea of a woman 'thinking her autobiography' is not, of course, what is tricky or postmodern about *The Stone Diaries*, since the form itself is fairly conventional, and, in Margaret Laurence's *The Stone Angel* (1964), finds a key modernist example of the type. Both novels are set in the Manitoba of a bygone century, though Laurence's Hagar Shipley seems to be coeval with the birth of the province, while Daisy Goodwill is born a generation later, in 1905. The story of each life is told in ten chapters, and the structure of each narrative is mostly linear. If anything, the chronology of *The Stone Angel* is more tricky, since the dramatic present of the narrator demands a series of flashbacks told in contrapuntal, yet chronological order, which gradually converge toward a moment of revelation in the teller's present circumstances. In *The Stone Diaries*, on the other hand, the teller's present is rarely dramatized, if its circumstances are implied; and the narrative structure follows the conventional pattern of linear history from 'Birth' and 'Childhood' through 'Marriage', 'Love', and 'Motherhood' to 'Work', 'Sorrow', and 'Ease', before ending in 'Illness and Decline' and 'Death'.

And yet the form of these two 'cogitative' autobiographies, with so much overlap between them of place and time and structure, could hardly be more dissimilar. For the ninety-year-old heroine of Laurence's novel is never really absent from her own story. Her memories occupy and organize the narrative of her final weeks, much as Shirley Douglas in James W. Nichol's theatrical adaptation of Hagar's story occupies the stage of past and present alike. Laurence's elderly protagonist is still so incapable of detachment, or of looking beyond the self, that she fails for a long time to see herself repeating many of the mistakes she made in her youth. Hagar's story – told to *herself* in the novel, if not on the stage – constitutes her final attempt 'to tell away the threat of endings' (Williams 90), not in order to possess the totality of her life or the truth about her past, but in order to preserve her integrity as an inviolate subject. In fact, this refusal of an audience is so crucial to Hagar's narrative that it undermines from the outset the stage adaptation with its generic requirement of an internal audience for its dramatic monologue. For Hagar's fanatical privacy, like her earlier refusals to reveal herself to any friend or family, works in the novel to keep an inward core of her forever private: 'I didn't let him know. I never spoke aloud, and I made certain that the trembling was all inner ... I prided myself upon keeping my pride intact, like some maidenhead' (*Angel* 81). Only when she confesses her part in her son's death to the stranger Murray Ferney Lees in her narrative present does Hagar surrender her hard-won subjectivity to a community of fellow sufferers in a hospital ward.

In a literary sense, this sort of privacy comes to us from the very origins of the English novel which both document and develop an expanding sphere of subjectivity in English society after the Restoration. As John J. Richetti remarks of *Moll Flanders*, 'Defoe's great achievement in this book was to communicate something important in the structure of eighteenth-century feeling. *Moll Flanders* is especially a part of the century's expanding literature of privacy' (Richetti 139). In a crucial way, Hagar is more like Moll than we have realized: '"More to hide" – the expression reveals a truth about the self in *Moll Flanders* and Defoe's other narratives: their confessional mode is a sign that selfhood is a matter of secrecy; the more characters have to "reveal" the more they may be said to exist' (Richetti 128). For Moll, who confesses everything, confesses nothing, since she doesn't even tell us her true name. Hagar, by contrast, clings to her name as the guarantor of her identity: 'Stupid old baggage, who do you think you are? *Hagar*. There's no one like me in this world' (*Angel* 250). But the less she lets slip out, or the more she holds her story in, the more she feels she possesses herself in private, away from the public domain. Such privacy has for several centuries now been the basis of liberal society, founded on the freedom of the individual. 'I think; therefore I am', the philosopher first announced as the subjective ground of epistemology; but in so doing, he also offered the private subject as the ground of religion, politics, and social organization throughout the modern era.

In *The Stone Diaries*, by contrast, a question mark is put over the whole field of subjectivity. For a reader soon notices that the autobiographer's story of 'Childhood, 1916' elides the child, beginning instead with the story of her guardian, 'Barker Flett at thirty-three' (41), and pursuing the life of her natural father, Cuyler Goodwill, who has built a great tower as 'a monument to lost love' (71). So, too, the autobiographer's thoughts in a chapter on 'Marriage, 1927' only marginally concern the bride. The usual conventions of wedding narrative, rooted in figures of transformation – the social, legal, psychological, and physical changes wrought through marriage, are declined in favor of the life changes wrought in the stories of four men. Cuyler Goodwill moves from being a Manitoba stonecutter to a silver-tongued Indiana businessman: 'And he is oddly unapologetic about his several metamorphoses, rarely looking back, and never for a minute giving in to the waste and foolishness of nostalgia. "People change," he's been heard to say, or "Such and such was only a chapter in my life"' (92). In similar fashion, 'Magnus Flett of Tyndall, Manitoba, retired quarry worker' reverses his life's journey by going '"home" to the Orkney Islands' (94), still unable to account for his wife's desertion of him and the alienation of his sons. One of these sons, Barker Flett, is also portrayed as repressing his shame of lust for an eleven-year-old Daisy and becoming a 'self-occupied' (112) bachelor, though he sends the bride-to-be a bank draft for $10,000 as a wedding gift from his deceased mother's estate. Finally, there is the bridegroom, Harold A. Hoad, whose life has been utterly corrupted by the suicide of his father, and whose marriage ends after two weeks in his drunken plunge through a window to his death on the paving stones below. Only for a few pages do the autobiographer's thoughts linger on impending changes in the life of the bride: first, in an improbable three-page monologue of do's and don't's in the voice of the mother-in-law; then in three pages of conversation by Daisy and her bridesmaids speculating on sex. But in the end, the marriage is never consummated; whether this is due to the groom's drunkenness, or seasickness, or disinterest is never certain. All that is certain is the irony of the title; for this 'Marriage' is no marriage whatsoever, and the bride herself is 'virtually absent' from her own memoir.

What is truly postmodern, then, about *The Stone Diaries* may be its use of the form of autobiography to decentre the figure of an autonomous subject, or to question the metaphysics of identity. In the three decades which have elapsed since publication of *The Stone Angel*, both the structuralist and poststructuralist critiques of identity seem to have altered the usual landmarks of autobiography, making it impossible any more to write unproblematically, or even un-self-consciously, of the self. The most obvious context for explaining this sea-change in the currents of life writing would have to be Jacques Derrida's critique of the metaphysics of self-presence – the idea 'of a full speech that was fully *present* (present to itself, to its signified, to the other)' (8), or the commonsense notion that consciousness was ever fully present to itself in the act of hearing/understanding oneself speak.

And yet Shields' novel would seem to shrug off deconstruction as a context for the life story of her autobiographer who is 'virtually absent'. As Daisy's daughters remark on her absence from her life – or as Daisy imagines them remarking on that absence after her death – she was apparently

'Afraid to look inside herself. In case there was nothing there.'
'Isn't that what Buddhists try so hard to get to?'
'The Buddhists?'
'Wanting to arrive at a state of nothingness?' (356)

A subject who seems to have 'arrive[d] at a state of nothingness' at the end of her life is nonetheless still alive and still imagining such conversations at the end of her story. All nine chapters which precede the final chapter, 'Death', are carefully dated, while the tenth is not. Even the obituary which opens this final chapter has yet to record the date of her demise 'on – , in the month of – in the year 199 – ' (343). The daughters, it is true, do speak of their mother in this final chapter as if her life were over; but suddenly Daisy appears out of a collection of various recipes and lists which document her life to speak in the first person: 'I'm still here, inside the (powdery, splintery) bones, ankles, the sockets of my eyes, shoulder, hip, teeth, I'm still here, oh, oh' (352). Ultimately, a third-person narrator even tells us that 'Daisy Goodwill, in her final illness, the illness she is reputed to have borne with such patience, was left with only her death to contemplate' (357-58). The absent subject is somehow still present as well; absence is not the whole of the story.

Still here, the autobiographer insists, though Daisy now seems to look back at her life from a point beyond her impending death. By what means, then, is she able to detach herself from her own existence to reach a Buddhist-like 'state of nothingness'? At the end, she has to find some way to stand outside as well as inside her life, knowing 'that what lies ahead of her must be concluded by the efforts of her imagination and not by the straight-faced recital of a throttled and unlit history' (340). And yet this stance of being outside as well as inside her life is hardly new to her. For Daisy, the twenty-two-year-old bride who was widowed more than sixty years ago, has apparently always known how to get outside herself: 'You might like to believe that Daisy has no gaiety left in her, but this is not true, since she lives outside her story as well as inside' (123). We might only wonder who is this narrator who addresses us in the second person? Yet chances are that it is Daisy speaking, since any form of second-person narration implies the direct address of a first person. And, given that the novel is coded as autobiography from its opening sentence – 'My mother's name was Mercy Stone Goodwill' (1) – the code of autobiography remains in effect in the presence of an implicit first person.

But such transpositions of voice also reveal a means by which the 'I' might get outside itself, or step back from its own discourse, in effect unvoicing itself. At the end of Daisy's life story, a third-person narrator intervenes to say that 'All she's trying to do is keep things straight in her head. To keep the weight of her memories evenly distributed. To hold the chapters of her life in order ... Words are more and more required. And the question arises: what is the story of a life? A chronicle of fact or a skillfully wrought impression?' (340). The question is all the more pertinent for the way that Daisy, the first-person narrator who relates the story of her 'Birth, 1905', has situated herself in her narrative as an adult who is present at her own nativity. Even as she 'sees' it happening, she says, 'It is a temptation to rush to the bloodied bundle pushing out between my mother's legs, and to place my hand on my own beating heart, my flattened head and infant arms amid the mess of glistening pulp' (23).

Later, in her narrative of 'Motherhood, 1947', Daisy will describe her own children as being likewise 'awestruck by the doubleness of memory, the hold it has on them, as mysterious as telephone wires or the halo around the head of the baby Jesus' (175). They are naturally fascinated by any doubling of the self through memory, as well as by the presence of another time in the moment. But none of them is quite so literally doubled as the self of this child Daisy who seems to be both a mother to the woman and a woman wishing to mother this child. Already present in the scene of memory as a tiny infant body, she presents herself as a second, adult body – the midwife, as it were, to her own arrival in the world. Of course, such corporeal doubling only makes more graphically evident the sort of temporal doublings endemic to autobiography. Any self who looks back may assume a single name and speak as one person, but various bodies appearing under the same sign are obviously multiple. Thus, even though successive times may be collapsed into the same moment of telling, successive beings who go by the same name cannot be collapsed into the same body. The 'I' is split from the outset by time, though memory (in this case 'memories' which are patently not the child's own, but must be supplied by others) is meant to bridge the gap between temporally different selves.

And yet 'what is the story of a life' after it becomes apparent that such gaps of time cannot be crossed? Longing to be present at her birth, to touch the mother who will be absent for the rest of her life, the adult narrator has to confess that she cannot do so. Even the possessive pronouns which mark the text until the moment of the mother's death – 'Light from the doorway fell on my mother's broad face, giving it a look of luster. My father was leaning toward her, his hand covering hers' (17) – have to be surrendered after the moment of catastrophe, as if to mark the dispossession of the motherless child: 'Where, you ask, is the Malvern pudding [with which the narrative opened], weighted with its ancient stone? It has been set aside, as has my mother's cookery book. They will not be seen again in this story. I am swaddled in – what? – a kitchen towel. Or something, perhaps, yanked from Clarentine Flett's clothesline, a pillowslip dried stiff and sour in the Manitoba sun' (38-9). This rupture in the life of the child is ultimately foregrounded as a rupture in the very plot of autobiography: the absence of the mother begets this absence in the subject. As the narrator says of the child who becomes that woman, 'I have said that Mrs. Flett recovered from the nervous torment she suffered some years ago, and yet a kind of rancor underlies her existence still. ...

Perhaps that's why she is forever "ruminating" about her past life, those two lost fathers of hers, and hurling herself at the emptiness she was handed at birth' (281).

The absent mother is not, however, a sufficient cause of such emptiness or 'virtual absence' in the self. Other causes which are far less accidental, are in fact systemic, present themselves. Recalling the isolation she felt as a girl with measles, the adult now refers to herself in a curious trinity of grammatical persons:

> She could only stare at this absence inside herself for a few minutes at a time. It was like looking at the sun.
>
> Well, you might say, it was doubtless the fever that disoriented me, and it is true that I suffered strange delusions in that dark place, and that my swollen eyes in the twilight room invited frightening visions.
>
> The long days of isolation, of silence, the torment of boredom – all these pressed down on me, on young Daisy Goodwill, and emptied her out.
>
> Her autobiography, if such a thing were imaginable, would be, if such a thing were ever to be written, an assemblage of dark voids and unbridgeable gaps. (75-6)

What makes *auto*-biography unimaginable, or at least profoundly problematic, to this 'woman thinking her autobiography' are precisely such transpositions of voice from first- to second- to third-person. For the 'dark voids and unbridgeable gaps' are not just between differing moments in time – the fascinating 'doubleness of memory' – but between differing subject positions in language, 'the inescapable duality of the grammatical "person"' (Lejeune 33) which, linguists argue, makes it impossible to resolve such contradictions into a unity.

The problem for autobiography, then, from the standpoint of linguistics, is that the subject is inevitably split by language. For one thing, an unavoidable lexical gap comes between the subject of the utterance (the one spoken about) and the subject of the enunciation (the one speaking). As Philippe Lejeune suggests, 'At the lexical level, it is "resolved" by the class of "proper names," to which in the final analysis the personal pronouns refer. The name is the guarantor of the unity of our multiplicity: it federates our complexity in the moment and our change in time. The subject of enunciation and that of utterance are indeed "the same," since they have the same name!' (34). So, for example, Daisy begins her account of 'Love, 1936' in the first person: 'The real troubles in this world tend to settle on the misalignment between men and women – that's my opinion, my humble opinion, as I long ago learned to say' (121). That this first-person narration belongs to a retrospective narrator, looking back on her younger self, is borne out by the topic sentence of the second paragraph: 'Men, it seemed to me in those days, were uniquely honored by the stories that erupted in their lives, whereas women were more likely to be smothered by theirs'. But by the third paragraph, Daisy the narrator gives up the pretense that she and the widowed bride share the same name, the name, at least, of the same pronoun: 'Her poor heart must be broken, people say, but it isn't true' (122). Here, the subject of enunciation, 'I', explicitly denies that the subject of utterance, 'she', can be identical to one another. For, 'wherever she goes, her story marches ahead of her. Announces her. Declares and cancels her true self'. The 'true self' is in fact simultaneously announced by an 'I' and canceled by a 'she', 'so that she's able to disappear, you might say, from her own life' (123-4). And so this 'I' who writes of 'her' is dramatically split into two persons as a seemingly new narrator intervenes between the first and us to speak in an impersonal third person, or what linguists call the 'non-person'. One of the 'unbridgeable gaps' of autobiography is made transparent, if no less problematic, once we see how the 'I' is no more than a mask for this fictitious unity in the self.

Another gap opens as well in the same passage within the subject of enunciation, in the form of a split between addressor and addressee. As the implicit first-person subject of enunciation speaks of the subject of utterance in the third person, there is another transposition of voice to the second person: 'There's something touching, in fact, about the way she's learned to announce pain and dismiss it – all in the same breath, so that she's able to disappear, you might say, from her own life. She has a talent for self-obliteration' (123-4). Here, the 'you' masks a split in an immediate audience addressed by the subject of enunciation, since, literally speaking, no one can be present to the writer but an imagined (or eventual) reader. And so the subject of enunciation must also speak to itself, or function as the immediate audience as well as subject of the utterance. Just as 'I' masks 'the gap that exists between the subject of enunciation and that of utterance' (Lejeune 35), so 'you' masks the gap between external and internal addressees.

'From these thoughts', Lejeune concludes, 'we can formulate the idea that when an autobiographer talks to us about himself in the third person or talks to *himself* about himself in the second, this is no doubt a figure with regard to accepted usages, but that this figure arranges a return to a fundamental situation, which we find tolerable only if we imagine that it is figurative. In general, these gaps, these divisions, these encounters are both expressed and masked by the use of a single "I"' (34). We rarely notice the multiplicity of persons passing under the same name, 'so much does the "I" always tend to recombine in our eyes the fictitious unity that it imposes as a signifier' (34-5). For that reason, it can be said that the autobiographical 'first person always conceals ... a secret third person' (35).

Is it any wonder, then, that Daisy the autobiographer would say in the first person that 'The recounting of a life is a cheat, of course; I admit the truth of this' (28). In context, she means only to say how the 'unimaginable gap' of twelve years in the life of her father, before he met and married her mother, must falsify her act of biography. But the 'inside' story of her own life is 'a cheat' in another sense, not just by virtue of omission but also of commission.

For, in her thoughts on 'Motherhood, 1947', she sees how 'The narrative maze opens and permits her to pass through. She may be crowded out of her own life – she knows this for a fact and has always known it – but she possesses, as a compensatory gift, the startling ability to draft alternate versions' (190). Autobiographical 'fact', it would seem, is inevitably permeated by autobiographical 'fiction'. It has even 'occurred to her that there are millions, billions, of other men and women in the world who wake up early in their separate beds, greedy for the substance of their own lives, but obliged every day to reinvent themselves' (283). Aware of an emptiness within an emptiness within an emptiness within the self, the autobiographer is obliged to invent alternate versions, or other selves, which she might have been.

In her imagined fiction of Clarentine Flett – whom she portrays as being alienated from her own life by a masculine world of husband and sons – her surrogate mother comes to anticipate the duplicity of Daisy's own experience. It seems that the woman who raised her for the first eleven years of Daisy's life has the same compensatory gift: 'It is frightening, and also exhilarating, her ability to deceive those around her; this is something new, her lost hours, her vivid dreams and shreds of language, as though she'd been given two lives instead of one, the alternate life cloaked in secret' (12). Estranged from her 'real' life, or 'crowded out of' it, each of these woman is able to invent an 'alternate life'. Thus, secrecy and deceit, those first parents of subjectivity in *Moll Flanders*, reappear in a story about the absence of subjectivity. The very existence of a private self, let alone the recounting of a life, is based on a cheat. Necessity, as they say, is the mother of invention.

'Motherhood', however, may figure more prominently still in this act of drafting alternate versions of a life. For the trope of a 'narrative maze' which 'opens and permits her to pass through', which crowds her 'out of her own life', suggests a womb-like space of narrative out of which the subject is forced to emerge. In the most literal sense, the narratives of Daisy's three children which people this chapter on 'Motherhood' are the mother's own creation; she gives 'birth' to these distinct third-person points of view which comprise her own story of being a mother. In strictly narratological terms, the projected subjectivity of 'Alice' (165-8), 'Warren' (168-71), and 'Joan' (172-3) is not their own, but the construction of a third person who contains them. Daisy's first person is transparently a third person which contains other subjectivities than her own.

The sort of 'cheat' involved in 'recounting' fictive thoughts of various witnesses is finally confessed in a later section of 'Motherhood', subtitled 'Mrs. Flett's Old School Friend'. For the thoughts of Fraidy Hoyt on a visit from Indiana to Ottawa are much too provisional to have come from her:

While she was there she thought: here is Daisy Goodwill with a distinguished husband and a large well-managed house and three beautiful children. Daisy's got all that any of us ever wanted. Whereas I've missed out on everything. ... Or else Fraidy Hoyt thought:

oh, poor Daisy. My God, she's gone fat. And respectable. Although who could be respectable going around in one of those godawful dirndl skirts – should I say something? (184).

Here, Daisy's first person is fully exposed as a third person speaking other voices than her own. She thus gives dramatic substance to the linguistic principle that 'the first person always conceals a secret third person'.

Of course, 'The construction of the fictitious posture of the "witness" is finally only the alibi for a presentation of the self. ... On the one hand, he puts himself inside others in order to understand how they see him; on the other hand, he puts himself outside his self in order to see that self as if he were someone else' (Lejeune 47, 49). The reason may be as simple as a human inability to see the back of one's head; one has to look with other eyes to see what otherwise must always be behind us. As Daisy imagines her father thinking: 'A person would have to wiggle and squirm in front of a double mirror, and even then there were parts of your body you'd never get a glimpse of. There are bits of your body you carry around all your life but never really own' (274). This inability to possess oneself as a totality thus requires one to think with other minds, as it were, than one's own.

In this way, Daisy clearly puts herself inside others to express an idea she has of the idea which others may have of her; but she also makes use of 'fictitious witnesses' to put herself outside herself, to see herself as if she really were someone else. As she phrases it in the first person early in her story, 'Life is an endless recruiting of witnesses. It seems we need to be observed in our postures of extravagance or shame, we need attention paid to us' (36-7). One way of 'hurling herself at the emptiness she was handed at birth' is to pay attention to herself through these many fictive witnesses who remind her that we cannot possess all the parts of ourselves, and so are never the autonomous identities we like to think we are.

If these witnesses, on the other hand, fail to become more than an 'alibi for a presentation of the self', then their invention could be a 'cheat' verging on solipsism. Perhaps for this reason, a host of documentary witnesses is summoned in 'Work, 1955-64', the chapter which follows 'Motherhood, 1947', to play host to Daisy in a series of sixty letters. These social documents are written by everyone from family and friends to solicitors and editors in order to chronicle from outside Daisy's second widowhood, her blossoming career as a newspaper columnist, and the sundry departures and milestones in her children's lives. Several mini-narratives of new loves and new babies in the household are told on the slant by those who are absent from, or at least not residing at, 583 The Driveway, the Flett's home in Ottawa. In every case, Daisy is the recipient, and not the writer, of these chronicles of her sixth decade in life. While letters speak for Daisy as much as they speak to her, they also show how an autobiographer who contains other voices and other stories in her narrative must also be contained by them. As such, they reverse the centripetal direction of an autobiography which threatens to be self-absorbed as well as self-absorbing. In their modest way, they help to offset the 'cheat' of conventional autobiography by reminding us that our lives are not merely our private property.

But there could be another sort of 'cheat' in 'alternate versions' which exist solely in the subject's imagination, lacking any social reality. 'Maybe now is the time to tell you that Daisy Goodwill has a little trouble with getting things straight; with the truth, that is. ... She is not always reliable when it comes to the details of her life; much of what she has to say is speculative, exaggerated, wildly unlikely' (148). What social value do we place on a life which is imagined over against a life which is actually lived? Can both lives ever be more than contiguous to one another? Or might they overlap and even inform one another?

Daisy offers her own defense of fiction as a part of life, a defense which underwrites the social value of writing a fictional autobiography such as Carol Shields has done: 'She understood that if she was going to hold on to her life at all, she would have to rescue it by a primary act of imagination, supplementing, modifying, summoning up the necessary connections, conjuring the pastoral or heroic or whatever, even dreaming a limestone tower into existence, getting the details wrong occasionally, exaggerating or lying outright, inventing letters or conversations of impossible gentility, or casting conjecture in a pretty light' (76-7). By the time we realize that Cuyler Goodwill's limestone tower may have no substance in the story of Daisy's life, we are ready to believe that existence itself may be a form of fiction, or that imagination might be the only sure ground of subjectivity. 'I can imagine my life; therefore I am': Daisy's implicit credo resituates the absent subject in the space of the imagination. We can imagine Daisy's life; therefore she is.

The acceptance of this imaginative principle in life writing changes the question of what is a life story to a question of who owns a life story, or even who lives the life and how many lives can be lived at a time? Here, Daisy's own psychological absence through depression in a chapter called 'Sorrow, 1965' reveals more than 'a bitter and blaming estrangement from those around her, her children and grandchildren, her many good friends and acquaintances' (229). For social existence, like nature, abhors a vacuum; and others may be drawn in to this absence. Now everyone but Daisy has a theory about her paralyzing sorrow: 'Surely no one would expect Mrs. Flett to come up with a theory about her own suffering – the poor thing's so emptied out and lost in her mind she can't summon sufficient energy to brush her hair, let alone organize a theory. Theorizing is done inside a neat calm head, and Mrs. Flett's head is crammed with rage and disappointment' (261). Inside other heads, however, Daisy's sorrow appears to take life in ways which suggest that our lives are never merely our own, but are always a product of social dialogue.

Daisy's daughter Alice theorizes that 'The self is not a thing carved on entablature' (231). Having altered her own life, she concludes that 'my life, therefore, was alterable' (233). She assumes that, when her mother lost her husband, 'she went slack and heavy as though she were gasping for air through an impermeable membrane, her history, her marriage, everything gone down the chute. But then, presto, she became Mrs. Green Thumb. Her old self slipped off her like an oversized jacket' (239). Daisy's old friend, Fraidy Hoyt, still takes 'issue with Betty Friedan's exaltation of work as salvation' (242). As she protests to us: 'You don't expect Alice Flett Downing to believe in her mother's real existence, do you?' – apparently holding to the idea of an essential self, though adopting a metaphor from science in the place of a metaphor from religion. 'The self is curved like space' (247), she insists, still refusing the idea of soul or some spiritual essence, but clinging nonetheless to another dimension beyond matter.

Though Fraidy believes some deep sexual yearning, long repressed from adolescence, has come round again to haunt Daisy's being, other witnesses offer their own conjectures for the return of other repressed feelings. 'The poor motherless thing' (255), says Cora-Mae Milltown, a black housekeeper once employed by Daisy's father; 'I'm all she's got. I'm not even half a mama, but I'm all the mama she's ever going to get. How's she going to find her way? How's she going to be happy in her life?' (257). But by the time we come to 'Skoot Skutari's Theory', the grandson of the Jewish peddlar who attended Daisy's birth, we recognize the improbability of this unlikely witness who would hardly know of a distant woman's depression, much less be able to theorize of it that it is the 'infant's loneliness', sensed by the peddlar who 'himself had suffered since leaving home at eighteen' (260), now returned to haunt the sorrowing woman. The increasingly fictitious character of these witnesses suggests that each of their theories is a product of Daisy's own imagination, and that imagination itself is the key to her renewed 'self-possession'. As Daisy, the subject of enunciation says in the first person about the absent, or depressed, subject of utterance, 'In a sense I see her as one of life's fortunates, a woman born with a voice that lacks a tragic register. Someone who's learned to dig a hole in her own life story' (263). Clearly, her ability to dig an imaginative hole permits her escape from the cell of psychological isolation, leading her back to a social world of other lives. But at the same time, her escape from self-absorption is paradoxically a way back to self-possession. 'I can be imagined by others; therefore I am', she might say. And so imagination is revealed as the bond that enables social being.

In the final analysis, Daisy's ability to imagine other lives is equally vital to their existence – at least in her life story. For instance, her profound sense of identification with Magnus Flett, the deserted husband, projects him as 'the wanderer, the suffering modern man – that was how she'd thought of him all these years. Romantically. And believing herself to be a wanderer too, with an orphan's heart and a wistful longing for refuge, for a door marked with her own name' (305). Even in her story of the bride in 'Marriage, 1927', she remains fixated on this figure of the wanderer returning to his childhood home. In his turn, the 'suffering modern man' seems to be fixated on a photograph of his wife who 'seems irreverently happy' when she is away from him: 'Magnus Flett has looked at this photograph of the Ladies Rhythm and Movement Club a thousand times, searching from face to face, moving from left to right, from top to bottom, and always he comes down to this: the proven fact of his wife's happiness' (97). Clearly, out of sight does not mean out of mind, for the imagination of this deserted husband binds him more closely to his wife than he was ever bound to her in life: 'If this talky foolishness was her greatest need, he would be prepared to meet her, a pump primed with words full of softness and acknowledgment. ... Or if these utterances proved too difficult for him, as he suspected they would, he would simply gaze into her eyes and pronounce her name: Clarentine. ... Saying it softly at first, the way you calm a tetchy creature, forcing his voice to remain gentle, speaking straight out toward that face that belonged forever to the Ladies Rhythm and Movement Club, but not to him, that dear staring face. Clarentine. Clarentine' (101).

And yet, by the time Daisy catches up with a man in the Orkneys named Magnus Flett, now aged 115 years, there is no proof that he is the same man she has tried to imagine all her life. In fact, there is no proof that she has even seen the photo before which the nurse now shows to her, this image of a happy wife which was supposed to have fuelled a lonely husband's imagination:

'What a pity it was folded, the faces all cracked. Oh. They're lovely though, what I can make out. Oh.'
. . .'There's something written on the back.'
'Oh, yes. It says . . . it says, "The Ladies Rhythm and Movement Club." But there's no date.'
'Early in the century, I should think. From the looks of those dresses.'
'A long time ago.' (304-5)

The absence of any recognition scene, either during Daisy's examination of the photo or in her inconclusive meeting with the confused old man, points to her later invention of the story of a repentant husband to explain a picture which she first encounters in Scotland. This narrative of a brutish man who changes his ways too late, who memorizes the whole of *Jane Eyre* to be ready for sensitive conversation with his wife should she ever return, may well be Daisy's retroactive, and wholly romantic, reconstruction of events to suit her own heart's desire. For Daisy's *good will* itself demands this story of the man redeemed by his own suffering. 'Naturally it will take some time for her to absorb all she's discovered. A conscious revisioning will be required of her:

accommodation, adjustment. Certain stray elements which are anomalous in nature, even irrational, will have to be tapped in with a jeweler's hammer. Reworked. Propped up with guesswork. Balanced. Defended. But she's willing, and isn't that what counts?' (307).

But even the best will in the world cannot be enough to satisfy the heart's desire for life at the end of life. Knowing 'that what lies ahead of her must be concluded by the efforts of her imagination' (340), Daisy confronts heroically the thought of her own extinction. She has been 'left with only her death to contemplate – and she approached it with all the concerted weakness and failure of her body' (357-8). She lingers neither in regret nor in nostalgia for the past: 'What pressed on her eyelids, instead, was a series of mutable transparencies gesturing not backward in time but forward – forward toward her own death. You might say that she breathed it into existence, then fell in love with it' (358). Of course, the narrator's transposition to a second-person voice reminds us that it is still Daisy, the implied first person, who speaks. And the image which she finally imagines for herself is surely monumental in character:

> Stone is how she finally sees herself, her living cells replaced by the insentience of mineral deposition. It's easy enough to let it claim her. She lies, in her last dreams, flat on her back on a thick slab, as hugely imposing as the bishops and saints she'd seen years earlier in the great pink cathedral of Kirkwall.
> It wasn't good enough for them, and it isn't for her either, but the image is, at the very least, contained. (358-9)

One troubling question at the end of *The Stone Diaries* must be whether the contained image of life is more, after all, than that figure of self-containment which the narrative has simultaneously announced and canceled all along? That is to say, Daisy's imagining of other lives in the place of her own life was always more than an alibi for self-presentation; it also opened up her life for a theatrical presentation of the other. So, given the social power of imagination throughout her life story, was the absent autobiographer ever really so absent? Or was her virtual absence more likely a sign of her omnipresence as a third-person omniscient narrator? To put it most bluntly, does Daisy's story of the decentred subject end after all in a figure of unified identity? How, in aesthetic terms, could an otherwise 'postmodern' narrative which questions autonomous identity adopt a modernist form of closure to resolve all contradictions into a formal unity? Finally, in social terms, how might the 'contained' image of a saint or a bishop offer more than a formal figure, or an aesthetic object, to offset the human fear of mortality?

Daisy's story of the life, much less the death, of her father does not augur well for merely formal values. 'Such-and-such was only a chapter in my life' (92), her father used to say, implying a real lack of connection, or design, between the chapters. This man, who in his twenties was 'a captive or Eros', later 'belonged to God' in his thirties, 'and, still later, to Art. Now, in his fifties, he champions Commerce' (91-2). But which is the 'real' Cuyler Goodwill? At one point, he had himself anticipated such a question by intending to present his dead wife's wedding ring to his only child, 'making a ceremony of it, a moment of illumination in which he would for once join the separate threads of his life' (182-3). Yet he had always failed to do so, and in the end, as he lies dying, he can't even remember his first wife's name, let alone where he has buried the ring which was to have brought his life full circle. Or at least so his daughter imagines: 'The thought of his only daughter either did or did not occur to him in his final moments' (279). Even his final monument to his life – a miniature version of the Great Pyramid of Cheops – is left incomplete, a great mess which he chooses to abandon. As far as Daisy is concerned, there can be little consolation to the dying in aesthetic form, or in the formal unity of a well-told story.

Neither is there any consolation to the dying Daisy in religion: 'Committees and bazaars, weddings and baptisms, yes, yes, but never for Mrs. Flett the queasy hills and valleys of guilt and salvation. ... Jesu, Joy of Man's Desiring. It was all rather baffling, but not in the least troubling' (321). In fact, the ninth chapter of her story, 'Illness and Decline, 1985', offers an extended parody of the sort of story of redemption which is found in *The Stone Angel*. One recalls that in the ninth chapter of the ten-part story of Hagar Shipley's life, the old woman enters a hospital and begins her gradual, if grudging, progress from private pain to shared suffering, 'surrounded by this mewling nursery of old ladies. Of whom I'm one. It rarely strikes a person that way' (*Angel* 264). So, too, Daisy 'lives now in the wide-open arena of pain, surrounded by row on row of spectators' (*Diaries* 310). She is even visited by a minister, evidently recalling Hagar's Reverend Mr. Troy, though Reverend Rick does not appear to shrive Daisy Goodwill, or even to teach her to rejoice. Instead, he confides to her the secret of his homosexuality that he cannot confess to his mother. And, when he asks her whether he should tell his mother, Daisy turns *The Stone Angel*'s drama of self-revelation upside down: '"Let me put it this way. Your mother half-knows. Soon she will fully know. She'll work it out. People do. It's not something the two of you will ever have to discuss if you don't want to. Not ever." (She can't help feeling just a little proud of this speech)' (334-5). And neither, it would seem, can Shields help but share her pride; for Daisy's speech amounts to a polite refusal of the novel of confession informing the whole of *The Stone Angel*. Deathbed conversions in the social world of *The Stone Diaries* are evidently in bad taste.

A few more scenes from *The Stone Angel*, echoed and repeated in Daisy's autobiography, serve to limn the full dimensions of the parody. 'She's a wonder', her daughter Alice says in the hospital, 'she's a real inspiration' (323). Alice appears to take the words right out of the mouth of Hagar's son Marvin: '"She's a holy terror," he says' (*Angel* 304), after Hagar has confessed to him her fear of dying, and he has received his mother's long-withheld blessing. But the words which leave Hagar feeling herself blessed, or even feeling 'like it is more than I could now reasonably have expected out of life' (*Angel* 305), do not come as a blessing to Daisy. Rather, they come at the end of a series of similar nominations which prove to be more of a burden than a blessing:

> 'A fighter,' Mrs. Dorre, the head nurse says. 'A fighter, but not a complainer, thank God.'
> 'A sweetheart, a pet,' says Dr. Scott.
> 'A real lady,' says the physiotherapist, Russell Latterby, 'of the old-fashioned school.'
> Which is why Mrs. Flett forgets about the existence of Daisy Goodwill from moment to moment, even from day to day, and about that even earlier tuber-like state that preceded Daisy Goodwill; she's kept so busy during her hospital stay being an old sweetie-pie, a fighter, a real lady, a non-complainer. (322)

Such witnesses to a life story are trustworthy only so long as they confirm a general social image of the self; but once they start naming the woman into their own projections of self, or once they try to define her in terms of their own social needs, the self is inevitably corrupted into the image of the other. And so the recognition scene which marks the climax of *The Stone Angel* – the moment when Hagar acknowledges Marvin as her true son – turns into a scene of mistaken identities in this novel, identities which are forced, through a series of social constructions, on to an all-too social subject, still too willing to please.

Even the form of closure which Laurence finds for *The Stone Angel* – the metaphor of a stone angel turned to flesh, that totalizing metaphor which redeems Hagar's whole life – is undercut in *The Stone Diaries*. For the last word of Daisy's story is given to her daughters whom she imagines having recognized too late the symbol of continuance which would have completed her funeral:

> 'Somehow, I expected to see a huge bank of daisies.'
> 'Daisies, yes.'
> 'Someone should have thought of daisies.'
> 'Yes.'
> 'Ah, well.' (361)

Those very final, flat monosyllables echo the final sentence of Hagar's life story: 'And then – ' (*Angel* 308) – but without the possibility of continuance, of a life beyond life. The daughters' note of regret at their missed opportunity speaks of an unhappy sense of incompletion, so different from the hint of incompletion in a life everlasting.

The only other metaphor at the end of Daisy's autobiography likewise speaks of incompletion. An allusion to stone figures recalled from Keats' Grecian urn hints neither at the perfection of 'unheard melodies' nor at the eternal character of art, but only at the limits of human speech:

> From out of her impassive face the eyes stare icy as marbles, wide open but seeing nothing, nothing, that is, but the deep, shared common distress of men and women, and how little they are allowed, finally to say.
> Her final posture, then, is Grecian. Quiet. Timeless. Classic.
> She has always suspected she had this potential. (359)

What lingers at the end of Daisy's life story is not Keats' sense of a 'silent form' which 'dost tease us out of thought,/ As doth eternity' (Bush 208), but a sense of silent lives of desperation which cannot avoid disquieting thoughts.

One other loose end at the end of the novel, the last imagined word of its protagonist, also denies aesthetic resolution:

> 'I am not at peace.'
> Daisy Goodwill's final (unspoken) words. (361)

In the end, what this unquiet ghost has to say, but what she cannot say, will haunt the reader long after the book is closed. Now, oddly enough, it is only after the autobiographer is conclusively absent that she seems most present. For her inability to rest in peace becomes our own inability to rest in the aesthetic object, or to adopt a romantic faith in beauty as truth, truth beauty. Daisy's quiet distress lives on in the common distress, in our deeply shared sense, finally, of how little we all are allowed to say. Art may not be not enough for any of us; but in the end, there is no place else to go, beyond the organic record traced in stone.

REFERENCES

Bush, Douglas, (ed.), *John Keats: Selected Poems and Letters*. Boston: Riverside P, 1959.

Derrida, Jacques, *Of Grammatology*, Translated by Gayatri Chakravorty Spivak. Baltimore and London: The Johns Hopkins University Press, 1976.

Laurence, Margaret, *The Stone Angel*. Toronto: McClelland and Stewart, 1964.

Lejeune, Philippe, *On Autobiography*, Translated by Katherine Leary. Minneapolis: University of Minnesota Press, 1989.

Richetti, John J, *Defoe's Narratives: Situations and Structures*. Oxford: Clarendon Press, 1975.

Shields, Carol, *The Stone Diaries*. Toronto: Vintage Books, 1993.

Thomas, Joan, "'The Golden Book'': An Interview with Carol Shields', *Prairie Fire* 14, Winter 1993-4, 56-62.

Williams, David, *Confessional Fictions: A Portrait of the Artist in the Canadian Novel*. Toronto: University of Toronto Press, 1991.

Wake-Pick Weavers: Laura G. Salverson and Kristjana Gunnars

Gudrun Gudsteins

Alertness to the power of literature in cultural politics and to the vision that destructive dichotomies need to be resolved through constructive acceptance of their binary interdependence characterizes the writing of both Laura Goodman Salverson and Kristjana Gunnars. Salverson was a Canadian born to Icelandic immigrants. She moved with her family to America during her formative years, but returned to Canada as a young woman. In her works she responded to the pressure on immigrants to assimilate to the Anglo-Canadian cultural heritage during the settlement of Western Canada early in this century. Salverson resisted the idea of unquestioning adoption of the established hierarchy of power and values, on the grounds that freedom and national unity could not be accomplished except by granting equal status to all immigrants and to women and men alike. The vision she offered as an alternative to the ideal of piety, which she saw as paradigmatic in Anglo-American culture, involved recognition of the constructive potential of impurity: good contained within evil, destruction within construction, past within present, progress within resistance to change, masculinity within femininity.

In her early works, Gunnars, like Salverson, deals with the immigrant experience. A landed immigrant in Canada since 1969, Gunnars was born in Iceland to an Icelandic father and a Danish mother, but the family moved to America when she was sixteen. Both in *Wake-Pick Poems* and in *The Prowler* she picks up themes and motifs from Salverson and lends them a wider application, presenting the tensions arising from the immigrant experience and male/female power politics as essentially exaggerated manifestations of tensions grounded in human nature and existence. Like most of Gunnars' works, *Wake-Pick Poems* is a generic mixture that defies the borders between autobiography, history, fiction, poetry, prose, current literary and cultural theory and criticism. Her strategy of resisting divisions is rooted in the outlook on politics and writing that characterizes all of her works; in *Wake-Pick Poems* she uses the image of wake-picks and textile production to affirm that a clear vision of the constructive potential in violent dichotomies is as necessary as the determination to mend destructive ruptures.

Salverson's *The Viking Heart* was her first significant effort to promote the vision that national and individual independence is dependent upon equality and cultural continuity. In 'The Literature of Immigrants' Terrance Craigh agrees with Eric Thompson in 'Prairie Mosaic: The Immigrant Novel in the West' that in the cultural policy for the development of the Canadian West the ideal of cultural continuity was of primary importance – that is, of the Anglo-Canadian heritage which Thompson describes as 'British to the core', yet modified by 'exposure to the West' by the experience of 'actually living there' (238). Craigh observes that the vision of Canadian nationality proffered by novelists such as John Murray Gibbon, Rev. Charles Gordon (Ralph Connor), Nellie McClung, and Robert J.C. Stead presumed that all immigrants were to participate in preserving Anglo-Celtic cultural values by sacrificing their own; 'assimilation' meant that '"foreignness"' was to be 'moulded into English-Canadianness, politically, morally, linguistically, and even at times religiously' (46).

Alison Hopwood points out in her introduction to *The Viking Heart* that until the novel's publication 'in 1923, fiction about the Canadian west had dealt almost exclusively with English-speaking immigrants from Britain, Ontario, or the United States' (ix). She notes the 'exception' of 'Ralph Connor's *The Foreigner* (1909), about Galicians in Winnipeg', and stresses that the 'bias of the times' is evident in the way that 'Connor's Galician sheds language, family, religion, and is triumphantly transformed into an imitation Presbyterian Scot' (ix). 'By contrast', Hopwood adds, '*The Viking Heart* describes Icelanders who have a culture of which they are proud, and who become a part of their new country without losing their identity' (ix).

Salverson's autobiography *Confessions of an Immigrant's Daughter* reveals that her life was fraught with tensions between seemingly irreconcilable differences. Her first entry into American society at the age of ten, after being raised in an exclusively Icelandic environment, added cultural conflicts to those between her mother's and father's widely disparate temperaments and ancestral backgrounds – womanhood and the inferior employment possibilities available to uneducated women finally compounding the complications. She confesses her eager 'conversion' to 'the pleasant myth' that 'in the land of liberty' they 'were all free and equal' (247). Yet as an immigrant she was counted among 'the assorted savages' that needed to be 'elevated' at school by adopting the ideal of 'piety' that the 'meritorious fraternity' of the 'Pilgrim Fathers' 'stamped upon the fabric of the nation' (247-48). She indicates that in the name of piety – 'the mainspring' of American civilization – patriarchy was established and maintained by 'rules' and 'prohibitions', 'taming' equally 'the wilderness', 'obstreperous youth', 'the wild turkey', and 'women' to make them domestically 'useful' and thereby defeating the aims of 'freedom and equality' (248-49).

Salverson exposes piety as a strategy of self-elevation divorced from self-valuation. Salverson does not dismiss lightly the lure of the 'tremendously flattering' idea that 'one's self' is 'the chosen elect of an all-powerful dictator' (268) and the expediency of a 'piety' that 'seldom quarrels with the sources of money' (276). As an immigrant's daughter whose poverty debars her from education and professional training, she repeatedly has to resist devaluation of herself. During her teens 'respectable scruples' put 'under a fearful ban' the diverse cultural peculiarities of her own people and other immigrants, which previously had 'romantic flavour', even when 'existence' was 'at its worst'; in the light of piety they became 'robust vulgarities', 'scandalously unprogressive' (245-46). The most painful consequence of her determination to resist this pressure to deny her background when she reaches womanhood is being jilted; the Irish 'minister's son' whom she 'loved without rhyme or reason, to the exclusion of everything else under the sun' (366) was 'secretly proud' of his pious background and 'an awful snob: he was ashamed of my nationality, ashamed of the place I called home; ashamed of my work' (367).

Salverson's low status tests her value of herself as an individual in various ways: working as a maid, she comes under suspicion when valuables go missing and the son of the household wants her to be 'a bit friendly' (336); working as a seamstress she gets an offer from her superior of 'more agreeable ways of – well, being independent' and her wages are withheld when she resigns to avoid continued harassment (364); and marrying for money is a tempting, 'sensible' solution to poverty (337). Salverson refuses to differentiate between the different exchanges of value of money in place of self: she describes marriage for money as 'selling' oneself 'to the fleshpots' in *The Viking Heart* and as socially acceptable prostitution in *When Sparrows Fall*. Eventually Salverson married George Salverson, a Norwegian who 'had been the main support of his family' from the age of twelve and left his family what money he had to feel free to get married (374). In *The Viking Heart* Salverson develops through the central images of 'gold' and 'tinsel' the basic tension between the totality of self-possession, self-value, self-command as opposed to the lure of material possessions, appearances, and command of others.

Confessions, Salverson's most open discussion of the underpinnings of her thought, would seem to substantiate complaints that she failed to resolve fundamental conflicts in the ideals she promoted. On the one hand she emphasized the value of individualism, on the other the value of collective effort; she criticized her fellow Canadians for failing to unite in national pride while at the same time she promoted multiculturalism; she extolled the virtues of her Icelandic ancestors and their Nordic heritage, yet she felt 'rooted' (357) in 'the golden west' (375); she was a staunch pacifist on the grounds that 'organized warfare, like any other organized human institution, camouflaged ulterior' socio-economic 'motives' (376), yet in both *The Viking Heart* and *The Dark Weaver* she presents the view that immigrants paid for their Canadian citizenship by sacrificing their most hopeful sons in World War I; she openly attacked the socio-economic system, the offspring of 'slave-bred civilizations', for treating immigrants, and especially women, as 'slaves' at times worth less regard than livestock (83), while at the same time she uncompromisingly rejected the idea that dire economic straits could exonerate any sacrifice of self-respect or self-value, be it by theft from a rich man's table or by marrying for money, as in *When Sparrows Fall*.

Salverson does resolve the seeming conflict in her ideals. Her primary value is self-value – the hard earned possession of self that takes pride in its own totality, good and evil, past, present, and future potential, upon which national unity and pride are also dependent. She recalls her 'profound discovery' that the tales her parents told her from their 'ancestral' past were immediately relevant to her by evidencing her father's insistence upon 'the immortality of the right effort. That which people accomplished, whether good or evil, was the true substance of themselves, and could not perish. It went on and on, born in memory and the hearts of later generations' (214-15). The idea of the 'immortality' of 'right effort', 'good or evil', is basic to all of Salverson's works, and she offers this vision of the totality of human nature as essentially a more rewarding ideal for celebrating Canadian nationality than the American ideal of piety.

In *The Viking Heart*, Salverson's most popular and best known novel, she introduces through the history of Icelandic settlers her central image of the national fabric as woven from threads of tinsel shot through with gold, of sensibility and weakness supported by coarse strength, of life renewed by death, demonstrative of the immortality of the 'right effort', whereby evil may arise out of desire for good, just as of good may ensue from evil. Every 'right effort' in *The Viking Heart* is rooted in recognition of the intrinsic value of self and other. Salverson indicates that the rightness of individual effort may not be obvious until regarded in a broader context. Sjera Bjarni is the character who most clearly formulates Salverson's vision of individual effort as it relates to collective value: 'Those who live close to nature know that there is no waste in the universe though much appears so. All growth is painful, all progress fraught with distress' (104). The young minister's words at Thor Lindal's memorial service, that Thor's effort is not wasted because he 'lives on in the life of our nation', reinforces this idea which Salverson dramatizes in the mutual recognition between the minister and Borga Lindal that although he is 'an Englishman, she an Icelander', in Canada they have a 'common heritage' (321-22).

Thor Lindal's efforts to become a surgeon, only to be killed in World War I, are more obviously 'right' than those of his sister Ninna and Loki Fjalsted, but essentially similar. Thor's death forces his mother Borga to accept that although born in Iceland, she has been claimed by Canada through her various sacrifices to the land. Thor's death also gives his fiancée Margaret the determination to realize her own dream and potential by joining the medical profession instead of fulfilling her mother's dream by becoming a teacher. Thereby Thor's effort is salvaged on a personal level in addition to the national. And the novel concludes with news that Thor's sister Elizabeth and Balder Fjalsted have named their newborn son Thor the second; Borga's response to this renewal of hope is to start knitting to prepare for the future of her grandchild.

Salverson's depiction of the means by which evil redeems itself by 'the right effort' has been largely misunderstood. In 'Pioneers, Patriarchs, and Peer Gynts', for instance, Hallvard Dahlie describes Ninna Lindal as 'simply silly and selfish' (86). He also points out that Balder Fjalsted represents the 'fair' in human nature, but his father Loki the at times amoral, 'cunning, elusive and complex' aspect, thus corresponding to their namesakes in Nordic mythology (86). But he fails to recognize how Salverson dissolves and reconstructs the positive/negative dichotomy.

Ninna opts for tinsel when she eventually marries for money, comfort and power, and renounces her own family and background to keep up false appearances. But earlier in the novel Ninna's golden hair, beauty, and strong presence also became Balder Fjalsted's musical inspiration. And her determination to capture him was a recognition of his value; when she demonstrated that she did not love him by jilting him, the pain gave him the emotional depth necessary to make his music great. Elizabeth also benefited from her sister Ninna's example, however mixed her motives. When Ninna captured Balder from under her nose, Elizabeth recognized the value of self-affirmation in Ninna's initiative. The self-presence and insight into image making that enabled Ninna to establish herself as Dr. Whitman's secretary, and would have made her a great actress, inspired Elizabeth to shake her own timidity, boldly strike out with a proposal that launched her career as a fashion designer, and bring out the best in her own modest good looks.

Balder unites his father's toughness and his mother's sensibilities; his music transforms and redeems his father's streak of cruelty and his mother's madness. Anna's madness is caused by her loss of faith in Loki's inherent value as much as by his final attempt to teach her toughness and make her recognize the value of his toughness by having her help him kill a calf. And the inheritance of money that Loki leaves Anna upon his death, saved up to have her cured, enables Balder to realize his musical inheritance from her. Balder's musical compositions draw upon the fragmented songs Anna sang hauntingly in her madness, in search of her lost lover – Loki as he was when they first fell in love. When he treats his wife and son unkindly, Loki's action represents in itself a succumbing to evil, just as Anna's lack of faith in his potential for good, Ninna's preference for tinsel rather than gold, and Thor's

146

untimely death are in themselves defeats. But their individual actions, demonstrative of the 'right effort', leave a heritage of lasting values to others.

Failure to understand Salverson's vision of the interdependence of evil and good, weakness and strength, man and woman noticeably affects readings of her *Dark Weaver*, where her title calls special attention to her central image of the mysterious transformations that occur in the web of humanity, the web of the national fabric. Her title is in full: *The Dark Weaver; Against the Sombre Background of the Old Generations Flame the Banners of the New.* In 'Prairie Mosaic: The Immigrant Novel in the Canadian West' Thompson 'questions whether' the characters have any free will at all and whether Salverson's vision of a better life for her immigrants is only illusory' (244). In 'Pioneers, Patriarchs, and Peer Gynts' Dahlie finds 'the note of fatalism or determinism, suggested by the novel's title' at confusing odds with Salverson's 'optimism' and her 'amelioration of' the 'legacies' of 'sins of the fathers' (92). He notes that in both *The Viking Heart* and in *The Dark Weaver* 'Salverson creates stronger women than men ...., seeing them not only as stronger individuals in their own right but associating them, too, with the power of the new land to shape its flawed men' (91).

Dahlie's confusion lies in the assumption that the Dark Weaver refers exclusively to Fate or God, and not to Salverson's vision of Canada as the land of possibilities. Salverson presents Canada as a country where the legacy of materialistic patriarchy yields to greater equality by collective effort – where women are recognized as no less significant 'weavers' and 'webs' than men are in the national fabric. Indeed, in the conclusion of her *Confessions* Salverson addresses a young immigrant daughter who might want to mine the 'gold' of language and experience 'to justify her race' and 'lay' her 'burnt offering upon the altar of her New Country' (414). Salverson, pointing to her own example, asserts that even if difficult, 'It can be done', and encourages the hypothetical daughter to pick up the thread and weave tales of her own experience, hopes, and dreams into the variegated fabric of their culture (414).

It is probably Salverson's emphasis on the clashes between her own Icelandic or Nordic background and the British legacy in North America to develop the dichotomy between a vision of inner values, freedom and equality, as opposed to materialism and oppression, that diverts attention from the more subtle aspects of her depiction of humanity. Exclusive attention to Salverson as an 'ethnic' writer leads Thompson, in 'Prairie Mosaic: The Immigrant Novel in the Canadian West', to classify her as one of the early '"folk novelists"' whose 'uplifting stories of simple people whose ideal (and ordeal) of group settlement is crowned by success' (246). Thompson finds Salverson's writing 'a closed, in-group kind of narrative', neither broad nor realistic enough to depict the immigrant experience (246).

Craigh's estimate of Salverson in 'The Literature of Immigrants' is altogether different from Thompson's. Craigh notes that by insisting upon

Western Canadian cultural 'existence and difference' from the Anglo-Canadian East, Salverson claimed 'a position of critical authority within – not outside – Canadian nationality' (45). And he observes that in her awareness 'of the English-Canadian pressure to assimilate', Salverson 'made some of her novels a battleground where the issue could be fought' (46). Salverson's development of Ninna in relation to other characters in *The Viking Heart* is a particularly relevant example of the terms she envisioned for assimilation. Ninna sacrifices the value of her own totality to materialism, whereas Balder and Elizabeth resolve the tension between the values of their cultural background and materialism by adopting the ambition and initiative embedded in materialism for the constructive ends of enhancing their own natural and cultural heritage.

Whereas Salverson's critics note her ameliorating tendencies, reviewers of Gunnars' *Wake-Pick Poems* who assume that she intends to give a factual rendering of Iceland and Denmark find it negative or odd. Margaret Harry says in 'Empty and Unnamed: Settlement Poems from Western Canada' that 'What emerges' in *Wake-Pick Poems* is Gunnars' 'rejection of her roots' (117). In 'New Stars in the Galaxy of Canadian Poetry' Rosemary Aubert, on the other hand, confesses 'curiosity rather than full understanding' of 'the strange world' depicted in the poems (30). Gunnars' use of place to indicate a state of being or emotion has been more readily recognized in her subsequent works than in *Wake-Pick Poems*, especially in her later works set in Canada, *Zero Hour* and *The Substance of Forgetting*. *The Prowler*, although primarily set in Iceland, has also been recognized as having a bearing upon a Canadian situation, probably in part because to some extent it directs its own reading, unlike *Wake-Pick Poems* where Gunnars leaves it to the reader to make the broader connections embedded in her structural arrangement. *The Prowler* marks the end of Gunnars' concern with the immigrant experience; she reviews and, to a considerable degree, explicates through the prism of post-colonialism the interrelations of the main themes she explored in her earlier books of poetry, using Salverson's *Confessions* as a dialogizing background to an affirmation of textuality governed by reason and organic values rather than destructive drives aiming to kill.

In his entry 'Kristjana Gunnars' in *Dictionary of Literary Biography*, Travis M. Lane points out that the three cycles in *Wake-Pick Poems* are best understood as depiction of the stages in human growth:

'Changeling Poems' depicts the gradual humanization of a child from birth to preadolescence. 'Monkshood Poems' represents a young girl growing into adult understanding. 'Wake-Pick Poems' is spoken in the voice of a mature woman dedicated to her community. The pervading themes of all three cycles are the growing understanding of and acceptance of mortality as well as of human community. (97)

As Lane himself points out in his entry on Gunnars, his own are among the most interesting reviews of her books of poetry. In 'Troll Turning: Poetic

148

Voice in the Poetry of Kristjana Gunnars' Lane examines *Wake-Pick Poems* in greater detail and in the context of her earlier books, *One-Eyed Moon Maps* and *Settlement Poems I & II*. He notes that in 'Changeling' and 'Monkshood' the speaker resists 'identification with the family' but 'grows to accept and proclaim her rootedness in family' (65). He observes that the 'two closing poems of 'Monkshood' are 'spoken by a grown woman' whose 'maturity seems to be going ahead ... towards death – not the trip resisted, but the trip rejoiced in' (65). Lane sees the mature 'pre-modern woman' speaker in 'Wake-Pick' as heroic in 'her own choice' of self-sacrifice, 'surviving and supporting others by arduously carding, spinning, weaving, fulling, and knitting' (65-66). Lane's reading can be fruitfully aligned with a reading of *Wake-Pick Poems* as a study of the immigrant experience, because through her parallel development Gunnars reveals that the pattern of disruption, alienation, and assimilation in the immigrant experience is an exaggeration of the pattern inherent in the natural process of growth.

But Lane's linear reading in 'Troll Turning: Poetic Voice in the Poetry of Kristjana Gunnars' leaves out the wider context of duality in *Wake-Pick Poems*. Lane de-emphasizes the significance of 'herbs, charms and rituals', except as these relate to 'the magical and transitional world of the child becoming human' in 'Changeling' and to 'tradition' in 'Monkshood' and 'Wake-Pick' (63-64). He also dismisses the possibility of a connection between magic and the 'Wake-Pick' figure's work: 'Her heroism has mythic reference and literary tradition, but her power is not magic – it is only handiwork' (66). His failure to see the connections that Gunnars makes through structural movements brings him to the misleading conclusion in his entry on her in *Dictionary of Literary Biography* that her use of 'folkloric fantasies' and 'medieval fantasy' is 'an integral part of experienced history', but altogether divorced from the 'Judeo-Christian' tradition and 'unrelated to church and social morality' (98). Contrary to Lane's assumption, the dialectic relationship between these 'fantasies' and Christianity is central to the Gunnars' juxtaposition of the heritage of the Father and the Mother in the context of myth, history, and spirituality.

Gunnars' formulation of her longpoem poetics in 'Avoidance and Confrontation: Excerpts from Notes on a Longpoem Poetics' provides helpful insight into her structural development in *Wake-Pick Poems*. Gunnars says:

> The poem should be evasive and indirect, because directness kills a poem.... Poetry should be hard to understand, impossible to cope with, and full of lies, but underneath, or above, such 'barbed wire' communication, there should be a yielding and vulnerable, but distant, signal ... to the effect that we are in touch and have a strategy in mind. (185)

Gunnars says in her article that 'as much as' her poetry is '"about" anything' it is 'a groping for a basic (perhaps "natural" as opposed to "civilized") *reason* in the midst of our (often perfunctory) desire to act out our "craziness"' or 'destructiveness of modern life' (182). In *Wake-Pick Poems* Gunnars uses what she calls in her article 'Double Counterpoint':

> you not only have two major 'top voices,' but they can easily be inverted, taking turns being primary and secondary. This occurs aside from all the 'lower voices' which are inevitably there throughout. The lower parts should, theoretically, be without much tune themselves, but should accompany the major parts. (183)

Gunnars also points out her preference for Pablo Neruda's use of borrowed motifs: "'objects touched by human hands'" (179). Through the borrowed motifs she identifies or 'names' the different aspects and literary authors of the cultural heritage.

The autobiographical markers in Gunnars' *Wake-Pick Poems* stress her dual descent, Icelandic and Danish, but her development transcends the historical markers in the poems and lends them mythic significance. In 'Changeling Poems' Gunnars recalls her childhood in Iceland, in the 'The Birthmark' section in her 'Monkshood Poems' she recalls her summer visit to her maternal family in Copenhagen when she was a child, and in the 'Spindletree' section her stay at a Danish school for young women. The background to Gunnars' personal and cultural history is predominantly mythic in 'Changeling' but historical in 'Monkshood.' In 'Wake-Pick', however, the background is predominantly historical – a pre-industrial farm in Iceland – but the speaker is a mythic embodiment of Gunnars' cultural heritage within the Canadian context.

In *Wake-Pick Poems* Gunnars suggests that the inherent duality in man's nature is manifested in an invidious hierarchy that needs to be dismantled and reconstructed to bring out the constructive potential of a destructive pattern. In her contrapuntal development of this schism Gunnars uses her own dual background, paternal in Iceland and maternal in Denmark, to establish exaggerated representative types of natural and civilized existence to develop the dichotomy between body and spirit, life and death, past and present, male and female, destruction and construction. Through 'Double Counterpoint' she resolves the tensions between opposites on the one hand through parallel development, but on the other by destabilizing the relationship between signifiers and signified through inversion and fusion. Rather than examine *Wake-Pick Poems* thematically, I will examine Gunnars' contrapuntal development by following the order of the cycle to demonstrate how she traces the different roots and branches of Western cultural heritage, and places herself within that context.

In her development of the innate duality of human nature in 'Changeling', Gunnars uses the motif of Icelandic elf lore that Salverson describes at length in *Confessions of an Immigrant's Daughter*. Salverson explains that the Icelandic term *huldufolk* for elves means the 'hidden people', in reference to a folk-tale where God unexpectedly visited Adam and Eve on earth after the

Fall and, not to be found wanting a second time, Eve hid those of her children who were dirty, and presented clean and tidy Cain and Abel as her only children. When she swore they were her only children, God pronounced that the children she hid would remain hidden for ever. In the opening of 'Changeling', on the other hand, the elves are pure and innocent, but the trolls are dirty, insect infested and 'take away your innocence' (27). However, rather than remaining stable, this binary correspondence between purity and dirt, spirit and body, innocence and experience starts merging towards the end of the 'Changeling Poems'.

Belief in elves, charms, and other forms of superstition that the 'Changeling' speaker relies on are usually seen as the surviving traces of pre-Christian Nature worship. The verbal magic that the speaker resorts to in the second 'changeling' poem in her attempts to get rid of the snot-nosed troll children that are to be her companions sounds like primitive exorcism: 'i place them in a tub of water/ wash them out of my eyes/ i don't want them to be born, to lie/ in snowpools, in knolls somewhere/ ... i want to get rid of the trolls/ want to hang them from a slime-thread/ from a tree/ drop them on the rocks/ sail them out the fjord' (8). Poetry is rooted in this kind of chanting, prevalent in 'Changeling' and into the opening of 'Monkshood.' Although practised through the ages by men and women alike, the different forms of Nature worship are usually seen as belonging to the feminine – to the heritage of the Earth Mother.

Once the speaker begins 'to feel at home' and has 'a name' she sits up 'when trolls sleep' to 'write poems about jupiter' (21) but resists the 'huldufolk', the 'folk from jupiter' (22), and 'the blue-throated elf' who 'sings like a nightingale/ ... of wanderer-stars' (25). Her perception of the earthiness of the troll environment also changes. She learns to prefer natural earthly beauty rather than ideal purity: 'you don't have to wash/ i learn to prefer honey-coloured nature' (26). She learns to see earthiness as a part of natural individuality: trolls are happy when they're dirty/ i'm dirty/ it's good enough/ ... trolls don't want to wash/ away uniqueness, walk on floors/ that aren't impressed (26). And she learns to accept continuity in time – experience – and the timeliness of contemplating and facing the inner darkness in human nature: 'it's important to darken the room/ to go into mountain/ to adjust your eyes in time/ adjust your taste/ to time' (26).

In the last two 'Changeling Poems' the imagery identifying the elf and the troll start merging. One of the things the speaker does to assist and teach the 'younger ones' is to 'pick sticky stars from their hair', the image of 'sticky stars' combining the grubbiness of the trolls and the stars of the elves (29-30). When the speaker learns that she is about to be sent away by her family, she protests vociferously against being sent into exile and rejected. Her appeals affirm on the one hand her ties to troll-hood: 'i'm rooted in rock/ ... can't be gotten rid of/ i'm here to stay, to remember' (31). But on the other hand her appeals to her family affirm her ties to the elves: 'i grew in the scrub/ hosted my innocence away to elves in the scrub/ gave myself away to you' (32). Here elf and troll have become one. The speaker's concluding statement in 'Changeling' evokes Salverson's childhood fancy in *Confessions of an Immigrant's Daughter* that her creative mind marked her as a changeling – a human child substituted for an elf. Gunnars' 'Changeling' speaker says: 'if foreigners see my shadow dig up/ desert treasures/ it isn't me/ it's my changeling they see' (32).

The speaker's adjustment to the trolls 'who begin you again' is her initiation into the heritage of the Father (27). On autobiographical level Gunnars' christening, being given her 'great grandmother's' name Kristjana, is her initiation into the culture of her father Gunnar (16). As such, a male presence that the speaker 'met first' at her 'birth' suggests her father. The voice responding to her rebellious outcries, that she is 'a foreigner' and 'won't act like one of' the dirty trolls points out that 'it's no worse elsewhere/ foreigners are dirty too' and that she was 'raised out of a bog' (9). But the male presence is someone the speaker recognizes 'from antiquity' and Gunnars' references to dirt, earth, suggest the Holy Spirit's creation of Man from earth or dust (9). Gunnars reinforces her allusion to Christ in her use of the symbol of water and in her suggestive word division when the speaker says: 'i remember him/ remember the deep water/ of a peat bog, remember sin-/ king' (9). The troll's rootedness in rock also parallels the traditional motif of the Christian church as founded upon rock.

Gunnars also evokes literary father figures. The 'Changeling' speaker sounds strikingly similar to William Blake's rebellious infant in 'Infant Sorrow' from *Songs of Experience* and the central tension in 'Changeling' is indeed between innocence and experience. Gunnars reinforces her reference to Blake by having her infant speaker struggle against the heritage of the father 'who wants to lay' her 'in swaddles' and 'wrap around' her 'chest/ again', like the father in 'Infant Sorrow' (9). Gunnars' allusion points to Blake's ideas about the Higher Innocence reached when innocence has been tempered and united with experience.

The image of the 'bog' from which the speaker was raised suggests another literary father, Stephan G. Stephansson, whose works Gunnars translated in *Stephan G. Stephansson: Selected Prose & Poetry*. Gunnars does not fully 'name' him or identify her allusions to him until she does so in 'Wake-Pick Poems', but the speaker shares his turn of thought in 'Changeling' when she insists that adjustment to darkness is necessary for a vision through time. The 'Changeling' speaker's impression that her fatherland is stamped upon her, even if she becomes an exile, is central to the poem by Stephansson that Gunnars calls 'The Exile' in her translation. Stephansson regrets in the poem that he has 'no father land' because he cannot 'recognize the face' of his 'ancestral soul' among 'relatives and friends' in Canada, his 'foster nurse' (75-

76). Gunnars' evocation of the heritage of the Father as acceptance of earthy trollhood in 'Changeling' thus works on different levels simultaneously: as cultural conditioning during the speaker's formative years; as initiation into Christian or Earth Father acceptance of sin as a part of the human heritage; and as 'naming' of literary Fathers.

The setting of mythic nature in 'Changeling' is in contrast to the civilized setting of 'Monkshood Poems', underlining the opposition between the concern with acceptance of life in the former and death in the latter. 'Birthmark' introduces the heritage of death, history, and the taint of blood and body that the speaker must accept as a part of her maternal inheritance. In the opening the speaker proclaims that her soul escaped during the passage by ship to Copenhagen and that her mother's family will simply have to take her 'body/ a necessary pain' (36). The speaker's maternal family resists the elements that were accepted by the paternal trolls. Instead of retreating into darkness to face and welcome time, they darken their windows haunted by memories of 'the war' (37). Likewise, they try to erase 'unwashed, unfortunate' 'uncle jørgen' whom they 'don't say much about' yet they are 'afraid' that 'a memory' may 'walk/ through a door' – that it may not be enough to 'tie a thought in a bag/ if it gives you trouble/ ... toss it out the window' (38). And in contrast to the speaker's vocal command in 'Changeling', she finds herself locked out by language, her 'dead tongue' when she needs to name things (45).

In 'Birthmark' the speaker recognizes the dual heritage of the body and the continuity of family despite individual death. She describes a trip 'through a medieval city' of Copenhagen to visit 'the round tower with birte', imagining herself a 'prisoner led to execution' (42). While overlooking the city she envisions 'beggars rub spurge leaves on legs/ display sores for copper pieces/ women drink spurge juice/ to disappear/ moles, warts, corns, hair/ all go up here for beheading' and recognizes her kinship with them: 'it's body/ bliss in body/ pain in body/ in both places' (42). In the following poem the speaker also recognizes her kinship with 'lise' who is 'orphaned at fifteen' and 'looks after herself' (43). Together they discover that the 'the root for a view/ of the family rests/ in heathen times/ trace it back, you'll see/ it meanders along a path/ like a mosquito's flight trail' (43). The speaker recognizes that, like Lise, 'one is always orphaned' and the toxic 'baneberry', or 'toadroot', signals that death is their common heritage or 'root' (43).

Through her grandfather the speaker learns to accept the redeeming aspect of resistance. Her recognition that 'someday' her old grandfather will die, 'his seat will stay empty/ & unnamed', puts her dilemma of alienation in perspective (45). The speaker's grandfather teaches her to 'get used to' death when yet 'again' he 'lies in a heap on the floor', seemingly dead, but recovers and 'whispers/ 'damn well thought i was dead'' (46). His example teaches her the necessity of resisting death: 'so long as you're travelling/ you can keep returning/ it's when you get where you're going/ you can't come back/

grandpa knows that/ shuffles anywhere there's support' because once 'you've left your muscles .../ ... you won't get them back again' (49). By his resistance of death the speaker's grandfather stands in contrast to the entropy implied in the stone imagery associated with the trolls in 'Changeling', yet his capacity to overcome death also evokes the Christian associations of the troll.

The structural unity between the 'Changeling' and the 'Birthmark' poems that runs counter to their division into different sections is important. They focus on the natural life and death of the body and the theme of exile. The speaker's relative 'kirsten' in 'Birthmark' keeps telling her that she is 'a replica of' her 'mother', making her stumble 'uncoordinated' to 'the mirror/ to look at' herself: 'the birthmark at my ear just like hers' (49). The bitterness and sense of betrayal that the speaker recognizes as underlying Kirsten's recollections of the time before 'tove' left her family and moved to another country – the feeling that 'she should never have left them/ in silence like that' – also mirrors the speaker's own feeling when she was sent away from home to visit her mother's family in Denmark (49).

The birthmark points to the double bind of betrayal – to the mark of Cain, and Gunnars' reconsideration of the heritage of Eve: death, exile, sin. The birthmark unites the central theme in 'Changeling' that darkness illumines the purity tainted with experience in human life and nature, and the central theme in 'Birthmark' that history not only shadows but illumines the present, and that the most meaningful acceptance of death is to be found in its resistance. The birthmark, like the troll motif, identifies Gunnars' personal heritage of her mother Tove and the pull of blood that cannot be resisted. But it functions also as a symbolic motif for the heritage of the Mother as Gunnars develops it in the following section, 'Spindletree'. On a mythic level the birthmark is the mark of Eve's – the first Mother's – betrayal: the Fall that cast her and Adam into exile from Eden.

Through point, counterpoint development, the 'Spindletree' section of the 'Monkshood Poems' works in continuation of previous sections, picking up their motifs and bringing the basic tensions to an affirmative resolution. In counterpoint to the pattern of the speaker's initial resistance but eventual acceptance of her natural heritage in 'Changeling' and 'Birthmark', the speaker initially yields to the heritage of the cultivated lady in 'Spindletree', but eventually she resists it as invidious. In 'Spindletree' Gunnars brings again into the foreground the ancient tradition of Nature or Mother Goddess worship thought to underlie elf lore and witch lore alike. 'Spindletree' adds a twist to the association between elves and the speaker's initial desire for ideal spiritual purity and pleasure in 'Changeling.' In 'Birthmark' the association between death and baneberry succeeds the speaker's vision of medieval use of herbs to cure the body and remove physical blemishes, showing death as part of the natural life of the body. In 'Spindletree', however, Gunnars uses imagery of highly toxic and sedative plants to show that our cultivated heritage specifically cultivates appearances and death through destructive sacrifice of self.

The emphasis on virginal purity that Gunnars brings out in 'Spindletree' is a part of the heritage of both the Father and the Mother. The heritage of the Pater that Gunnars places in the foreground in the opening of 'Spindletree' overlaps with the heritage of the Puritan Father which she brings into the foreground as the section progresses through allusions to John Milton's *Paradise Lost*. In its emphasis on virgin purity, the paternal heritage in 'Spindletree' is in diametric opposition to the heritage of the Earth Father in 'Changeling.' The maternal heritage in 'Spindletree' splits into binary branches: that of Our Virgin Lady and that of the Earth Mother – the witch. The Earth Mother heritage splits again into binary branches: the witch who uses her herbal arts for destructive purposes, and the healer. Gunnars resolves the dichotomy between the paternal heritage of purity and the maternal heritage of earthiness in 'Spindletree' through their common value of charity, cancelling out the destructive aspects rooted in both.

It is not only a boarding school in Sjælland that Gunnars went to as a teenager, but every woman's school of life, that is headed by a man. And the cult of the Lady is based on cultivation of appearances. The speaker does her best 'to be a lady/ hang like a lady/ blister like a lady' but fears that 'sometime, someone'll notice/ it's not a lady in those sharp heels' (58). The main lessons are: 'we're all girls/ it's hammered in: daphne/ you've got no shell, no skull/ ... you are spurge olive/ dwarf, dwarf/ small/ insignificant/ ... notice: natural beauty/ this is what you're here for' (67).

Through her imagery of herbs and trees, Gunnars stresses the covert noxiousness of role shaping that denies women self-value. By convention both the monkshood plant in the title of the whole cycle and the spindletree in the title of the section refer to women. Witches used aconite and belladonna for their flying ointments and the term 'spindle-side' refers to the female line of descent. But Gunnars unsettles the conventional association and emphasizes in the opening poem of the cycle that the cult of the Lady continues the monastic ideal of purity, in rejection of women. The 'rektor' of the school welcomes the young women 'in a monkhood' and refers them to the roots of classical learning, naming especially authorities on the need to suppress women: 'st. augustine' and 'cicero's letter/ to his son/ the terrible one' (51). Monkshood, a common garden plant in Scandinavia and seemingly innocuous, produces the deadly poisonous aconite, especially in the root.

The speaker's initiation into the community of the Lady in 'Spindletree' stands in ironic parallel to her initiation into the community of the Father in 'Changeling.' When she is christened in 'Changeling' 'they pour water on' her 'head' and raise 'goblets' to 'drink' her health in celebration (15). In her second baptism, into the community of the Lady, she is being purified by being deloused, because she is 'not smooth/ & downy like' the other girls sitting 'by the spindle tree' and has 'lice/ bites on' her 'scalp' (52). The rektor, like a knight dedicated to the chivalric cult of Our Lady, 'brings the grail' to sprinkle 'prickwood leaf powder' that he keeps in the 'gunpowder room' on her 'louse-infested head', bringing on the 'symptoms' of 'nausea, fever', and 'hallucinations' of 'deep skewerwoods' (52-53). Prickwood and skewerwood are alternative names for spindlewood, also named *Euonymous*. The leaves of the spindletree have strongly injurious chemical properties if not ministered with caution. *Euonymous* refers to the Furies, the spirits of uncompromising justice and vengeance who were addressed as the *Eumenides*, or the kindly ones, in hope of soothing conciliation.

Having been initiated into the community of the Lady, the speaker embraces the potentially destructive heritage of the witch. Gunnars indicates that the initial pull is akin to the desire for ideal purity in 'Changeling.' After breaking away one night with 'gitte' and 'jytte' for the 'thrill' of roller coasters, dancing, cigarettes, and beer that leaves a 'putrid' aftertaste of 'cold ashes', she wants 'to start over' (55). She wants to 'dance/ faster, farther away/ into fields of deadmen's bells' and 'hunt/ in the foxglove' (55). But Gunnars also signals that although rooted in pre-Christian nature worship, the ideal promised by the lore of the Lady is different in kind from that of the fairy lore in 'Changeling.' The speaker wants to 'learn, little by little/ about fairy caps that break off/ at a touch/ about virgin's gloves that won't come/ off/ about foxes shuffling around/ chicken coops with gloves on' (55). Fairy caps, dead men's bells, gloves of Our Lady, Virgin's gloves, all these are alternative names for the foxglove plant. According to one branch of folklore, the spots on the flowers are the fingerprints of elves to warn of their poisonous nature; according to another, perverted elves give the flowers to the fox to use as gloves when he sneaks into the chicken coop. One alternative to the foxglove name which Gunnars does not thread into the poem is witches' gloves, but that aspect signifies later.

Gunnars suggests that emphasis on purity breeds destructive duplicity and complicity. When 'gitte' 'wants to give birth/ to a miscarriage, three months', the speaker gives her 'henbane seeds' and assures herself that they will not be 'burned' unless they are found out (57). And the speaker reasons that 'it's harmless' to get 'high' on the 'fool's hemlock' of having 'a skeleton in the closet/ not for use, but it's supposed to/ be there, to exist/ ... to resort to' after 'dancing on the green grass' and 'singing' (59). When it is her 'turn to cook' she uses a 'twelfth century/ recipe' with 'this spice from dioscorides/ theophrastus: dog mercury, they say, dried/ determines the sex of the unborn' (60). The narcotic effect of Dog Mercury on 'forty fine female hands' is as insidious as the duplicity engendered by the command that they are not to 'wave at young men/ from the balcony, it's not allowed/ don't wave'; their reaction is: 'quiet, lean over the railing/ arm, hand, a flag at half mast –/ an ancient spectre' (61).

156

The culmination of Gunnars' development of imagery of toxins and death points heavily to her observation in her article about longpoem poetics that modern life cultivates craziness and destructiveness. Towards the end of 'Spindletree' there is an escalation in imagery of death and destruction, culminating in the future threat of massive human self-destruction 'under the white-laced hemlock net' of an atomic bomb (71). Gunnars builds up towards this orgiastic image of self-sacrifice through her imagery of the young women being trained in sacrificing their natural impulses and their sense of themselves in the school of life – to see themselves as 'insignificant', as 'martyrs' (67). Gunnars indicates that in effect girls are being reshaped in the image of monks. She echoes Salverson's observation on the Pilgrim Fathers' determination to tame obstreperous youth and women when the speaker says, 'youth is monkshood'; 'an afternoon/ numb with monkshood/ aconite waiting'; 'girls' in 'purple hood' 'read friar's cap texts/ on wolfbane benches' (62-63).

And in addition to this training in alienation from a living, gendered self, Gunnars' school of life provides training in alienation from death. Through her depiction of the school's visit to a slaughterhouse where pigs are being killed by 'push-button death' she suggests that modern man has developed a convenient system of enjoying death from a mechanical distance without feeling responsible: 'we walk in the blood of pigs/ this is the stony center of the cherry/ & then we can leave the stonehouse behind/ sit under the cherry laurel at last/ in the white-flowered perfume/ in the sun of our hidden spite' (69). In contrast to this cultivation of alienated sacrifice, the 'tollund man' was sacrificed in 'heathen' times 'to bring on spring' but he 'rose again in 1950' (66).

The turning point in 'Monkshood' is the speaker's encounter with the constructive, life-affirming aspect of the tradition upon which civilization rests. The speaker discovers these 'roots' where she 'least' expected them. Her visit 'at kari's farm', where 'mustard & curry are sprinkled like lice' on 'the spindle table', comments ironically on her initiation into the cult of the Virgin Lady (70). Kari has 'a gray alder bowl' that 'is brimming with honey', and since gunpowder was made from the charcoal of alder branches, she stands in further ironic contrast to the 'rektor' and his gunpowder room. Instead of using herbs to drug or kill, Kari uses herbs curatively, 'wears ivy leaves in her shoe/ to soak away corns' and 'in her ivy wood goblets/ the infusion of white wine has a sore taste/ an ivy bush in bloom/ stands covered with bees' (70). In her presence the speaker's 'own fingers/ grasp at things like ivy roots' (70). Kari's association with Earth Mother acceptance of impurity and with the healing witchcraft of the ivy, the emblem of poetry, suggests Karen Blixen, Isak Dinesen, who specifically resisted idealization of purity and suppression of natural physical existence by singling out the redemptive aspects of fallen femininity.

In subsequent poems Gunnars plays upon the concepts of blindness and vision to affirm that modern mankind must blind itself to the lure of destruction – to clear its inner vision and learn from the life-giving roots of its own past. All of the herbs Gunnars mentions in 'Spindletree' have curative as well as toxic, irritant, and narcotic properties. The speaker pleads, 'blind me to the shadow of what's to be', when she envisions further 'threading through clumps of poison parsley', and a possible end of all life 'under' the atomic bomb's 'hemlock net' (71). The answer to her pleas parallels the male voice that speaks out in response to the infant's rebellion against earthiness and experience in 'Changeling': 'hemlock leaves drop on my eyes/ an unfamiliar hand strokes my brow/ in an unknown country/ a mother i never knew responds/ with words i never heard' (71).

The associations that Gunnars sets up in the immediately preceding 'kari' poem identifies Salverson as the unknown 'mother' who restores the speaker's vision by blinding it to the lure of destruction. In Salverson's *The Dove* a Danish witch teaches her half-Danish, half-Icelandic foster-daughter the art of healing through the use of herbs. And the very name Kari not only suggests Karen but *caritas*, charity, the generous kind of love of self and other that both Dinesen and Salverson envisioned in their writing. *Caritas* is the kind of love that is the expressed central theme in Salverson's *When Sparrows Fall*. Even if Gunnars goes far beyond Salverson in scope, education, and command of her medium, she agrees with her that the way out of the deadlock system of inequality and destructiveness is to be found by mining the gold of our cultural past and present to recover the 'right effort.'

But the mother who brings a vision of a new hope also points to the second Eve, the Virgin Mary, and Milton's *Paradise Lost*. Milton's Fallen Eve, intoxicated on the taste of the forbidden fruit, corresponds to the toxic aspects of the heritage of the Lady that the speaker is initiated into in 'Spindletree.' The subservient gender role that the young women are intended to accept for themselves also corresponds to the way that Eve is to accept Adam as her lord and master. The speaker's celebration of the intoxicating pull of fox-glove/Virgin glove pleasures after the worldly pleasures that tasted like ashes on her stolen night out echo Eve's praises, in 'Book Nine' of *Paradise Lost*, of the heady powers of the forbidden fruit, as being second only to experience. The pleasures that taste like ashes, on the other hand, echo the discovery of the Fallen Angels when they throng to the illusory trees of forbidden fruit that appear in Hell after their transformation into snakes, to assuage their raging thirst and hunger, but finding every bite turn to ashes. Gunnars' play upon blindness and vision towards the end of 'Spindletree' reinforces her reference to Milton and the speaker's unexpected discovery of the healing ministrations of 'kari' points to Milton's second Eve as well as Salverson as the mother 'in an unknown country.' In the conclusion of *Paradise Lost* Michael emphasizes that in thought and in deed Adam and Eve must practice the love called charity, embodied in Christ, the second Adam, born to Mary, the second Eve. Gunnars recovers the signification of the Earth Father in 'Changeling' through the Earth Mother in 'Spindletree'; the speaker's discovery of a common constructive value in charity and resistance of the destructive aspects of her paternal and maternal roots resolves the tension between the heritage of the Father and that of the Mother.

The speaker arrived as a ghost in the opening of 'Monkshood Poems' and leaves as a ghost by stepping into 'the open death' in the Viking spirit of the Icelandic poet 'egill skallagrimsson' (74). The phrase also echoes the allusion in 'Changeling' to Blake's 'Infant Sorrow', where the rebellious infant leapt into a dangerous world, because to 'get going into the open death' is an Icelandic turn of phrase which means to face life fully aware of its hazards. Gunnars thus recovers the meaning of spirit in her references to ghosts in 'Monkshood' and affirms that due to the power of memory she can revisit the Denmark she loves best, 'when dew swells upon the sjælland farms', and see her mother there 'draw water from the well/ & she won't see me' (73). Through memory the speaker's vow at the end of 'Changeling', that she is 'here to stay, to remember' (31), is reconciled with her assertion at the end of 'Birthmark', that 'you're not bound to any place' (49). Like Adam and Eve who left the eastern part of Paradise for the western part, she preserves within the happiest aspects of places to which she will not return.

The speaker in 'Wake-Pick Poems' is a woman in time – a woman labouring at an Icelandic farm in the historical past – yet she is also Woman through time, labouring under oppression and stigma, uniting a clear vision of inequalities and injustice in her past and present with a regenerative vision of the future. Hers is a life of hardship and drudgery: 'service in a stranger's home' (87). She participates in 'the knitting wake' that was a part of the Christmas advent in Iceland when times were hard: 'over night knitting/ over enough socks to pay for christmas/ before christmas/ with wake-picks on my eyelids/ not to fall asleep while working' (94-95). But she does not reap the benefits of nights of work with her 'eyelids nailed open' in her 'forehead' (94): 'the men go to trade their quilts/ carpets & saddle cloth/ in town for wealth/ the women put their hands in water/ rinse their faces before church' but 'they leave' her 'on death-watch legs' (89). The speaker is determined to claim equal rights for the downtrodden, those assigned the sinister role of the left hand instead of the privileges of the right, but not by cutting off her 'right hand' because it 'offends' her: 'how do i work without a hand?' (86). Above all she wants to right women's lot in life: 'i want to break the law/ i want to break the distaff/ ... & because i believe freedom is spun/ out of restrictions/ i won't go by the law/ ... there is no law for me/ woman breaking distaff heads in solitude' (81). The distaff side of a family is the female branch, and the speaker's words point back to the 'Changeling' speaker's claim that she can only remain a troll if 'a distaff' does not 'touch' her 'head' (12).

Through her imagery Gunnars retraces women's inherited roles of rebellion, error, retribution, oppression, kept alive through the authority of the Scriptures, but by lending her mythical figure the redeeming values of unbounded capacity for forgiveness, charity, self-sacrifice for the good of others, Gunnars makes Christian spirituality accessible to women. Gunnars fuses the Christian symbol of the rock and the biblical account of God turning Lot's wife into a pillar of salt, in punishment for her disobedience. Thereby she brings out the redeeming qualities in biblical references to salt and adds the patriarchal possibility of rebirth to female spirituality: 'tonight again i pretend/ to be salt/ i separate myself again/ fine from coarse/ die another death tonight/ & when i'm dead/ .../ i turn to stone' (77); 'we need to live & breathe darkness/ again turn into pillars of salt' (84). The 'Wake-Pick' figure speaks in full awareness of her own duality – her capacity for destruction in her desire for advancement: 'i've wanted better/ than i've been given/ .../ i've wanted evil more than sufferance/ .../ wanted scythe-shaped wings/ ... wanted instant change' (93). But she draws upon the determination of the Furies or the Harpies, instead of their vengeance, and combines it with Christian charity: 'i'll turn the other eye/ i'll give all my eye' (95). Gunnars likewise transforms the idea that women's nature is warped by accepting the term on constructive premises as the supportive strands in the web of humanity: 'the strength of a woman is an evergreen spreading/ a cedar of lebanon/ an ancient warp' (88). The spindle recovers the constructive aspect of the spindletree.

Gunnars concludes her cycle by affirming the continuity of the spirit of female strength and revival, reliant on yet transcendent of individual effort. The 'Wake-Pick' speaker reinforces the thrust of the whole cycle. Akin to the way she disentangles 'soft ... fibre from coarse hairs', she has the capacity and determination to cull the constructive aspects of human nature from the destructive (77). She has a 'wake-picked' vision of past and present but also a vision of the self gained through her self-sacrificing efforts; a fisher of women, she offers herself as the 'bait' 'for them all to gain life' and as the spindle hook 'where women bite the future/ bite my failure for life' (96).

The 'Wake-Pick' speaker continues Gunnars' dialogue between the heritage of the Father and the Mother within a Canadian context – between the Anglo-Canadian and the Icelandic Canadian literary heritage. The 'Wake-Pick' figure embodies Gunnars' response to Milton's justification of the ways of God to *men* in counterpoint to Salverson's encouragement in *Confessions* to a future immigrant daughter to 'justify' her 'race' by placing her 'burnt' offerings on the altar of her new country: 'i create incense/ to mend the scavenger's life'; '& i burn the earth's debris/ until it smells good' (86).

Gunnars' development of imagery of plant and animal life of primitive wilderness in 'Changeling' and cultivation in 'Monkshood' is parallel to the prevalent motif of tension between wilderness and cultivation in Canadian literature. The tree imagery in 'Wake-Pick' concludes Gunnars' development in a dialogue with Stephansson that parallels Margaret Atwood's dialogue with Susanna Moodie. In her image of woman's strength as an evergreen Cedar of Lebanon, Gunnars draws upon her translation of 'The Spruce Forest' where Stephansson celebrates the capacity of the 'hardy spruce' to survive, 'greenest of all woods', through the 'gusts of winter' that leave the 'oak' 'frostbitten, bare' and 'twisted'; an emblem of perseverance, the evergreen's 'roots of hope' thrive 'concealed' in 'the bottomless bog' of social injustice and inequality (55-57).

The 'Wake-Pick' speaker's vow, 'when i'm dead i'll be bait' so that 'grave-dug' trees can 'gain life' (96), responds to Stephansson's 'Evening' translated by Jakobina Johnson in *Stephan G. Stephansson: Selected Translations from Andvökur*. In 'Evening' Stephansson welcomes darkness and night as the time when his 'thoughts', 'longings', and 'dreams' can soar into the 'songs' that 'day' and 'labour' 'startled' away. But nightmare visions of 'the foundlings of life' upon whom 'Greed' 'thrives' like 'Disease at the heart of our trees' keep him 'sleepless at night' (62-63). Stephansson resolves the tension between his hopes for a 'dawn of advancement' and the 'ghastly' visions of 'masses bereft of their reason and will', baited and governed by' greedy oppressors, by insisting that the dawn 'Transforming their' and his 'arduous day' is only perceptible when regarded in historical context, through time (62-63). He concludes by affirming that his 'sleeplessness' is amply rewarded in his poetry: 'The best that was in me for ever shall live,/ The sun over darkness prevail' (64). Gunnars 'names' Johnson's contribution as a translator of Stephansson by alluding to her title 'At Close of Day' when the 'Wake-Pick' speaker wants 'close of day/ all pick week through' (95); Gunnars' title for his more optimistic celebration of the power of poetry than in 'Evening' is 'At Labour's End.'

The premises for Salverson's social criticism in *Confessions* are in clear continuation of Stephansson's resistance of a destructive hierarchy of power and values; Gunnars aligns their resistance with that of Canadian women authors on sexual politics. Gunnars unites Stephansson's image of the evergreen with Salverson's image of a warp for weaving, and the image of the spindle-hook is a variation upon the hook or double hook image that recurs in writing by Canadian women in resistance to the heritage of patriarchal oppression. Margaret Atwood's poem 'you fit into me', where she uses the image of man as a fish hook caught in woman's open eye, is a striking response to the convention that women's hooks are destructive, hooked into man's flesh, instead of redemptive as fishers of men.

But above all, Gunnars' 'Wake-Pick' figure resolves these tensions. With her tasselled cap she is the 'ancestral soul' of Iceland the 'fatherland' that Stephansson found missing in 'The Exile', enjoined with the ancestral spirit of Canada the 'foster nurse' (75-77). Her 'wake-pick' vision harkens back to Milton as a patriarchal representative and recovers the value of his emphasis on a vision of good and evil guided by reason, but through imagery and on terms set by Stephansson in his emphasis on a sleepless social conscience. In *The Prowler* Gunnars picks up threads from her determination in *Wake-Pick Poems* to weave together some of the 'right efforts' from which Canadian literature draws its vitality. Her observation in *The Prowler* that in 'literature' and 'politics', 'only that which kills is thought significant' (129) so that a 'detective story' signals the intention of finding the 'enemy' instead of detecting the allies (47) has an obvious bearing upon her literary politics in *Wake-Pick Poems*.

Textile imagery in 'Wake-Pick Poems' is central to both the content and the form of the whole cycle. In her tracing of the levels of duality in the heritage of Western culture to recover constructive values from both the paternal and the maternal roots Gunnars evokes the linguistic roots from which the word 'textile' derives. The Greek word *techne* is cognate with the Latin word *texere*. *Techne* signifies art, craft, skill, construction, and its derivatives include the words technology, technique, and detection. *Texere* means to weave and takes derivatives such as text, context, textile, texture, and the Latin *textus*, signifying both the Scriptures and an account. All of these levels of meaning come into constructive play in Gunnars' text. In the same manner she weaves the alternative names for the different plants into her text so that they become a natural part of the imagery and gain dual function, such as her use of the alternative name 'dead tongue' for 'dropwort' to indicate her inability to speak Danish as a child.

The very principle of 'Double Counterpoint' in Gunnars' structural development in *Wake-Pick Poems* suggests weaving: the deconstruction or unravelling of a web of violent dichotomies for reconstruction on the old warp. She weaves organic imagery into that of human artifact and construction; she weaves together history, myth, folklore, and fantasy; she weaves together the paternal and the maternal heritage; and she weaves the textuality of the past into her own construct of Canadian literature that breaks ground for a better future. Salverson uses the web predominantly as a symbol to define the fabric of the Canadian nation. Canada, as a dark weaver, magically transforms the coarse fibres of the immigrant past into banners of gold, by opening up new possibilities through cultural interaction and through recognition of women as the mainstay of family, as professional contributors, and as interpreters of Canadian reality. In her own efforts to settle within a Canadian context, Gunnars affirms Salverson's vision yet transcends it to lend it wider application and to emphasize the 'wake-pick' power of literature to settle and resolve cultural tensions rooted in the duality in human nature but exaggerated by Canada's immigrant history.

REFERENCES

Aubert, Rosemary, 'New Stars in the Galaxy of Canadian Poetry', *Quill & Quire* 48/4, 1982, 30.

Craigh, Terrance, 'The Literature of Immigrants', in: Jørn Carlsen and Bengt Streijffert (eds.), *Essays in Canadian Literature: Proceedings from the Second International Conference of the Nordic Association for Canadian Studies, University of Lund 1987.* Lund: The Nordic Association for Canadian Studies, 1989, 43-50.

Dahlie, Hallvard, 'Pioneers, Patriarchs and Peer Gynts: The Nordic Figure in Canadian Literature', in: Jørn Carlsen and Bengt Streijffert (eds.), *Canada and the Nordic Countries: Proceedings from the Second International Conference of the Nordic Association for Canadian Studies, University of Lund, 1987.* Lund: Lund University Press, 1988, 83-101.

Gunnars, Kristjana, 'Avoidance and Confrontation: Excerpts from Notes on a Longpoem Poetics', in: Birk Sproxton (ed.), *Trace: Prairie Writers on Writing.* Winnipeg, Manitoba: Turnstone Press, 1986, 179-86.

Gunnars, Kristjana, 'The Exile', in: *Stephan G. Stephansson: Selected Prose & Poetry*, 75-77.

Gunnars, Kristjana, *The Prowler.* Red Deer, Canada: Red Deer College Press, 1989.

Gunnars, Kristjana, 'The Spruce Forest', in: *Stephan G. Stephansson: Selected Prose & Poetry.* 55-59.

Gunnars, Kristjana, *Stephan G. Stephansson: Selected Prose & Poetry.* Red Deer, Canada: Red Deer College Press, 1988.

Gunnars, Kristjana, *Wake-Pick Poems.* Toronto: Anansi, 1981.

Harry, Margaret, 'Empty and Unnamed: Settlement Poems from Western Canada', *The Fiddlehead* 135, January 1983, 117-18.

Hopwood, Alison. Introduction, *The Viking Heart*, New Canadian Library No. 116. Toronto: McClelland and Stewart Ltd., 1975.

Johnson, Jakobina, trans., 'Evening'. *Stephan G. Stephansson: Selected Translations from Andvökur.* Edmonton, Canada: The Stephan G. Stephansson Homestead Restoration Committee, 1982, 62-64.

Lane, M. Travis, 'Kristjana Gunnars', in: *Dictionary of Literary Biography.* 1987, 96-100.

Lane, M. Travis, 'Troll Turning: Poetic Voice in the Poetry of Kristjana Gunnars', *Canadian Literature* 105. Vancouver: August, 1985. 59-68.

Salverson, Laura Goodman, *Confessions of an Immigrant's Daughter*, 1939. Toronto: University of Toronto Press, 1981.

Salverson, Laura Goodman, *The Viking Heart*, New Canadian Library No. 116, 1923. Toronto: McClelland and Stewart Ltd., 1975.

Thompson, Eric, 'Prairie Mosaic: The Immigrant Novel in the Canadian West', *Studies in Canadian Literature* 5/2, 1980, 236-59.

Painting Canada

Bengt Streijffert

1. Introduction

Canadian Studies, or 'the study of Canada outside Canada', is a subject pursued at universities all over the world. The International Council for Canadian Studies has 20 affiliates – in the Nordic countries (NACS/ANEC), Brazil, Korea, Russia and many others. Centers for Canadian Studies are being developed at a number of universities.

The pursuit of Canadian Studies has often been spurred by the study of Canadian literature, or of some social studies subject like geography or economics. These subjects, plus others including ethnicity, are very often those that support the development of interdisciplinary Canadian Studies. It is very rare that Canadian art is included in these contexts. The number of articles concerning Canadian art in Canadian Studies journals is minimal as compared with those about other disciplines, and this observation applies equally well to the papers presented at international conferences.

Canadian art is not the subject that has attracted university teachers and students around the world to concentrate on Canada. That impulse has rather been primarily provided by the impact of Canadian literature during the 1960s and 1970s, undoubtedly succored by the tension between Anglophones and Francophones and the desire to think about an alternative, in North America, to the U.S.A.

Another reason contributing to this neglect is naturally the limited availability of material on Canadian art outside Canada. Generally speaking, one can observe that amazingly little on this subject has been published, regarding both general overviews and monographs. The extant objects for such studies are to be found in Canadian museums – not at universities around the world. It is even difficult to obtain slides of representative works – whereas one can find examples of Canadian literature in bookshops and at airports all over the world.

It is regrettable, albeit understandable, that art is so little employed in interdisciplinary studies of Canada. There is indeed a branch of art that must be recognized as 'Canadian art'. And it can also be employed by students who are not primarily interested in art *per se* as an illustration of the history and development of Canada. For example, the society of Quebec prior to the

British occupation can be delineated with the help of religious art; visualizing the Hudson's Bay Company and the conquest of the prairie is aided by painters like Rindisbacher and Kane; perhaps the Quiet Revolution can be better understood by observing the work of Paul-Emile Borduas. Folkloric painters such as Cornelius Krieghoff are outstanding illustrators of an older Canadian reality. Canadian art over time is far from being the least useful material available for seminars devoted to the development of Canada from colonialism to nationalism. The late 18th and early 19th century epigones so firmly entrenched in European attitudes can be contrasted with the early 20th century Canadian nationalists from the Group of Seven. And finally, and above all, it is difficult to imagine studying the indigenous peoples without access to artistic illustrations, both their own and others showing how they were seen by their invaders down through the centuries.

There is a wall running through Canadian culture, albeit a wall with some portals, between Anglophones and Francophones. We have two literatures – and two silences. The separation between these two cultures is not at all as clear in the realm of art. Linguistic differences, which make the division between the literatures so obvious, do not exist in art. Other patterns emerge instead. The division of Canada, which seems so apparent to us, is by no means so obvious in art. Although the difference between Quebec and ROC (Rest of Canada, to employ contemporary terms) ought to be toned down – at least in this context – it is nevertheless quite possible to distinguish characteristic features in the artistic development of Quebec that differ from those in the rest of Canada. Some typical – but not particularly surprising – features can be mentioned here: the ecclesiastical dominance up to the 1940s, the umbilical relationship with French art and culture, and, hence, the greater receptability to influences from Paris and a different, more political, nationalism than in other parts of Canada.

With this by way of prologue, I will attempt to provide a brief introduction to the art of Anglophone Canada. My theme is *painting Canada*, i.e. artists working with Canadian motifs, and how Canada and Canadians emerge on the artists' canvasses. Note that the focus is on the English-speaking, European Canada, and not the land of the 'Indians' or the Inuits.

2. A Colony and a Company: 1759-1867

Upper and Lower Canada

Early Canada rested on two pillars: the Catholic Church and the British Army. As I mentioned in passing above, the Church dominates the art of French Canada. Logically, then, the British Army dominates the art of English Canada. It had both artists and buyers in its ranks. The first painters in British North America at the end of the 18th and beginning of the 19th centuries were often Army officers educated in England, at the Woolwich military academy, in drawing and map making, which were skills required for war in the days before cameras and satellite reconnaissance. They were also British gentlemen who wanted cultural pastimes in the colonial outback. Nature painting was an excellent way to combine business with pleasure. One could maintain military preparedness while painting watercolors of one's exotic outpost. From this period, we have a relatively large number of landscape paintings from both Upper and Lower Canada. They wash the Canadian landscape in European and idyllic tones to enhance their attraction for collectors; there was as yet no market for untamed Nature. Many of these canvasses found buyers on the other side of the Atlantic or accompanied the soldiers back to Britain.

Another genre near at hand for the military society in Canada – which after all was defending the British colors against the Americans, the Fenians, other Republicans and perhaps even unruly French Canadians – was battle paintings and the glorification of heroes. Here we must mention Benjamin West's famous painting *The Death of Wolfe*, which depicts the British general's heroic demise after the battle at the Plains of Abraham in 1759. William Berczy's 1805 portrait of the Mohawk chieftain *Joseph Brant* is typical and well-known. Joseph Brant is represented here as the Neoclassical hero, replete with toga and lap-dog, leading his people from New England to Upper Canada; with a magnificent gesture he embraces the land given to his Mohawks by the British. He had fought on the British side in the American War of Independence and, like other Loyalists, had to flee from the U.S.A. after peace was negotiated.

Cornelius Krieghoff (1815-1872) depicted another Canada. He painted the rocky, forested and usually snow-covered Quebec, and the Indians and *habitants* (the impoverished French-speaking peasants) so exotic to the British. The landscape is picturesque and very different from the earlier landscape painters' 'European' Canada. The people in the paintings, the Indians and *habitants*, are folkloric, i.e. portrayed humorously and anecdotally at their daily tasks or on festive or ceremonial occasions, and quite frequently with special attention paid to diverse bodily anomalies. Krieghoff's clientele, however, is the same as before. British officers and civil servants bought his paintings as mementos of their service in the citadel of Quebec, the Gibraltar of North America. Les Québécois did not approve of his paintings, which they regarded as caricatures and manifestations of colonialism. Krieghoff's paintings add something new and exciting to the Canadian scene. His training and experiences at the Düsseldorf school and its genre painting worked very well in the milieu – Quebec and its inhabitants – he had chosen. Krieghoff created a new, albeit somewhat caricatured, image of the mid-19th century Canadian reality, an image still encountered on Christmas cards and in advertisements.

The West and Hudson's Bay Company

From the arrival of the Europeans in North America and up to the 1860s, Western Canada was the domain of the fur trading companies. From the beginning of the 19th century, Hudson's Bay Company was the only enterprise and controlled a vast empire from Western Ontario to the Pacific Ocean. The company created an efficient machine that produced hides of various kinds for the European market. The Indians had their place in the chain of production as trappers, the halfbreeds (*les métis*) as buffalo hunters at the trading posts, the French Canadians as transport workers in their canoes and the Scots as storekeepers. This multiethnic chain worked in Canada. The weak link was the fashion market in Europe, whose vagaries caused a ripple effect in the chain that ultimately meant a blow to the Indians. Pioneers and outsiders were not welcome in the company's territory. Cultivation could drive away the game, and the Indians could be 'debased' by the encroachment of whites. Nor was Western Canada easily accessible; you could get there either on one of the company's ships from Britain via the Hudson Bay, or by canoe over the lakes and rivers.

The first artist in this gigantic territory – or west of the Great Lakes, for that matter – was a young Swiss named Peter Rindisbacher (1806-1834). He arrived at the Red River Colony, at today's Winnipeg, in 1821, and painted Indians, *les métis*, merchants and the very special hybrid culture that resulted from the meeting of Europeans and Indians at the Hudson's Bay Company forts. His naive and untutored pictures give us a very interesting and stimulating insight into the life of the Canadian West. Although he sold his paintings to the local merchants, he moved to the U.S. to find a larger and more profitable market, but died young.

Another 25 years or so went by before the Canadian West acquired a major pictorial artist. Paul Kane (1810-1871) was born in Ireland and came to Toronto as a child. After training as a painter and several years in the profession, he went first to the U.S.A., where he saved up money as a portrait painter, and then embarked on the great educational journey to Europe. He visited Italy and France before arriving in London in the fall of 1842. While there, he visited an exhibition of the great recorder of American Indians George Catlin, who had painted Indian tribes while travelling in the American West as far as the Rocky Mountains. He had painted them in true Romantic fashion to illustrate for posterity the destruction of valiant people of nature, that we might reflect on this phenomenon.

Kane recognized his destiny. He would be the Canadian Catlin, only better. His enthusiasm for the West knew no bounds. A New World had opened up for artists, not only for pioneers and settlers. The American drive to the west appeared unstoppable. The dominance of the Hudson's Bay Company over northwestern North America could not continue much longer, and a great vacuum would emerge. Would the U.S.A. under President Polk push north? As

White Mud Portage, Winnipeg River. c. 1851-1856. Paul Kane. Oil on canvas. National Gallery of Canada, Ottawa, no. 138. Transferred from the Parliament of Canada, 1888.

we know, this question was answered by The Oregon Treaty, and the U.S. took over Texas, California, etc. from Mexico instead.

Kane's ambitions were different from Catlin's. He wanted to conquer the Canadian West for Canada through art, not fuss over valiant but dying peoples. He wanted to incorporate the 'principal chiefs' and 'the scenery' of the West into the Canadian mythology and show Canadians what fine, exotic new Canadians were to be found there. It is important to remember that Kane's Indians are different from Catlin's. The American Indians were guerrilla fighters struggling for the land against superior numbers; Kane's Indians were colleagues of the Hudson's Bay Company and had lived for a hundred years in peaceful contact with the whites.

This is what Kane himself says about his task in his 1859 travel narrative *Wanderings of an Artist among the Indians of North America.*

> I determined to devote whatever talents and proficiency I possessed to the painting of a series of pictures illustrative of the North American Indians and scenery.... The principal object in my undertaking was to sketch pictures of the principal chiefs, and their original costumes, to illustrate their manners and customs, and to represent the scenery of an almost unknown country.

He returned to North America via two years in the U.S.A. On June 17th, 1845, he set out on his first trip with 'no companion but my portfolio and box of paints, my gun and a stock of ammunition.' He wanted to paint the Ojibwa tribe who lived around the Great Lakes. He spent the winter of 1845/46 in Toronto and, working from sketches, prepared a number of paintings from the Ojibwa. One famous portrait is *Ojibwa Chief Mani-tow-Wah-Bay [He-Devil]* from Manitoulin Island. This is how Kane describes the Chief's reactions in his book:

> He anxiously inquiered what I wanted the likeness for. In order to induce him to sit, I told him that they [the sketches] were going home to his great mother, the Queen. He said that he had heard of her, and was very desirous of seeing her, and that had he the time and means, he would pay her a visit. It pleased him much that his second self would have an opportunity of seeing her. He told me, with some pride, that he had been a successful warrior, and had taken nine scalps in his warfare. He was very fond of liquour, and, when under its influence, was one of the most violent and unmanageable among them.

Kane yearned to go farther west into Hudson's Bay Company territory. After writing letters and paying calls on the company offices, he finally received permission from Sir George Simpson (the CEO for the entire Hudson's Bay Company and, in reality, the ruler of what is now Manitoba, Saskatchewan, Alberta, British Columbia and the northwestern U.S.A.) to accompany the trading canoes westward and enjoy the full hospitality of the Hudson's Bay Company's forts. Now he could set forth on his Great Journey. He was transported primarily by canoe, and in the first year he reached Fort Vancouver. The following winter was spent at Fort Edmonton. In 1848 he returned to Toronto with a huge hoard of sketches.

Kane had made a voyage unmatched by any previous artist. Few people in eastern North America had seen what he had seen. Over a period of six years he painted some one hundred pictures from sketches and memory. They caused a sensation when they were exhibited in Toronto in the 1850s. Eastern Canadians realized what was to be found in the West. Kane provided them with a new Canada. Now, that which existed west of Ontario was no longer the private domain of the Hudson's Bay Company; now, it was revelation. A new Canadian mythology had been created.

Kane's Indians are peaceful and usually noble, and painted with ethno-graphic credibility. His paintings may be regarded as a monument to the Hudson's Bay Company's Indian policy – mutually beneficial cooperation for winnings fairly shared. These paintings have also reinforced the notion that Canada treated 'its' Indians better than the U.S.A. treated 'its' indigenous population. It is interesting to compare Kane with the American portrayers of Indians, who tend to present their subjects as aggressive, teeming with power and violence, and preoccupied with tribal warfare. In this case, art can be said to have reflected the disparity between, on the one hand, the strife between Indian and white for possession of the land and, on the other hand, the peaceful cooperation – albeit on different conditions – within the fur trade enterprise in Canada.

3. A Dominion: 1867-1914

The Dominion of Canada was created in 1867, involving Ontario, Quebec, New Brunswick and Nova Scotia. Over the next five years, British Columbia, Prince Edward Island and the Hudson's Bay Company territory (including the Arctic regions) were joined to the nation in North America. We cannot be certain whether The Dominion of Canada was based on the need for a state for the railroads, on the threat from the south, on colonies' natural emancipation process – and it really didn't matter for the proud, new Canadians. The New Dominion grew rapidly. There was great enthusiasm, and the nation procured the necessary institutions and apparatuses that a nation must have. Among these, naturally, was a cultural identity, including literature and art. The 'confederation poets' flourished. Stephen Leacock, Robert Service and Lucy Ann Montgomery achieved international reputations. The latter two were immediately translated into Swedish – although for two entirely different readerships! The first Canadian symphony orchestra was founded in 1902.

Naturally, art follows suit. The art market grows. No longer does one paint for British officers. Toronto gradually emerges as an important center for the art world outside Montreal. Artists, and painting, in Canada had long been 'decentralized'. The immigrating artists had settled down in the countryside; that was where they most often found a market for their productions. For a long time, Toronto had not been interested. But things change. Ontario's rapid growth and industrialization transform Toronto into a major regional center with vast ambitions. The Ontario School of Art is founded in 1872. The Ontario Society of Artists presents its first exhibition in 1873. The National Gallery of Canada is established in 1880.

These are exciting years in Canada. Railway construction reaches its apex. There are radical improvements in communications with both the U.S.A. and Europe. The country enters upon its industrialization phase. There is an explosion of immigration. The prairie region goes under the plow and new provinces are created. Louis Riel and *les métis* revolt in Manitoba and Alberta. How do artists paint Canada now?

By and large, art is still essentially documentary. It is still the enormous, magnificent and, at times, terrifying landscape that fascinates the artist. Yet there is also an attraction exercised by the new and growing cities, and their harbors accommodating steamships and immigrants. The railways provide new opportunities for viewing the land. It is no longer the adventure of a lifetime to voyage to the West Coast. Yet, at the same time, art is amazingly conventional, conservative. There is no evidence of the new, dynamic Canada. Nor can we observe the great developments in the West, or any desire to create something explicitly 'Canadian'. Canada is still being viewed through the old European lenses. Just as Paul Kane used Italian Renaissance horses and Dutch skies over the prairie, and Cornelius Krieghoff applied Düsseldorf techniques to *les habitants*, now we see pre-Raphaelite Indians, German High Romanticism and reflections of the American Hudson River School – sometimes referred to as Luminism. It is above all important to be recognized as a good and accepted artist within established genres and styles, rather than to attempt creating something new and personal. Perhaps this is natural for a new country, uncertain of its identity and even of its status as a nation. A parallel can be drawn with the big railway hotels now being constructed by the Canadian Pacific Railway in Banff, Quebec City and other places in the so-called French chateau style, a style that has nothing to do with Canada.

Lucius O'Brien (1832-1899) is the best-known Luminist and may be used as a representative of the nature painting of the period. His beautiful and poetic paintings from the Rocky Mountains during the 1880s are typical. The wild, magnificent landscape that was opened up by the railway is rendered in a restrained, conservative manner. O'Brien stays well within the framework of European taste established thirty years earlier. In his famous *Sunrise on the Saguenay* (1880) he makes effective use of the painting-against-the-light approach, but he stays within the older, established European techniques.

Improved communications meant faster access to impulses from abroad. Immigration at the end of the 19th century, as before, brought with it artists as well as craftspeople and farmers. Three German painters, Otto Jacobi, William Raphael and Adolphe Vogt, arrived in Canada in the 1860s, attracted by the possibilities of gaining the support of wealthy patrons. They were skilled painters, and brought their German training with them. Raphael carried on the Krieghoff tradition, painting genre pictures from the 'low life' of Montreal. His *Behind Bonsecours Market* is interesting and appreciably more advanced than Krieghoff's studies 20 years earlier. Like O'Brien, Jacobi and Vogt painted the beautiful natural environment, but with a greater degree of realism and photographic accuracy. In a way new to Canada, they dared to venture beyond the prevailing conventions. Vogt's beautiful *Niagara Falls* is worthy of special mention.

However, it was not the German influence that was to carry the day. From the close of the 19th century, thanks to the railway and steamship, France, and Paris, lay within the reach of Canadian artists. To be trained in Paris, to experience the art world there, the salons and schools, became a necessity for the Canadians. The first artists to return home introduced new practices. Studio painting became popular. Paul Peel's *A Venetian Bather* was the first nude study exhibited publicly in Canada (Toronto, 1890). The diversity of the Parisian art world provided a multiplicity of impulses for the Canadian painters. Conservatism, Modernism, Impressionism – all made their way westward with the returning artists, and were practiced in the Canadian milieu with somewhat mixed results. George Read's *Mortgaging the Homestead* (1890) nicely combines French and American training (Read had studied in both Paris and Philadelphia) with a Canadian motif – the shame of being forced to pawn your farm.

Most interesting of them all, and the best harbinger of the future, was James Wilson Morrice (1865-1924). Morrice came from a wealthy family. He studied law in Toronto but tired of it and succeeded in persuading his father to finance art studies in Paris. He went to France in 1890 and returned to Canada only for brief visits. Morrice became a member of the international art world in Paris and was a good friend, for example, of Somerset Maugham. Morrice belongs to two artistic worlds – Canada and Europe. He was the first Canadian artist to become known in Europe, and he was the first Canadian modernistic artist. Stylistically, he moved from Impressionism towards a Matisse-inspired apprehension of color, space and sensuality. His Canadian art emerged from his annual visits to Quebec City, where he painted the snow, the river, the mountains and the winter. His 1907 *The Ferry* is regarded as one of the most significant Canadian paintings ever produced. The cold northern light and the pure, austere forms belong to Canada. The balance, rhythm and the cool colors harmonize with the content. This is Late Impressionism in Canada.

4. A Nation and a Group: 1914-1935

The 1900s would be the Canadian century, according to Sir Wilfred Laurier, Canada's Liberal Prime Minister at the turn of the century. The land was populated, the prairie territories had become provinces and self-confidence was on the rise. Canada was no longer an unknown newcomer among nations, uncertain of its status. World War I created a common destiny for the country. The enormous, tragic losses in Europe turned attention inward, towards Canada itself, away from the Europe that had caused so much suffering. The cities grew. Toronto became the most important city for English Canada. The country – or at least Toronto and Ontario – was ripe for a national art.

The Group of Seven
Several artists met and became friends in Toronto around 1910. They sensed a feeling of community in their approach to art. It was important, they thought, to communicate in your art with the beholder, not be obliged to express your personal feelings. And if you want to communicate through artistic media in Canada, your motifs should be Canadian, not Dutch cows or Italian Renaissance horses. Art should ideally obtain its motifs from nature, the vast Canadian wilderness. Exhibitions of the work of two of these friends, J.E.H. MacDonald and Lawren Harris, in Toronto in 1911 and 1912, pointed the way forward. The following year, they visited an exhibition of Scandinavian art in Buffalo, New York. There they saw the light – just as when Paul Kane looked at Catlin in London in 1842.

172

The group began to coalesce and formulate an ideology. Their art was to be 'true souvenirs of that mystic north around which we all revolve' (Dennis Reid, *The Group of Seven*, Ottawa, 1970, p. 33). It should not imitate traditional European art, particularly not Dutch art, which had become particularly odious. They were questing for the soul of Canada. It was 'the true north, strong and free' that was to be revealed in art. Canada was no temperate middle European country with cattle grazing peacefully and yeomen plowing. Canada belonged to the north, it was wilderness, forests, lakes and cliffs – in other words, the Canadian Shield landscape with strong colors and, for Canadians, deep symbolic value. This harsh, grave northern land would constitute a synthesis with the spirit of the nation and of the world through art.

The experiences and training of these friends were different from those of their predecessors. Lawren Harris had studied art for four years in Berlin, coming in contact with northern European nature painting, nature mysticism and symbolism. Most of them had received their educations at North American schools of graphic design, quite obviously with preoccupations entirely different from those of the Parisian academies. They also had commercial connections with design. Art Nouveau was their common background.

Their terrain, at least from the beginning, was the forested, rocky and lake-dotted Ontario extending to the northern shore of Lake Superior, a natural environment as far removed from England's cathedrals and France's fields of grain as one can imagine. As ambitions of creating a national art expanded, their territory was extended to include the Rocky Mountains and the Pacific Coast.

Nature – as they painted it – was far from dead. All of them, in varying degrees of intensity, were intrigued by the spiritual. Theosophy, popular at the time, had a strong influence on them. Included in their portfolios of interests were the Transcendentalism of Emerson and Thoreau and Scandinavian symbolism. Kandinsky's notions about Nature as a manifestation of spirit, implying that the task of art was to prefigure the spiritual, were important for them. Their work gradually became increasingly Expressionistic. After starting out as purely reproductive, they progressively revealed the artist's inner feelings at the expense of the realistic element in art.

This group of kindred artistic spirits in Toronto around the outbreak of World War I thus had entirely different aspirations and experiences *vis-à-vis* those previously found in Canada. They also had a definite goal: 'An Art must grow and flower in the land before a country will be a real home for its people', and this art must belong to the country, i.e. be Canadian.

Beginning in 1914 and continuing during the first melancholy years of the war, they exhibited individually or collectively. Gradually, however, they were in different ways absorbed into the war apparatus. After the war was over, they consolidated their group – The Group of Seven – and held their first collective exhibition in 1920, in The Art Gallery of Toronto. Their membership was composed of A.Y. Jackson , Lawren Harris, Frank Carmichael, Franz Johnston, Arthur Lismer, J.E.H. MacDonald and F.H. Varley. Some other artists became affiliated over time.

The critical reception of their work before and during the war was rather lukewarm, if not downright negative. Their opponents referred to their work as Hot Mush. But after the 1920 exhibition, the resistance was negligible; they were accepted. All the while, they had enjoyed the support of The National Gallery, under the guidance of Eric Brown, who was also in quest of a national art. In 1924, they were taken along to the magnificent Empire Exhibition in Wembley, London. The Tate Gallery purchased one of the group's paintings, A.Y. Jackson's *Entrance to Halifax Harbour*. Their influence grew, and the next generation of painters was wholly dependent on The Group of Seven. They were also, eventually, appraised as what they had wanted to be from the beginning, the creators of a domestic *national* art that could be hung in public galleries and civic spaces. They were major contributors to the creation of a Canadian identity, or myth.

The myth runs something like this. The Canadian nation belongs to the North, with all the associations attributable to the words 'North' and 'Northern'. The nation is a wilderness, the people are imprinted by the wilderness, and it is the wilderness which expresses Canada's inmost character. This is an identity which makes it possible for an urban dweller in Toronto to feel kinship with the Canadian frontier, which in turn has survived the decades and which has possibly contributed to the tightening of the contacts between Canada and Scandinavia. The Group of Seven are, aside from *les automatistes* in Montreal, the only artists, by and large, who are generally known outside of Canada. This group came, as indicated, to dominate the artistic life of Canada (at least outside of Quebec) for many years. We should not be surprised to discover that the breakthrough of Abstract Art in Canada occurred in French Montreal in the 1940s, where the influence of the Group was for obvious reasons limited, and not in English Canada.

Despite great individual differences, which increased over time, they belong together. They painted together (at least at the outset). They often spent their summers and autumns in the forests – Algonquin Park or even further off. During the winters they painted in their studios in Toronto. Their trees, lakes, cliffs and skies, as well as their choices of colors and shapes, were based on approximately the same blueprint. All of them, most often, also excluded people from their paintings. It is the barren landscape which fascinates them; they portray it in loud colors and new idioms. The 'classic' Group of Seven painting represents a lake, a rocky shoreline, a forest bathed by an autumn or winter sky. Although they went through individual development, they did so along partly similar lines. They expanded their reach. They began to include the Rocky Mountains, the Pacific coast and Quebec. Their paintings became more abstract, less representational, and more ethereal.

It would seem appropriate to take a closer look at the members of the Group.

Lawren Harris (1885 - 1970)

Lawren Harris was descended from a wealthy family in Brantford, Ontario, and received a solid art education, in Berlin among other places. The Swedish Art Nouveau artist and craftsman Gustaf Fjaestad exposed him to the world of Scandinavian art. Another influential person was Dr. Emil Bistram, leader of the American Transcendental Group of Painters in New Mexico. Harris became the ideologue for The Group of Seven. His artistic development moved from realistic nature paintings to a greater and greater degree of abstraction, where the cliffs, lakes and clouds were reduced to form and color. They also received a stronger undertone of spirituality. Harris became a dedicated follower of Theosophy. He moved further west by gradual stages and, following a period

Stormy Weather, Georgian Bay, c. 1920. F.H. Varley. Oil on canvas. National Gallery of Canada, Ottawa, no. 1814. Reproduced courtesy of Mrs. D. McKay/F.H. Varley Estate.

in Santa Fé, New Mexico, finally arrived in Vancouver in 1940. His paintings from 1940 to 1970 were entirely abstract and difficult to interpret, far from the Group's original ideal of a hard, Northern Canadian art. Harris nevertheless maintained his artistic leadership and became a central figure of the official cultural life on the West Coast.

Frederick Varley (1881-1961)

Varley was born in Sheffield, England, educated at The Sheffield School of Art, and arrived in Canada in 1912. He met The Group of Seven through his Sheffield colleague Arthur Lismer, and became one of its members from the start. Possibly because of his roots in England's industrial heartland, Varley was less enthusiastic than the other members of the Group about the Canadian wilderness, and preferred painting portraits. However, his nature paintings of the 1920s are well within the perimeters of The Group of Seven. *Stormy Weather, Georgian Bay* (1920) is among the best, and a typical early Group

Algoma, November, c. 1935. A.Y. Jackson. Oil on canvas. National Gallery of Canada, Ottawa, no. 4611. Gift of H.S. Southam, Ottawa. Reproduced by kind permission of Dr. Naomi Jackson Groves.

of Seven painting. The sea, the rocky shoreline and the windswept trees are all Group of Seven. The horizon that attracts our gaze to the distance is Varley's logo. In the early 30s he moved to Vancouver and tried to start an art school with J.E.H. MacDonald. The economic depression dashed its chances, and Varley returned to the East and a life of relative poverty and artistic drought.

A.Y. Jackson (1882 - 1974)

Jackson hailed from Montreal and received his education at commercial schools of design there and in Chicago. He wanted, however, to be a 'real' artist, and in 1913 he contacted some of the future Group members. By 1920 he was firmly established in The Group and became its mainstay. He never abandoned nature painting and never really altered his style. It was only new territories that were incorporated into his Canada. Nor did he ever venture west, like Harris and Valery, in quest of a new spirituality. Jackson remained a nationalistic landscape painter throughout his life. His landscapes are familiar to all Canadians: the curving, meandering lines, the harsh, solid cliffs, the cold water with its little waves, the clouds forecasting snowstorms and, above all, the warm skies. *Algoma, November* (1935) is an outstanding Jackson and a good example of late Group of Seven.

5. Regions and Individuals: 1910 - 1965

The Group of Seven came to dominate the Canadian art world but, as often happens with dominance, it triggered opposition and its influence waned. Nor did Ontario's dominance produce unrelieved jubilation in all parts of Canada. As time went by, new artists appeared on the scene. Like youth in general, they opposed the prevailing fashion and built new groups. The Canadian Group of Painters was one such rebellion against The Group of Seven, although continuing in its tradition. Other newcomers pursued their own paths.

It was really only Montreal and Toronto that were large enough to have an active artistic life that could support artists. Vancouver, with its dramatic scenery, its still viable indigenous culture and its 'proximity' to Oriental mysticism became a magnet for artists despite its crass materialistic pioneer spirit. Varley and MacDonald encountered failure with their art school, as did Emily Carr. The artistic life in the provinces was to be found at the universities and their Art departments. Teaching was what provided the economic wherewithal to keep art alive. The battle for professorships and teaching posts was often equivalent to the struggle for the means to keep on painting. If Montreal and Toronto were satellites of the major art metropolises during the first half of the 20th century, the provincial capitals were satellites of the satellites.

We will now look at four artists who transformed their regionality into a Canadian and universal reality. With the last two, William Kurelek and Alex Colville, we also bring our overview up to the present time.

Emily Carr (1871-1945)

Emily Carr was born in Victoria, Vancouver Island. She grew up in a middle-class home in this little city of some 8,000 inhabitants which, despite being the capital of British Columbia, lay at some distance from Canada – it was 6 hours by ferry to Vancouver. Victoria also lay in a cultural melting pot. The city was English, American, Canadian, Chinese and not least indigenous. In the Carr home there was one Chinese servant, Bong, and one Indian, Wash Mary.

Emily's heart was set on art. At 20, she went to San Francisco to study at The California School of Design, returning home after three years to teach art to the children of Victoria. She sojourned in England (1899 - 1904) and visited France in 1910, managing to fit in an extra trip to Sweden for further art studies. Her attempts to live on art by selling pictures, teaching or operating a gallery in Victoria failed. Instead, she opened a boarding house there, and spent most of her time from 1913 to 1928 running it.

Her artistic activity can be divided into three periods. The first embraces her watercolors in Europe and in Victoria and Vancouver. They are apprentice works, not very interesting. The next two periods contain her major achievements: the indigenous peoples and the natural scenery along the coast of British Columbia. The artistically impoverished years at the boarding house fall between these two periods.

As early as 1908, Emily Carr had begun to visit the small, dispersed Indian camps along the coast of Vancouver Island and farther north towards Queen Charlotte Islands every summer. She reached the Haida tribe on Queen Charlotte Islands in the summer of 1912. Large numbers of the Haidas had died of smallpox, and when Emily Carr arrived there were only about 600 survivors left. It was a dying culture and people she met. Yet their magnificent and fascinating monuments remained – totem poles, houses and masks. She had found her artistic métier, and painted and drew a great number of pictures from the disappearing culture. Now she was in a sense working in the same tradition as 19th century American Indian painters and her countryman Paul Kane – a tradition of ethnic paintings of an exotic culture, where the ethnic is more important than the artistic. Obviously, she could not live on these pictures, and had to devote herself to her boarding house. The spirit was not extinguished, however, and in 1928, at the age of 57, Emily Carr flared up again, producing a very impressive, important and totally unique collection of art during the following years up to 1937.

In 1927, Emily Carr was included in an exhibition of West Coast art at The National Gallery in Ottawa. She also received a train ticket to Toronto. There

Indian Hut, Queen Charlotte Islands, c. 1930. Emily Carr. Oil on canvas. National Gallery of Canada, Ottawa, no. 15470. Vincent Massey Bequest, 1968.

she met The Group of Seven. The journey had a deep effect on her. The Group's ideology suited her, their way of painting suited her, and far from least, she felt that she belonged in a wider context, that she was part of the network. In Vancouver she could converse with Lawren Harris and Frederick Varley. She was an established artist and found the courage to start again. The American art teacher from Seattle, Mark Tobey, spent three weeks in Victoria in 1928 and exercised a radical influence on Emily in terms of technique. It is sometimes referred to as 'cubo-futurist', and sometimes as 'cubo-expressionistic'.

At this point, her indigenous paintings took on a new character. They were no longer primarily ethnic. She painted like The Group of Seven, and by painting in her own country, the magnificent West Coast, she achieved a communion between the landscape and its people, the Haidas and Kwakiutls, and the Great Spirit. She included in her Canada 'the Indian fact'. It thus became a Western, more North American country than the Scandinavian-inspired Ontario of the Toronto painters. God, Nature and Art were to be united in her painting. God was 'real God, not the distant, mechanical theosophical one' (Emily Carr, *Hundreds and Thousands: The Journals of an Artist*, Clark Irwin, 1966).

After 1932 she began to pay less attention to indigenous subjects, focusing increasingly on purely natural motifs. Using bold colors and forms, she depicted the forests, coast and sky in British Columbia and her love of her land and creation. The energy of life can be seen in her trees, in the torrent of verdancy.

In 1937 Emily Carr suffered a heart attack, and the tempo of her painting slowed. Instead, she wrote a number of books of a partially autobiographical nature. Her *Klee Wyck* was awarded The Governor General's Award for Non-Fiction in 1942.

Emily Carr wanted to be a Canadian artist, and she portrayed British Columbia at a time when art did not rank high on the lists of priorities of the people there. At the same time, she is one of Canada's most international artists. In her art we find American Transcendentalism, Scandinavian Expressionism – there are similarities to the Norwegian painter Edvard Munch – and the formal influence of the Cubists.

Lionel Lemoine FitzGerald (1890-1956)

FitzGerald spent his whole life in Winnipeg, and was as devoted to that city as Emily Carr was to her West Coast. FitzGerald's artistic development was slow and steady. He educated himself in Winnipeg and, for a year, in New York, and received a teaching post at The Winnipeg School of Art, where he eventually became the principal. His primary medium was drawing. His early work was from the prairie. He captured the sky, the light, and the wide open spaces impressionistically. But the large-scale motifs were not the ones that best suited FitzGerald.

He worked with simple and formal shapes and diluted colors. He sometimes resembles Lawren Harris, but prefers the little world. Among his still lifes, *The Jar* (1938) is one of the best. His paintings with Canadian motifs are from Winnipeg, with titles like *Williamson's Garage* (1928) and the famous *Doc Snyder's House* (1931), which employs simple shapes and a limited range of colors to depict winter in Winnipeg – the naked trees, the deep snow and the frozen house. What is there, behind the window, inside in the warmth?

William Kurelek (1927-1977)

A generation after FitzGerald, William Kurelek emerged from the Ukrainian farmers on the steppes, the depression and the 30s in his blood. His East European background differed from that of the artists descended from a British tradition. Recovering from illness, and undergoing a religious conversion from Greek Orthodoxy to Roman Catholicism in 1957, Kurelek began to paint. His subjects included didactic religious themes, illustrations for very popular children's books with prairie motifs, and ingenuous symbolic paintings of life on the prairie, often including motifs from the lives and customs of the ethnic minorities. His most important works are the religious ones in which he takes inspiration from Bosch, Brueghel and Goya and uses modern Canada as the setting.

Manitoba Party (1964) employs a wide-angle format to depict a festive occasion he recalled from his boyhood village, Stonewall. We both participate in the merry-making and observe it from outside.

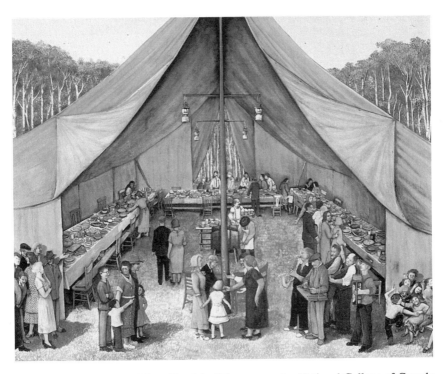

Manitoba Party, 1964. William Kurelek. Oil on masonite. National Gallery of Canada, Ottawa, no. 14761. Reproduced courtesy of The Isaacs Galllery, Toronto and William Kurelek Enterprises.

Alex Colville (1920-)

Canada is more than its metropolitan centers – Toronto, Montreal, Winnipeg, Vancouver. The Maritimes have their own culture. Sackville, New Brunswick and Mount Allison University have been offering art studies since 1893. Lawren P. Harris, son of Lawren Harris of The Group of Seven, became principal of the art school after World War II and revitalized it. He was soon joined by Alex Colville, fresh from military service and duties as an official illustrator of the war. Colville alternated his teaching assignments with painting. His paintings are uniquely Canadian, but also deeply rooted in the reality of The Maritimes. His motifs always come from his nearby surroundings: nature, animals, people, the ocean, boats, hunting, activities on the beach.

All of his works are very carefully composed and executed with geometric precision. Every detail in a painting is placed there with forethought and exactitude, and in the proper relationship to the whole. His paintings have a photographic acuity that freezes reality and life for a moment. He attempts to capture 'the magic moment'. Two phenomena are often combined, as in *To Prince Edward Island* (1965) where the man can be seen behind the woman with binoculars. The same technique is employed in *Couple on a Beach* (1957) and *Nude and Dummy* (1950). The people are never entirely clothed, but yet

To Prince Edward Island, 1965. Alex Colville. Acrylic emulsion on masonite. National Gallery of Canada, Ottawa, no. 14954.

in some way they are withdrawn and detached even when face to face with each other. What happens before and after the frozen moment is for us to ponder over. The resemblance to film is striking. There is a 'magic realism' as in Alfred Hitchcock. We do not know what secrets are concealed behind the canvass with the lightly clad tourists on Prince Edward Island, or who is observing whom. What Canada is the woman looking at through her binoculars?

Colville has attracted attention on the international art scene. He has even been exhibited in the little Swedish university city of Lund. His deep regional ties have become universal. Canada's art – like its literature – now belongs to the world.

REFERENCES

Carr, Emily, *Hundreds and Thousands: The Journals of an Artist.* Clarke Irwin, 1966.
Carr, Emily, *Klee Wyck.* Clarke Irwin, 1966.
Francis, Daniel, *The Imaginary Indian: The Image of the Indian in Canadian Culture.* Arsenal Pulp Press, 1992.
Kane, Paul, *Wanderings of an Artist among the Indians of North America,* 1859.
Reid, Dennis, *A Concise History of Canadian Painting,* 2nd ed. Oxford University Press, 1988.
Reid, Dennis, *The Group of Seven.* The National Gallery of Canada, 1970.
Russell Harper, J, *Painting in Canada: A History,* 2nd ed. University of Toronto Press, 1981.
Shadbolt, Doris, *The Art of Emily Carr.* Douglas and McIntyre, 1979.
Shadbolt, Doris, *Emily Carr.* Douglas and McIntyre, 1990.
Tippett, Maria, *Making Culture: English-Canadian Institutions and the Arts before the Massey Commission.* University of Toronto Press, 1990.

Cultural and Political Aspects of United States-Canada Relations

Marissa Quie

1. Introduction

The intention of this paper is to take a comparative stance on the analysis of the US-Canada 'relationship'. It will focus much more on the differences between the two nations and the current very noticeable interpenetration of both cultural and political identities than on their formal relationship. The formal links between the US and Canada is an area which is well documented, as is the American influence on Canadian culture, society and economy. A recent trend, which I think is of potentially greater interest, is the way in which the Canadian experience currently influences new orientations and substantive policy in the US. This is an important area for future research but, for reasons of space, this paper will confine itself to a discussion of multiculturalism and new conceptions of citizenship, democracy and freedom.

2. Multiculturalism in the US and Canada

Nations can most fully be understood only in comparative perspective. The more that what appears superficially to be similar is compared, the fuller is our appreciation of the deeper complexities. Looking intensively at both Canada and the US increases our understanding of both societies.

Societies vary in their organising principles, in their fundamental beliefs about sources of authority and values, and in their conception of the nature of their society. The two nations that once constituted British North America were separated by the outcome of the American Revolution, so that the unintended consequence of this revolution was not one nation, but two. Americans saw their nation as a *tabula rasa* on which to construct a new future. They saw themselves as constituting a new and a great civilisation which would achieve things to rival all that had gone before it, a civilisation which would constitute the land of the future. In contrast, Canada developed from a people who consciously, and with some considerable sacrifice, chose continuity as opposed to revolution. Could an evolutionary pattern engender originality? The history of Canadian development shows that it can, but in a different and perhaps more subtle manner. Creativity and originality have been defined in many ways. Koestler's 'Act of Creation' views creativity as the original combination of existing ideas. This conception is very applicable to Canada. The desire to embrace rather than reject the past has encouraged an attempt to create a society and a political system which continually reflects and reinterprets the past to create a better system which more closely integrates individual communities and national identity.

The circumstances surrounding the emergence of Canada as a nation meant that, as Northrop Frye has said, 'no-one could ever know what it meant to be 100% Canadian'. The framers of Confederation were confronted with the French fact. This meant that the path to national development was always shaped by heterogeneity by difference.

It has been said that America was the first 'new nation', the first colony to transform itself by means of revolution into independent statehood, after which a stable and democratic society developed. Eric Hobsbawm, one of the foremost theorists of nationalism, argued that the US was founded on a model of what he called 'revolutionary democratic' or liberal nationalism.[1] This, in contrast to most forms of nationalism, is not reliant on a homogenous conception of ethnicity. On the contrary, it seeks to extend the scale of human social and cultural units – to unify and expand, rather that restrict and separate. The United States has been called a 'nation of nations' because it is one of the most racially and ethnically diverse nations in the modern world. Although the English comprised the greatest proportion of the early colonial population, the middle colonies (N.Y., N.J., Pennsylvania and Delaware) were settled by substantial numbers of Germans, Dutch, Scotch-Irish, Scots, Swedes and French and Huguenots. These colonies had the greatest variety of European cultures in colonial America and therefore provide a context within which the first interethnic relations among European and Aboriginal peoples can be examined. It was here that the idea of America as a *'melting pot'* in which diverse cultures come together to form a new people was first formulated. In 1782 a Frenchman, Hector St. Jean de Crèvecoeur, wrote: 'What then is the American, this new man? ... Here [in America] individuals of all nations are melted into a new race of man, whose labourers and prosperity will one day cause great changes in the world'.[2]

The US escaped the divisiveness of a heterogeneous society through the creation of a new national identity. The point of America was not to preserve old cultures, but to forge a new *American Culture*. America's first president, George Washington, argued that 'by an intermixture of our peoples', immigrants will 'get assimilated to our customs, measures and laws: in a word, soon

185

become one people'. This was the ideal that, a century later, Israel Zangwill crystallised in the title of his popular 1908 play, *The Melting Pot*; an ideal which, until recently, Americans have fervently supported and transmitted to their progeny: *E pluribus unum* – out of the many, one. Today the balance is shifting from *unum* to *pluribus*.

For more than 200 years the American ideology of the melting pot was successful. When I say 'successful', I mean in a pragmatic and utilitarian way. Differences remained, repression and protest persisted. Yet the system functioned without being subject to extreme crisis. Today, some of the central components in the American gallery of national icons have received dramatic reworking. The elements which are currently the most contentious for Americans include the concept of the melting pot, of the US as the paramount place in the world where immigrants shed their past in order to forge their future. Another key area which is subject to intense debate is the emphasis on the principle core ideals that form part of the American experiment: that rights reside in the individual rather than with social or ethnic classes, and that all who come to the US shores can be assimilated by an open society that transforms disparate peoples into Americans. Instead, there is a new paradigm that emphasises the racial the ethnic diversity of American citizens and which views the many cultures that have converged there as being valuable in their own right and deserving of study and respect.

In the critical optic of this new 'multicultural' perspective, American history as it was once written – I refer to those often tedious treks from Christopher Columbus to Dwight Eisenhower – leaves out too much, namely everyone who, in the view of some of the melting pot's most severe critics, was not a 'dead white male'. Some adherents go even further, questioning whether the Western ideas and ideals which form the ideological foundations for America discriminate against people from other traditions. A more radical school argues that those values are no more than the ethnic expression of 'Eurocentric' culture and should be taught only as such.

What is interesting is that the spread of multicultural perspectives throughout America's schools has taken place without much notice because curriculum reviews, even sweeping ones, do not appear on local ballots. Yet it is important to note that these are not just academic disputes. In diverse, secular societies such as the US, a shared sense of the past – indeed, until now, a *coherent* sense of the past – plays a pivotal role in the way values and visions are transmitted from one generation to the next. No community can exist as a community without common experiences. In a modern nation such references are very dependant on a commonly held view of the past.

The issues now being raised in the US, although they are presented under a bland guise of syllabus reform, are much too crucial to be left to teachers, school administrators and social commentators. Everyone deserves a say, for the customs, beliefs and principles that have united the US for more than two centuries are being challenged with a ferocity not seen since the Civil War.

Put bluntly: do Americans still have faith in the vision of their country as a cradle of individual rights and liberties, or must they relinquish the teaching of some these freedoms to further the goals of the ethnic and other groups to which they belong? Could the political system be restructured in such a way as to enhance the freedom of US citizens and make it more democratic? Is America's social contract – a vision of self-determination that continues to reverberate around the world – fatally tainted by its origins, in particular, strands of Western European thought? What kind of people do Americans now think they are and what will they tell their children about that?

This supposedly educational debate shades over into a broader area – an area in which the Canadian experiment may prove a paradigm for the future. Canada is significant here, in that it has continually reflected, in a critical way (since 1982 in particular), on questions which are at the heart of democracy. The questions which Canadians have put to themselves are those which now confront their neighbours to the south. Can a democratic society treat all its members as equals and also recognise their specific cultural identities? Should it try to ensure the survival of specific cultural groups? Is political recognition of ethnicity or gender essential to a person's dignity? These are questions which rage at the heart of the debate over multiculturalism.

As in Canada, the character of US immigration has changed dramatically over the last several decades. The 1965 Immigration Act passed by the US Congress reversed the policy, which has been in place for 40 years, of favouring Europeans and making things difficult for other candidates. Between 1980 and 1990, the white non-Hispanic majority in Los Angeles county became a minority. In the US as a whole during the same decade the number of Hispanics increased by 53% to 22.4 million, approximately 9% of the population. The Dade County Florida School District, the fourth largest in the US, now includes students from 123 countries. In the contemporary period, most immigrants come from developing nations. As early as the 1890s new immigration resulted in questioning as to whether the US could assimilate so many people from diverse societies. Today, anxieties focus on the cultural results of changes in the immigrant population and, in particular, on the ability of newcomers to learn the English language. The relationship between language and culture is crucial. From the Romantic philosophy of the eighteenth century we derive the notion that men and women need a language in the broadest sense in order to discover their humanity. Because this language is something that we have access to through our community, it seems logical that the community defined by natural language should become one of the most important poles of identification and hence often a central pole of national identification. It therefore seems unsurprising that the movement to have English declared the 'official language' of the USA has grown and continues to gather momentum.

In the beginning, the anxieties generated by the changing character of immigration resulted in only remedial action. In 1968, existing bilingual educational programmes in primary schools were put under federal or state financing. In 1974 it was agreed that students could first be taught in their native tongues and then weaned onto English and, by 1986, 41 states had bilingual education programmes which were financed by the federal government. However, rising numbers of non-English speaking immigrants undermined the general agreement that this was the way to proceed. Opponents of these arrangements argued that bilingual education delayed the process by which immigrants learned the language and that, since learning it was an inescapable prerequisite to becoming an 'American', it should be accelerated by the government. Colorado Governor Richard D. Lamm spoke of English as the nation's 'social glue' and contended that while the US should be 'colour blind' it should not 'linguistically deaf'. The US could be a 'rainbow' but not a 'cacophony'. It should 'welcome different people'. This position was opposed by organisations like the Mexican American Legal Defence Group, which perceived nativist prejudice in the attempts to teach immigrants in English. Some referred to a 1985 RAND Corporation study which showed that 90% of first generation Mexican-Americans were already proficient in English and that 50% spoke no other language. From these statistics they concluded that the government need not intervene in the area of bilingual education.

However, increasing numbers of native-born Americans throughout the country remained unconvinced. They saw language as central to American identity and for that reason, as something which could not be left to chance. By the end of 1986, voters in Georgia, Illinois, Indiana, Kentucky, Nebraska and Virginia had accepted propositions to make English the 'Official Language' in their states. Republican Senator Steven Symms of Idaho spoke for them when he introduced a resolution into the US Senate in 1986 stating that 'the English language shall be the Official Language of the United States'. In 1980, Dade County, Florida, which includes the city of Miami, banned bilingualism. This meant that official publications were no longer sent out in Spanish and welfare hospital forms were often printed only in English. Government jobs could no longer be advertised in Spanish-language newspapers, and Dade County stopped financing the annual Spanish Heritage Festival. However, the realities of Dade's linguistic situation soon impinged on such policies, as officials found that it was impossible to abandon bilingualism in the emergency health and safety services, and that they had to continue to broadcast items such as hurricane warnings bilingually. In practice, therefore, government officials continued the use of bilingualism in matters of health, safety and tourism. This was in accordance with the realisation that whatever the intention for the future might be, much of the US population does not speak fluent English. Nonetheless, voters continued to support attempts to make English the Official Language.

Some of the insistence that English be made the official language of the US derives from the belief that multilingualism may become a reality in the not too distant future. In California, the debate over making English the official language was much affected by the publication in the late 1980s of a study by the California Population Research Unit which suggested that between 1985 and the year 2010, the proportion of whites in the State's population would decrease from 64% to 47%, while that of Hispanics and Asians would rise from 22% to 32% and that of Asians from 7% to 13%.

The movement against the repression and Anglo-conformity of the traditional 'melting pot' ideology began in the 1960s. The catalyst for this was the turbulence and intellectual stimulation provoked by the civil rights movement, women's liberation and by protests against the war in Vietnam.

Public institutions, including government agencies, schools and universities have now come under severe criticism for failing to recognise or respect the particular identities of citizens. This, of course is an issue which is not specific to just the United States or Canada. On the contrary, the current problems confronted by these two nations, are, I think, endemic to all liberal democracies.

The philosophical foundations of liberal democracy derive much from Rousseau's view on the nature of equality and the role of citizens in the public sphere. This perspective, as the Canadian political theorist Charles Taylor characterises it, is simultaneously suspicious of all social differentiation and receptive to the homogenising and repressive tendencies of a politics of *the* common good, where the common good reflects the identity of all citizens. The demand for *particular* recognition could be satisfied within this framework, but *only* after it has been socially and politically disciplined so that people pride themselves on being little more than equal citizens and expect to be recognised only as such. Taylor correctly argues that this is simply too high a price to pay for democracy. With some modification, however, this is the starting point for what American democracy is about.[3]

On the whole, the American state takes a position of political neutrality among diverse and often conflicting conceptions of the good life held by citizens of an inherently pluralistic society. The paradigm of this perspective is the American doctrine of the separation of church and state, where the state not only protects the religious freedom of all citizens but also avoids, as far as possible, identifying any of its own institutions with a particular religious tradition. When this was extended to the question of cultural pluralism, the melting pot ideal meant that cultural groups were free to fend for themselves, but not to enlist state support for particular cultural projects.

3. New Paths for Democracy

The Canadian policy, as Americans are now recognising, has for a long time been more reflective and innovative on the question of the accommodation of difference within democracy. I think the Canadian experiment goes further and achieves more in this area than any other democratic system. To make sense of this, we need to look at the democratic developments in democracy in Canada over the last three decades.

In 1965 the Royal Commission on Bilingualism and Biculturalism was formed as a response to unrest among French Canadians in Quebec, who called for the protection of their language and their culture and the opportunity to participate more fully in political and economic decision making. It was seen as a step towards ensuring wider recognition of the basic cultural dualism in Canada. The inquiry revealed that Francophones did not occupy in the economy, nor in the decision-making ranks of the government, the place warranted by their numbers and their position as one of Canada's Founding Peoples. Recommendations to address these and other weaknesses were quickly implemented. Educational authorities in all nine Anglophone provinces reformed regulations concerning French minority education and moved to improve the teaching of French as a second language with financial assistance from the federal government. New Brunswick declared itself officially bilingual; Ontario did not, but greatly extended its services in French. French language rights in the legislature and the courts in Manitoba, disallowed by statutes passed in the province in 1890, were restored by a decision of the Supreme Court of Canada in 1979. A federal Department of Multiculturalism was established. Institutional bilingualism became a fact with the passing of the Official Languages Act in 1969 and the appointment of a Commissioner of Official Languages. What the Royal Commission on Bilingualism and Biculturalism did not do, and what has now become a focus for national debate, was to examine the constitutional implications of this issue.

Multiculturalism was a term first used to counter the conception of biculturalism fostered by the Royal Commission. It is a term which is used in at least three ways: to refer to a society that is characterised by ethnic and cultural heterogeneity; to refer to an ideal of equality and mutual respect among a population's ethnic and cultural groups; and to refer to government policy proclaimed by the federal government in 1971 and subsequently by a number of provinces.

The work of the Commission on Bilingualism and Biculturalism, and the legislation attached to that, links up with a vision of Canada as a nation which has had relevance since Confederation in 1867. This is the vision of 'Two Founding Peoples': the English and the French. From this vision came the co-operative federalism approach to politics. What made this system so effective in its prime, when political and economic power resided in the centre, was how well it meshed with the traditional Canadian practice of parliamentary federalism. Even the existing Senate fits fully into this model, given the distribution of seats, the method of selection and the total domination by the two traditional parties.

The impressive accomplishments of this system of government are often taken for granted. Canadians pride themselves, for example, on having national social programmes which are far more generous than those of the United States (indeed, this is a key point for debate in the North American Free Trade Agreement). The question of the welfare state is central because it is central to Canadians' sense of identity, to the way in which they distinguish themselves from Americans. Yet, how can this be reconciled with the fact that Canada has a much more decentralised system of government than exists in the United States? Until the Meech Lake Accord of 1990, the answer was to be found in the genius of the underlying process of elite accommodation, and particularly in the fact that one of the provinces (Quebec) was a 'have not' province desirous of greater autonomy.

In 1982, Pierre Trudeau attempted to update this perspective with his vision of 'Renewed Federalism'. Renewed Federalism was formulated to counter the challenge posed by Quebec's demands for sovereignty in the 1980 referendum. The crux of this policy was the repatriation of the constitution and a Charter of Rights and Freedoms. Combined with the policy of Multiculturalism, the Charter conflicted with Quebec's demands for priority on the basis of the 'Two Founding Peoples' model. The Charter generated a pan-Canadian notion of equal citizenship which linked up with an older, Anglophone conception of Canada as one nation. Many outside of Quebec now perceived the country to be one of equal citizens and equal provinces. Quebec saw this is a revisionist model which homogenised rights and unacceptably placed them on the same level as other more significant collective interests.

Brian Mulroney's efforts at national reconciliation revolved around the 1987-1990 Meech Lake process and the 1992 Charlottetown Accord. Quebec's demands to be recognised as a distinct society, with the asymmetrical division of powers which that entailed, generated a spiral of demands from other groups who now embraced the Charter as the banner of their Canadianism. The 1982 Constitution Act greatly increased the cast of constitutional stakeholders; they now extend beyond governments to embrace a variety of charter constituencies and the Aboriginal peoples of Canada. The Charter gives constitutional recognition to non-territorial pluralism of women, 'multicultural' Canadians, official language minorities and Section 15 equality seekers among others. However, although the Charter embodies important collective rights, it is more fundamentally an individual-rights document grounded in British common law and incorporating the due-process aspects of the American Bill of Rights. Almost immediately, Canadians were faced with profoundly different conceptions of their nation. One was basically federal in nature, where the cleavages were territorial, provincial and interprovincial. The other was inherently non-territorial, pitting pan-Canadian Charter rights against powerful vested interests.

The 1990 Meech Accord failed to reconcile these different and signalled the beginning of new modes of political participation for the Canadian people. The electorate would no longer accept the traditional model of elite accommodation. Mulroney therefore laid the groundwork for a national referendum with the 1992 Charlottetown Accord.

Charlottetown was a bold attempt to move beyond the Rousseauist model of equal citizenship adopted by the US. In the United States, the government has made no effort to prioritise difference. Members of the Ku Klux Klan, anti-Semites, etc. are given the same measure of toleration in terms of the expression of their views as other citizens. There, what Isaiah Berlin called 'negative liberty' prevails. All groups, regardless of their objectives, can articulate their interests as long as they do not impinge upon the rights of others. Canadians, in contrast, have embraced a more 'positive' conception of liberty which seeks to rank societal difference and to apportion related powers. Charlottetown put forward an asymmetrical model of democracy which transcended simplistic ideas of representation such as the notion of 'one man one vote'.

Charlottetown also failed, yet the apocalyptic vision of the future which many commentators held regarding a nation without a national consensus has not materialised. Canadians are innovative where democracy is concerned, and have begun to deploy new mechanisms to achieve their goals.

Through Charlottetown, Canadians sent a clear message to their elected representatives that henceforth they should pay more attention to constituency and less to party. After Charlottetown may political commentators in Canada predicted a profound fragmentation of the traditional party system. In the recent federal election the ruling Progressive Conservational Party suffered a dramatic defeat at the hands of the electorate. They lost their status as a party, moving from 157 seats to 2. Out of the debris, a new political landscape has emerged with two fresh and potentially dangerous opponents: the Reform Party and the Bloc Québécois.

The Bloc Québécois, under former Conservative Cabinet Minister Lucien Bouchard, only became a party in 1990. They now constitute Canada's official opposition in the House of Commons. The Bloc provides a fascinating case study of theorists of nationalism, in that Bouchard is not an unreflective revolutionary. He has much experience in federal politics and is a committed democrat. The Quebec electorate demonstrated their political sophistication in choosing the Bloc, in that this choice effectively carries few risks. For many, its attraction was that it offered a change from the two traditional parties, holding out the promise of better economic times if Quebec's interest are given higher priority in Ottawa. In addition, the Bloc is in a strong position to achieve the devolution of political powers from Ottawa which Quebec failed to gain from constitutional reform. Eric Hobsbawm has called nationalism 'the political AIDS of our time'. Globalisation means increasing economic integration, but paradoxically also signifies the fragmentation of previously cohesive political systems. This is an issue which Canada has been dealing with in a peaceful, democratic and innovative way. In this sense it provides a constructive paradigm in a world riven by nationalist civil wars.

However, the phenomenon of the Reform Party is of potentially greater interest to the US at the present moment. Preston Manning, the leader of Reform, has been called the 'Ross Perot' of Canada. Manning capitalised on support from his Western constituencies, where there exists a long-standing resentment towards central Canada. Much of his platform is similar to that of Perot: (1) a focus on tough measures to cut the deficit, (2) a critical stance towards NAFTA, (3) a call to reduce expenditure on the welfare state, and (4) demands for the restructuring of the traditional political system. Both men call for a closer link between politicians and the electorate, and for higher levels of accountability from government officials. Their vision of citizenship is more resonant of the concept of being a shareholder in a private company than of the Aristotelian ideal of fulfilment within the political whole.

Manning and Perot see themselves as 'grass roots' politicians with a strong popularist base. This means they seek to transcend the cleavages of class, age, religion and so on. In common with other parties of this genre – Boris Yeltsin's party in Russia; the BNP in Britain; the BJP in India or Sinn Fein in Northern Ireland – they have a xenophobic dimension. In order to be 'all things to all people' they must paradoxically construct an 'other' against which the people can define themselves. Manning and Perot have more difficulty with this demand, given the inherently heterogeneous foundation of their societies. They therefore focus on the weaknesses of the 'politically correct' movement and on the production of so called objective accounts of the ramifications of immigration.

It remains unclear whether those who voted for Reform in Canada were actually supportive of the Party's objectives or whether they simply wished to register a protest against the inadequacies of the traditional party system. Most of Reform's candidates are political neophytes who have a dubious grasp of the workings of the Canadian federal system. Only time will tell whether this populist movement can sustain itself in the long term.

For the US, however, Canada's new experiment with democracy signals hope for a restructuring of the American system. Although Perot failed in November of 1992, polls show that there is potential for independent parties in the US within this context, it is important to note that a *Times Mirror* Poll taken just before the election showed that 29% of those aged 18-24 said it was 'time for politicians to step aside and make room for new leaders', and that no fewer than 49% of the influential aged 65 and over cohort said the same.[4]

Many Americans liked the anti-state, anti-bureaucracy dimensions of Perot's campaign. The increasing polarisation of the country in terms of race, religion and class could signal new paths for democracy in the future.

The 'Quebec question' has always been central to the more innovative ways in which Canada has approached the structuring of its democracy. The country's essential heterogeneity has always taken precedence over assimilation. The most recent challenge to a homogeneous conception of the nation-state came in the form of the provincial election of 12 September 1994. The results were strikingly different from the political revolution predicted by the Parti Québécois (PQ) leader Jacques Parizeau. In fact, the PQ fell dramatically short of widely accepted expectations. They received fewer than 80 seats and only 44.7% of the popular vote. This means that the federal option (albeit in a revised form) remains a very viable option for Quebec.

This argument is further substantiated when we look at the division of the vote in the election and at the recent political history of the province. The voting results did not demonstrate the ethnic/linguistic and geographic cleavages forecast by many analysts. From this it seems plausible that the proposed 1995/1996 referendum on some form of independence will not degenerate into a conflict between Anglophones and allophones versus Francophones. The fact that many Francophones voted Liberal in September has given the defeated Liberal leader, Daniel Johnson, some moral legitimacy. The 47 seats taken by his party in the National Assembly are also sufficient to ensure strong federal opposition within the provincial context.

Many commentators evaluated the election results in terms of a call for change rather than an initial step towards separation. An examination of the recent political history of Quebec would seem to verify this. Quebeckers have a history of limiting their provincial governments to two terms. This was the case when the Liberals were elected in 1960, the Union Nationale in 1966, the Liberals in 1970 and the PQ in 1976. Obstructing the possibility of a third term is the norm in Quebec, and the PQ itself experienced the ruthlessness of the electorate when it lost (after 2 terms) to the Liberals in 1985.

The Parizeau leadership *is*, however, different from that of René Lévesque, in that Parizeau is more avowedly separatist. He believes the referendum was lost by the PQ in 1980 because Lévesque waited too long after the 1976 election victory to hold it. In contrast, he proposes to hold a referendum by January of 1996. He has also said that he will not accept 'no' for an answer and would continue to hold referenda until Quebec becomes a separate country.[5]

Yet, Parizeau's interpretation of the election victory as the collective desire of the Québécois to take the initial step towards sovereignty is not born out by surveys of popular opinion. A *Globe and Mail* poll taken just prior to the election showed that 62% of voters believed Quebec would still be part of Canada in 4 years' time.[6] A closer look at levels of support for sovereignty over time shows that the failed Meech Lake Accord actually did more to catalyse separatist sentiment than any event in recent political history.

In the twenty-four years the PQ has been in existence as an electoral party, there has never been a direct correlation between the party's popularity and attitudes towards sovereignty/independence. In the elections of 1970 and 1973 PQ support peaked at 30% when the party made the argument that an electoral victory would be interpreted as a mandate for independence. It was only by separating its electoral performance from the question of independence and focusing on more 'mundane' provincial issues that the party won the election in 1976.

It is now generally accepted that the 1980 referendum severely undermined support for sovereignty for almost a decade. The issue regained its significance at the end of the 1980s and in the early 1990s as a consequence of several factors. Leon Dion, in his book *The End of Canada?*, contends that three elements were central to this revival: fear, confidence and rejection. First, the Supreme Court decision to reject a segment of the Quebec language law pertaining to signs exacerbated fears about the potential survival of French language and culture within Canada. At the same time, the cultural revolution and development of the Francophone business class begun in the 1960s with Lesage's call to become 'maîtres chez nous' engendered confidence that Quebec's 'projet de société' was viable within the international economic arena. Indeed, there was the belief that Quebec was in a better position to reap the benefits of NAFTA than the rest of Canada, because of its deep commitment to long term economic planning and reinvestment. Finally, the failed constitutional amendments which culminated in the Meech Lake debacle generated a strong feeling of rejection in Quebec. This, according to other analysts, did more than any single event to catalyse support for secession in the province.

In a 1992 book entitled *Le Virage*, Edouard Cloutier, Jean Guay and Daniel Latouche produced a detailed analysis of Quebec public opinion dating back to the 1960s. Their conclusion was that the Meech process had provided a turning point (hence the book's title) in the development of Québécois nationalism. Even before the failure to ratify the Meech Lake Accord in 1990, two-thirds of Francophones in Quebec were in favour of either sovereignty or independence – one third more than during the 1980 referendum. From this evidence the authors argued that the expansion of nationalism was now inevitable, rendering eventual independence a foregone conclusion. However, polls taken just after the provincial election undermine this view. On the contrary, they showed how Quebeckers' attitudes towards the concept of sovereignty/independence have come full circle and returned, almost to the decimal point, to the levels that defeated the Parti Québécois's first referendum in 1980.[7]

The analysis of nationalism, like that of other socio-political phenomena can never be objective, value-free and therefore completely predictive. The possibility of Quebec eventually choosing the option of independence cannot be discounted. Yet the information currently available seems to indicate the continuation of a united Canada. However, for this option to remain viable, a great deal will have to be accomplished in terms of a revision of the existing relationship between Quebec and the rest of Canada.

How might the existing relationship between Quebec and the rest of Canada be revised? Most of the proposals since the demise of Meech Lake revolve around the concepts of symmetry and asymmetry. In practical terms, symmetry implies progressive decentralisation, leaving the federal government with the most minimal powers of any nation-state in the world. Decentralisation might benefit the stronger and more populated provinces, such as Ontario, Alberta and British Columbia. However, the less populated and weaker provinces, including the Maritimes, Manitoba and Saskatchewan, would find it difficult to function on the level they currently achieve via federal funding for services and social programmes. This is why areas like the Maritimes have consistently argued for strong central government.

Decentralisation would further exacerbate existing economic and social inequalities in Canada. It is also unclear how this option would deal with the question of difference on a non-territorial level – for instance, gender, ethnicity and language. Thus far, proponents of decentralisation have produced interesting institutional solutions for regional problems but not for cultural or socio-economic cleavages. The demands which came out of Quebec's quest for recognition as a 'distinct society' are unlikely to be fulfilled by decentralisation, nor can the demands by Aboriginal peoples for self-government be met in this way.

The other alternative is asymmetry. This means dispensing with what Charles Taylor calls the 'Rousseauian politics of recognition' (cf. Taylor, *op. cit.*) which requires a homogenisation of difference and movement towards more enlightened forms of democracy and citizenship. In an institutional context, this would mean granting some sort of 'special status' to Quebec and developing new initiatives to implement the Aboriginal peoples' 'inherent right to self government'. Of course, this only touches the surface with regard to the reforms which will be necessary in the future. Both the Meech Lake and Charlottetown processes served to stimulate the demand for recognition of other forms of difference, including gender, and these will now require sustained consideration. What is most significant here is the reflective and civilised way in which Canada approaches the questions of difference, representation and citizenship. In a world riven by violence and fragmentation, Canada provides an important paradigm for the future.

4. Conclusion: Democracy, Globalisation and Postmodern States?

'Until our day', the anthropologist Peter Worsley has written, 'human society has never existed'.[8] What he means by this is that it is only in quite recent times that we can speak of forms of social association which span the earth. The world has become in many ways a single social system, as a result of growing ties of interdependence which now affect virtually everyone. The global system is therefore not an environment within which particular societies like the US and Canada develop and change. The social, political and economic connections which cross-cut borders between countries decisively condition the fate of those living in them.

It would be a mistake to think of globalisation simply as a process of the growth of world unity. Paradoxically, globalisation also engenders fragmentation, especially at the political level. This is principally because the process proceeds unevenly and has a differing impact on different societies and segments of those societies. Globalisation actually reinforces trends towards fragmentation, particularly the most divisive ideology of our time: nationalism. The central obstacle against the emergence of supranational government is the nation. It remains a largely mythological but potent source of individual and collective identity. The paradox is that although people may travel widely and live their lives within comparatively cosmopolitan environment, they still cling, as children do to a teddy-bear, to what Anderson calls the 'imagined community' of the nation.[9] Yet, such 'imagined communities' are fundamentally chimerical and, to a large extent, caricatures of reality.

The nation is an idea which enthrals us because of its promise of the symbolic unity we crave. This unity is impossible, and so the nation is a liminal image, an ambivalence that emerges from a growing awareness that despite the certainty with which historians speak of the 'origins' of the nation as a sign of the 'modernity' of society,[10] the cultural temporality of the nation inscribes a much more transitional social reality. Edward Said prescribes a kind of 'analytic pluralism' as the form of attention appropriate to the culture effects of the nation. He sees national culture, at its most productive position, as a force for 'subordination, fracturing, diffusing, reproducing, as much as producing, creating, forcing, guiding'.[11] The 'locality' of national culture, says Homi Bhabha, 'is neither unified nor unitary in relation to itself, nor must it be seen simply as "other" in relation to what is outside or beyond it. The boundary is Janus-faced and the problem of outside/inside must always itself be a process of hybridity, incorporating new "people" in relation to the body politic, generating other sites of meaning and, inevitably in the political process, producing unmanned sites of political representation'.[12]

In practical terms, our political boundaries are being redrawn at a pace which makes these changes difficult to grasp. New shapes are appearing on two levels: on high in the acronymic stratosphere, where people's lives are run by regional groupings of EC, CSCEs, ASEANs, NAFTAs and the like, and down below, in the basement world of Eritreas, Chechenyas, Bosnias and Tamil Eelams.

To anyone who had grown used to the old nation-state system, all of this seems rather sad: Athens to Greece to the European Union. This signifies the upward evolution of democracy from city-state or *polis* to nation state or supranational organisation. However, the opposing or downward trend towards increasingly smaller national units demonstrates that there is no natural end to the categorisation of difference as nationalists so fervently claim.

Globalisation means that economic space has begun to transcend political space. This is because it was originally the private as opposed to the public space which had begun to integrate on a global scale. The economic nation-state is responding to this process by passing some functions upwards through free trade agreements such as NAFTA and the European Accord. The GATT serves to propel the development of such agreements. The year 1994 saw the GATT bring its Uruguay Round to conclusion, and there is a growing recognition world-wide that issues such as trade, cross-border flows, direct investment and the environment require supranational co-ordination. This does not signify the arrival of a harmonious global consensus. National governments still strain to hold on to old powers and balk in reality at what globalisation entails in terms of a reduction of sovereignty.

What happens in practice is an intensification of the movement towards regional blocs, where groups of nations draw upon cultural affinities to create regional rules. It is obviously more pragmatic for Washington to assume control of North, Central and South America, in conjunction with the Caribbean, than to take a subordinate position in a world order based in Geneva. Nonetheless, objectives like this are still a knife in the heart of national sovereignty. Processes like the one described above enable subnational units like Quebec or the Aboriginals to champion their interests over larger national interests and to pursue the development of what Canadians call 'distinct societies'. Thus, what we see in Europe is a regional/international rather than a national *qua* nation conception of decision-making.

Theorists like Greenfeld simplify our current dilemmas through a championing of the existing nation-state.[13] In contrast, John Dunn eloquently expresses the need to rethink our current assumptions and to imagine new political possibilities when he writes: 'The search for a more intuitively plausible scale of community confronts us more than ever'.[14]

Canada is a place where this kind of imagining has thrived. William Thorsell (Editor-in-chief of *The Globe and Mail*) argues that Canada is 'not so much a country as it is a series of pragmatic arrangements'.[15] Strong nation-states (like the US) may consider this to be an anathema, but as we approach the twenty-first century 'this may prove the best way of running a country' (*ibid*). In a world of increasingly strong international governments, Canada's continual reflection is both prudent and progressive. The innovative solutions generated there may prove instructive for both the United States and other nations confronting a new international order.

The Canadian Federal system already offers more economic and cultural autonomy to its provinces than the American counterpart of the States. Much of what failed in the Charlottetown Accord will now be implemented politically. The existing constitution, for instance, provides an eminently workable framework for Aboriginal self-government, and negotiations on this issue are continuing with some success.

In April of 1994 the Innu of Labrador and the Government of Canada agreed to act on the basis of a Statement of Political Commitments. The Statement commits the government to negotiate self-government and a comprehensive land claim settlement, and to fund development work on policing and justice systems more sensitive to Innu traditions. It has also been agreed that existing federal programmes and funding should be devolved to Innu control.

In Manitoba, First Nations are increasingly assuming control of a wide range of areas, including schools, health care, child and family welfare services, and economic development. Another interesting example is the Yukon, where four First Nations, the Champagne and the Aishihik, the Teslin Tlingit Council and the Vantut Gwitchin of Nacho Nyak Dan have negotiated self-government agreements. As a consequence of this, the Yukon First Nations will have the capacity to pursue their own socio-economic priorities. They will be able to exercise law-making powers on a broad scale in areas such as health care, social services, training programmes, language and education, spiritual beliefs and culture, custody, estates, and revenue raising.

Many other examples of this type exist across Canada. Yet the most far-reaching attempt at Aboriginal self-government has begun to take shape in Nunavut. There, one-fifth of Canada's national territory is being taken over by the Inuit, who make up 80% of the population of the new territory. Complete implementation of the Nunavut project should be achieved in April of 1994. Examples like these may provide models for Aboriginal groups in the United States and South America.

Quebec currently retains more powers than any other subnational unit in the world. It controls education and nearly all of its linguistic policy, the foundations of national identity. It may now, with help of the Bloc Québécois, accomplish further devolution of the powers it was denied under the Charlottetown Accord. Through the instrument of the Charter, groups such as women and multicultural minorities will also press for more decentralisation – but on a non-territorial basis.

The Canadian political theorist Charles Taylor has said that both late modernity and postmodernity will call for new conceptualisations of citizenship and nationhood. He believes that we no longer require the holistic visions of the past. He sees these as being both repressive and largely rooted in mythologies which did not adequately reflect societal heterogeneity.

In opposition to Taylor's vision of diversity, the Pulitzer prize-winning historian Arthur Schlesinger argues that we must hold on to the sources which provided coherence in the past. The promise of America, he says, has always been a fresh start on an equal footing, and the classic image of the republic is that of the melting pot, where differences of race, wealth, relation and nationality are submerged in the pursuit and exercise of democracy.

Yet today the idea of the melting pot is under attack in the United States itself. The idea of assimilation is continually being undermined by the celebration of difference. Schlesinger concedes that this has had some healthy consequences, including long overdue recognition of the achievements of women, black Americans, Indians, Hispanics and Asians, among others. However, the cult of difference has its price, contends Schlesinger, and, pressed too far, poses this danger: 'fragmentation, resegregation and tribalisation of America life'.[16]

Schlesinger believes that the growing diversity of the American population makes the quest for unifying ideas and a common culture more urgent. In a world which is savagely riven by racial and ethnic antagonisms, the US must continue as an example of how a highly differentiated society holds itself together.

Taylor argues that holistic visions like this are also too high a price to pay for democracy. Even the old virtues of the American system such as toleration do not go far enough to meet the demands of today's heterogeneous societies. Taylor says we need to distinguish between toleration and respect for difference. Toleration extends to the widest range of views, so long as they stop short of threats and other discernible harms to individuals. What he advocates instead is a more positive conception of liberty based on what he calls respect. Respect, he says, is far more discriminating than toleration. Although we need not agree with a position in order to respect it, we must understand it as reflecting a moral point of view.

For Taylor, respect is not a static concept. Human identity is created dialogically, in response to our relations, including our actual dialogues with others. If human identity is dialogically created and constituted, then public recognition of our identity requires a politics that leaves room for us to deliberate publicly about those aspects of our identity that we share or potentially share with other citizens. A society that recognises individual identity will be a deliberative, democratic society, because individual identity is partly constituted by collective dialogues. Such a society will also be both critical and reflective. It must go beyond mere toleration to evaluate between differences and to rank them in accordance with this. In practical terms this signifies asymmetrical structuring of power and differing notions of what it means to be a citizen.

We have seen how Canada is much more advanced than the United States in its recognition of difference, its degree of decentralisation and in its willingness to experiment with new forms of democracy. The current political and demographic trends in the US point to a need for change in the system of government. Given the demands of the process of globalisation, Canada may prove a paradigm for the twenty-first century.

NOTES

1. Cf. Eric Hobsbawm, *Nations and Nationalism since 1780*, Canto ed. Cambridge: Cambridge University Press, 1990.
2. Hector St. Jean de Crèvecoeur, *Letters From an American Farmer*. N.Y.: E.P. Dutton, 1957, 39. Originally published 1782.
3. Cf. Charles Taylor, *Multiculturalism and 'The Politics of Recognition'*. Princeton: Princeton University Press, 1992.
4. Quoted in *The Economist*. London: The Economist Publications, October 31–November 6, 1992, 53.
5. *Montréal Gazette,* 21 September, 1994, 1.
6. Richard Mackie, 'Quebeckers don't expect split', *Globe and Mail*, 7 September 1994, 17.
7. Cf. Hugh Windsor, 'Many Point at Wrong Villain', *Globe and Mail*, September 13, 1994, 1-2.
8. Peter Worsley, *The Three Worlds – Culture and Development*. London: Weidenfeld and Nicolson, 1984, 1.
9. Benedict Anderson, *Imagined Communities*, 2nd ed. London: Verso, 1991.
10. Cf. Liah Greenfeld, *Nationalism: Five Roads to Modernity*. Cambridge, Mass.: Harvard University Press, 1992.
11. Edward Said, *The World, The Text and the Critic*. Cambridge, Mass.: Harvard University Press, 1983, 171.
12. Homi Bhabha (ed.) *Nation and Narration*. London: Routledge, 1991, 4.
13. Liah Greenfeld, *Nationalism: Five Roads to Modernity*. Cambridge, Mass.: Harvard University Press, 1992.
14. John Dunn, *Western Political Theory in the Face of the Future*. Cambridge: Cambridge University Press, 1993, 65.
15. In *The World in 1995*. London: The Economist Publications Ltd., 1994, 68.
16. Arthur Schlesinger, *The Disuniting of America*. New York, 1992, 1.

Differences between American and Canadian Studies

Hans Hauge

1. National Identity

Maintaining a Danish identity *vis-à-vis* our powerful southern neighbour, Germany, has been relatively easy, it seems, compared with maintaining a Canadian identity *vis-à-vis* its powerful southern neighbour, the United States. The Danish language made it easier. Even the Norwegians had the possibility of differentiating themselves from their southern, once powerful, colonial power, Denmark, because they could resurrect the old Norwegian language. The Americans had no such possibility of differentiating themselves from the English by means of a national language; they had to use other means: literature, for example. So Americans and Canadians have had the same identity problems so far as England was concerned. The Francophone Canadians were in as happy a situation as the Danes, since the Anglophone Canadians were their Germans.

Nineteenth century Danish literary historians urged the Danes to turn their backs on the south and face north. Their protective barrier against the south was their language; what they saw when they faced north was Scandinavia; the 'Nordic' in a mythological sense. The north was myth and poetry; the south German *Vernnuft*. Norwegians looking north, turning their backs on Denmark, saw only themselves and more mountains. When Canadians faced north they saw nothing, and they had nothing to protect them from southern cultural invasion, even though there has never been a strong American tradition for looking north; the Americans looked west, whilst the Canadians thought they were looking at them. When Canadians looked west, they could be fairly confident in themselves and call Canada a Dominion, but when they looked south they discovered the arbitrariness and unnaturalness of their nation and came to see Canada as a construction.

A national language functions partly as a bond and partly as a bar. It simultaneously includes and excludes. The French language is a bond amongst

Quebeckers and a bar towards English Canada. The English language is a bond that *unites* Canadians with the Americans and the English but it cannot act as a bar. It is almost impossible for Canada, as once a part of the Empire, to write back. In the absence of a national language as bond and bar, other things will have to perform the functions of a national language. A national language cannot be maintained without a national literature; a national literature is the national language's army and navy. A language without a national literature is a dialect. In Danish one does not have to worry much about such a thing as a Danish content. If a work of literature is written in Danish, it will remain Danish no matter what the content is. And once you have constructed a Danish national literature, even texts written in Latin or English create no serious problems. Karen Blixen's *Out of Africa* can be assimilated into Danish literature more easily than Margaret Laurence's African works can into Canadian. Even modernism, however international it is, can be nationalised into the paradoxical formation: national modernism. If one cannot invent a national language what then can replace it? Culture or literature are likely candidates, although neither of them are as efficient means of excluding the other as a national language. The great advantage of a poem written in Danish is that it cannot be translated, hence it can really be experienced as Danish property. A Canadian poem written in English cannot be kept behind bars; it travels abroad.

2. Studying the Other

What has all this to do with American Studies and Canadian Studies? So far very little. But the first lesson to be drawn from it is that it is easier, in all senses of the word, to study a literature if it is the literature of a European nation state with its own national language, than to study either America or Canada. In a university context, American and Canada simply do not fit in, because the university structure mirrors the structure of the old European nation states.

American and Canadian Studies as such appear to be unproblematic entities and they simply suggest that one can study America and Canada as objects. However, already here we should be aware of certain differences. To study Canada in Denmark is very different from studying Canada in Canada. Doing it in Canada means making oneself an object of study. They study themselves; we study them. And not only can American and Canadian Studies be seen as studying an object; they themselves can be made into objects of study. One can study an American Studies person whilst he or she is studying America.

Both Americans and Canadians appear to be quite happy about being made into objects of study. American and Canadian embassies bring gifts to us, if we study them. But how do they see us, while we look at them, since they even encourage and support us?

Everyone knows that if one is good-looking it can be, I guess, gratifying to be looked at and even studied in detail, especially or may be only, if it is the right person who looks and studies. If looked at, you may even come to believe that you are worth looking at. One can easily imagine a Canadian writer saying "Are you really looking at me? I thought you would never have noticed me, since there are so many much better looking writers such as Joyce or Proust or Baudelaire." Yet, sometimes you do not like being looked at. From an American point of view, there may be a difference between an Iranian doing American Studies and a Dane. The difference is that a Dane doing American Studies or Canadian Studies is cast in the role of ambassador, but an Iranian must be some kind of a spy. Nobody likes to be spied upon.

Anyone beginning to study either America or Canada – and can they study both without giving rise to jealousy? – is like a lover. One falls in love with Canada. Canada feels flattered and responds. A Canadian Studies person's first love may last. He will visit Canada, and his love will perhaps become stronger. He may return many times. And he may remain faithful to Canada and refrain from having English affairs. Yet he may also come to see her as she really is; he returns and becomes a critical Americanist or Canadianist. Now, I have a feeling that Americanists tend to be more critical of their chosen love-object than Canadianists, and perhaps the reason is that there is less to criticise about Canada. The reason for this could very well be, at least in a Scandinavian context, that they more or less do things in Canada the way we do them here.

My American Studies teacher told us to study America as a primitive culture, hence we should become *anthropologists*. I have never come across anything similar in Canadian Studies, although there is a sense in which a certain anthropological bias has recently entered Canadian Studies. If such a thing happens, that is to say, if you really study America in such a fashion, one can no longer be sure that the Americans like being studied. With regard to the anthropological bias in Canadian Studies I am referring to a widespread tendency to focus on minorities; especially Indians and Inuits – and women. I have attended – not many – but a fair number of Canadian Studies conferences and have heard countless lectures about Indians in Canadian literature but never one lecture about 19th century Canadian poetry. Is this, on the part of the non-Canadian Canadianist, a mild form of resistance? I love you, yes, but you have many faults.

So far I have discussed American and Canadian Studies together; the only difference I have mentioned is the presence of a more outspoken critical attitude among Americanists than Canadianists. This, again, may merely be a reflection of a general European intellectual tradition for being anti-American; a tradition, I would add, that is on the wane. Since Canadianists are less critical of their object, and thus more like lovers, Canadians tend not to mind being made into objects of study. Canadian Studies, as an academic field, seems not to be like what is called 'Orientalism', that is to say, Western scholarly and scientific studies of the Orientals. There has been a strong resistance amongst Orientals against being studied *as such* and thereby being made into objects. There is of course a similar resistance among Canadian Indians, but, as I said, not so much among white Canadians.

On the whole Canadian writers have had little fear of being appropriated by German university professors; they have rather seen it as an opportunity for travel grants. Yet there *are* critical voices inside Canada, and I restrict myself to creative writers and literary critics. The critique of Orientalism claims that when we in the West study them, we are really saying something about ourselves. Hence the Orientals can make a new science called Occidentalism in which they make us, or Orientalism, an object of study. This is a version of what is called 'the empire-writes-back-theory'. Such a critique is, as far as I know, non-existent in a Canadian Studies context. The explanation is the absence of power relations involved. There is no hierarchy between the one who studies and the one being studied. Canadians don't experience Canadian Studies as an act of appropriation, but rather as an act of seduction. This leads me back to where I began and to an incomplete sketch of a history of American and Canadian Studies. They have different histories and origins.

3. The Difference Between American and Canadian Studies

It appears to be relatively unproblematical to say that in Canadian Studies we study an object, already there, called Canada. We cannot study the whole, so we divide it up. American Studies, in contrast, at least in its early phase, before decline set in, did not divide America up in quite the same way. One could study America by focusing upon a set of shared myths and symbols that could stand for the whole. They are all well-known: the frontier, virgin land, the machine in the garden, the American Adam. One insisted upon the incomparability of America, its difference from Europe. And if America was different one needed a different method, a unique one, with which to study America. It just couldn't be studied the way one had traditionally studied, say, England or France. A new object required a new way of studying that object. One of the characteristics of American Studies was its combination of history and literary criticism. In a conference on the American and Canadian Wests, an observer noted that the Americans participating in the conference saw similarities between America and Canada, whereas the Canadians saw differences. So if Canada is as different from America as America is from Europe, we have the first explanation of why American Studies, as a programme, a theory, a discipline, cannot include or subsume Canada. One would overlook differences, barriers, borders. Canada would become invisible. So, Canadian Studies makes Canada visible.

But it is almost an empirical fact that many European academics in Canadian Studies originally came from American Studies. Since this is their background one may expect a certain transfer from that discipline to Canadian Studies, as if Canadian Studies was just American Studies with another object.

Yet Canada, or at least Canadian literature, was really first introduced in English Departments under the rubric of Commonwealth literature. It was of course the English language which made Commonwealth literature possible. Commonwealth Studies is, however, a monolingual institution which cannot really cope with other languages, be they French Canadian or Samoan. Although I have said that there seems to have been very little resistance on the part of Canadian writers and critics against being studied, there has been a resistance against categorising Canadian literature as Commonwealth literature, not only and understandably among Quebec writers. Quebec literature disappears, and Canadian critic Diana Brydon makes the point that Canadian critical discourse as a whole has been marginalised 'by its status as "Commonwealth literature"'. So in one sense Canadian Studies can be seen as an attempt to liberate, and make visible again, Canadian literature from Commonwealth literature. Canadian Studies helps to create a 'literature of one's own', but Canadian literature can, in its turn, become invisible again either if it is made a part of postcolonial literature or if it becomes just a cultural appendix in a Canadian Studies programme, since such programmes often make a point of being interdisciplinary.

One idea behind Canadian Studies is area studies. They originated in English missionary schools. If you were to send missionaries to a foreign country they had to know something of the areas' language, geography, history, and culture. This is, perhaps, the historical origin of why area studies are multidisciplinary.

Even if we take for granted that Canada can be studied in a discipline called Canadian Studies, it has to find a place, an institution, in which to exist. Either Canada can be studied in an independent research centre or in a university. At least in Europe the structure of the university constitutes a problem.

The most likely institute or department to study Canadian literature in is a department of English; it is almost never studied in Comparative Literature departments. In an English department outside an English-speaking country it will have to compete with several other literatures in English. It will be difficult to establish, anywhere, a Department of 'Canadian', an 'Institute' of Canadian Philology, even though there is in Beirut an Institute for Palestinian Studies.

The real name of Aarhus University's Department of English is the Department of English Philology (Institut for Engelsk Filologi). Now, why did we in Denmark begin to study English as an academic subject? In order to answer I return to my beginning. The creation of national philologies had the purpose of nationalising the citizens by means of the national language and its literature. This process began in the late nineteenth century in Denmark, Norway and Germany and in the beginning of this century in England. A European University's division into Nordic, German, Romance and English philologies mirrors Europe's division into nation states.

Canada did not establish similar institutions with the sole purpose of making Canadians Canadians; they studied English literature. But in the nineteenth century the English in England studied Greek and Latin literature. They did not study their own national literature. The reason why one began to study German, French and English in Denmark or elsewhere was the existence in these languages of classics. One could not begin to study one's own literature until that literature had classics as classical and good as Homer, Virgil and Horace. Germany had Goethe, France Racine, England Shakespeare and Milton; Denmark had none. In order to make it legitimate to study one's own literature one invented a national literature with national classics – the latter a contradiction in terms. A national literature is something which you don't share with others. It is your own. In other words: the way that part of the university which studies literature is organised reflects the division of Europe into nation states. Such a structure makes it extremely difficult to study Canadian literature in itself. It will for many years be an appendix to English literature and thus mirror the colonial expansion of Europe, not of course in terms of content but of the form of the university.

4. Frye and the Canadian Classic

Canada has no classics. Neither do we Danes. So if you just study literature without taking nationality into consideration there simply is no Canadian literature to study. One can make a long list of Canadian writers, it is true, but such a list is not a literary history; at most it is an encyclopedia of texts written in Canada. I am partly paraphrasing Northrop Frye's opening words in his 'Conclusion to a Literary History of Canada' when I say this, and I fully agree with him. Let me quote the following which, I would add, is both ironic and not-ironic: 'Canada has produced no author who is classic in the sense of possessing a vision greater in kind than that of his best readers'.[1] But then he adds that this is an advantage for Canadian literature:

> If no Canadian writer pulls us away from the Canadian context toward the centre of literary experience itself, then at every point we are aware of his social and historical setting. The conception of what is literary has to be greatly broadened for such a literature. The literary, in Canada, is often only an incidental quality of writings .... Even when it is literature in its orthodox genres of poetry and fiction, it is more significantly studied as a part of Canadian life than as a part of an autonomous world of literature.

What he says is that Canadian literature cannot be studied *as literature* but *as a part* of Canadian life, even though he also claims that 'many Canadian cultural phenomena are not peculiarly Canadian at all, but are typical of their wider North American and Western contexts' (279).

Many teachers of literature, Canadian or Danes, would welcome Frye's suggestion but misunderstand it. They believe that it is a good thing if literature can be studied in its social and historical context, whereas what Frye says about Canadian literature is that it has not managed to leave its context behind. Frye's other statement about content, on the other hand, could be read as a blueprint for studying Canada in a North American context, that is to say, as part of a North American Study Programme. The way Frye himself has dealt with Canadian literature is similar to the American Studies way. He has read it in terms of a specific Canadian mythology, in terms of the Bush Garden; and has inspired his most well-known pupil Margaret Atwood to develop such a method. There has been a movement within Canadian Studies which is very similar in intent and method to the American Studies myth and symbol school.

There is no doubt that because Canadian literature, since it is hardly literature but a cultural phenomenon, is so much a part of Canadian life it, has been able to integrate itself into that multidisciplinary discipline, Canadian Studies.

5. Understanding Canada

American Studies was a unified theory; a unique combination of history and literary theory. It was, I say. Then a process of Balkanisation set in. American Studies was split up into Southern Studies, Urban Studies, Afro-American Studies, Chicano Studies, Women's Studies, and today America is being studied only in parts. Canadian Studies, too, seems to divide Canada up, as I said earlier on, and to see the same entity from different perspectives. I base this on a particular book called *Understanding Canada*.[2] Its subtitle is 'A Multidisciplinary Introduction to Canadian Studies'. The idea was to have seven scholars 'view a nation through his own scholarly lens', and then to ask the question: what does Canada look like? The danger of such an undertaking could be seven different pictures of the same 'nation', some might even come up with the scholarly result that it wasn't a nation. What does Canada look like if you see it through all seven lenses? The answer, the Preface states, 'can be found in this rather unique book'. We don't have to wait for the answer until we have read all seven contributions, since we get the answer right after: 'What emerges is the story of people determined to build their own version of a distinctive nation in North America'. It is the whole book's contention – or at least that of the Preface – that the story it tells is about building a nation state. We find words such as national unity, national institutions, national economic policies, a national consciousness to be, as it says, 'reflected in Canadian literature'. Yet one of the lenses, the anthropological one, sees a multicultural society emerging. Where six lenses see one, the seventh sees many.

The seven perspectives are geography, history, political science, economics, anthropology, literary criticism and an international perspective in that order. This seems to be perspectives enough in order to tell one story of the birth of a nation. However neutral and scholarly Canadian Studies appears to be, it cannot be divorced from the problem of nation and narration. Donald Sutherland's contribution to the book is, I suppose, somewhat controversial. He tries to bridge the gap between the two cultures: the English Canadian and the French. His literary perspective is identical with the national. His claim is that the study of a national literature 'provides the key to understanding the character of the nation'. Sutherland's perspective makes it possible to study Canadian literature as such, but he could only do so by looking at it through a national lens. The establishing of Canadian Studies follows a period in the post-Diefenbaker years where observers had begun to fear that Canada as a nation had been defeated. I am referring to a book from 1965 by the Canadian philosopher George Grant called *Lament for a Nation*,[3] which carries the subtitle 'The Defeat of Canadian Nationalism'. Similarly, Frye has claimed that Canada leapt directly from a colonial or regional into a post-national phase.

One might ask whether these seven perspectives are contingent or whether Canada invites precisely these. One discipline always looms large in Canadian Studies in contrast to American: Geography. Geography is very seldom included in other multidisciplinary programmes. One explanation for its inclusion is the special character of the Canadian landscape. It has even led to what is called the geographic fallacy, which tries to explain for instance the distinctiveness of Canadian literature in terms of Canadian nature.

Let me try to sum up. The typical non-Canadian Canadian Studies person begins as a lover. He can remain a faithful lover, and in that capacity he will tell other people about his beloved. He becomes an ambassador or missionary for Canadian literature and life. He will try to find a room of Canada's own in his institution, although it is crowded. If he is a moralist he will have a tendency to study Quebec, Indians and immigrants. The typical American Studies person often suffers from a love-hate relationship to his object. He tends to be much more critical of America than the Canadianist is of Canada, while the Canadian Studies person will often share the American Studies person's fear of America. The Canadian Studies person is also a scholar. This may explain the emigration from American into Canadian Studies. Canada is virgin land for the scholar; the burden of history and tradition is not so heavy.

There are obvious advantages for the teacher of Canadian literature, since it has never managed to pull us away from its context. By studying its literature, you study its life. But what happens if a Canadian text actually manages to escape from the garrison context in which it has been imprisoned? Will it escape the grasp of Canadian Studies as well? If there is no trace of geography and therefore of place left? Can it still be studied? Now who has pulled us, or himself, away from the context? Northrop Frye himself, to mention one. What would it mean to read his *Anatomy of Criticism* in a Canadian context? Another one is Marshall McLuhan; what is Canadian about *The Medium is the Message?* There is Harold Innis, a theorist of communication; and one could go on. There is a Roman Catholic philosopher, Bernard Lonergan, whom nobody knows is a Canadian and who lived in the Vatican in Rome. Even if we knew he was Canadian it wouldn't make much of a difference. I would also mention Margaret Atwood and Robertson Davies as creative writers who have pulled themselves away from the context.

There have been made attempts to recontextualise some of these figures. A book by Arthur Kroker, a Canadian sociologist, is called *Technology and the Canadian Mind: Innis, McLuhan, Grant.*[4] One of Kroker's points is in fact that 'Canada's principal contribution to North American thought consists of a highly original, comprehensive, and eloquent discourse on technology'.

Frye has a somewhat similar point: 'It is in the inarticulate part of communication, railways and bridges and canals and highways, that Canada, one of whose symbols is the taciturn beaver, has shown its real strength'. Frye divides Canadian culture's use of language into two, a division which roughly corresponds to the nineteenth and the twentieth centuries. The first use is rhetorical, argumentative, assertive: language as weapon. Canadian writing of the nineteenth century is philosophy, theology, sermons, psychology, history. The second use of language is poetical. But then comes the really interesting thing in Frye's Conclusion: 'We notice that scholarship in Canada has so often been written with more conviction and authority, and has attracted wider recognition, than the literature itself'. Notice his 'we notice that'. Frye himself, of course, is one of the many Canadians who has written with conviction and authority and has attracted wider recognition than Canadian literature itself. The reason is that scholarly writing, as he goes on to say, is 'more easily attached to its [Canada's] central tradition'. If that rhetorical, communicative, philosophical tradition is really the central Canadian one, it is surely significant that it is not represented in the multidisciplinary *Understanding Canada*.

6. Why do you study Canada?

Let me conclude with some remarks about the differences between American and Canadian Studies in terms of *why* we teach them outside of the two nations and what they *do* to us when we study and teach them. I have briefly tried to argue that Canadian Studies as such is inseparable from the idea of nationality. *It began after a period where serious doubts had been voiced about whether Canada was still a nation.* It helped recreate and reinvent Canadian nationality, a national literature, a national political culture. American Studies contributed to creating an image of the United States as unique, different, new, incomparable. The import of American Studies into Europe just after the war was an antidote to Marxism-Leninism and was meant to strengthen European democracy and act as an ideal for Europe; but we were never meant to copy it. When one studies Canada in that special way which is called 'Canadian Studies' one is already, always involved in a comparative undertaking. Inevitably, one begins to reflect on one's own nation, on one's own national literature and on nation building. There is a certain reciprocity present, whereas in the case of American Studies one realises differences between the new and the old world. The unique American experience and way, its myths and symbols, can never as such be emulated, shared or imitated. American and Canadian Studies in both cases lead to a reflection on one's own country: on one's difference from America and on a certain similarity to Canada. It is obvious why Canadian Studies in Germany has a politological bias; studying Canadian federalism illuminates German federalism. In the Danish case, getting involved in Canadian Studies rediscovers Greenland for us, and this is helpful since we tend to forget it. Reading about how Canadians have treated the Inuits is an ethical act, not because it is ethically better to read such literature instead of novels written by white, male, English-speaking Canadians but because it reveals that we do not read 'our own' literature about 'our own' Indians. Reading Inuit Canadian literature is an act of *not* reading our own. Seeing the other is seeing oneself in a slightly different light – never a better light.

NOTES

1. Northrop Frye, 'Conclusion to *A Literary History of Canada*', in: *The Stubborn Structure*. London: Methuen, 1970, 278.
2. William Metcalfe (ed.), *Understanding Canada: A Multidisciplinary Introduction to Canadian Studies*. New York and London: New York University Press, 1982, xiii.
3. George Grant, *Lament for a Nation*, Carlton Library no. 50. Toronto: 1965, 1978.
4. Arthur Kroker, *Technology and the Canadian Mind*. Montreal: New World Perspectives, 1984, 7.

Notes on Contributors

Charlotte Beyer is a graduate of the University of Aarhus, and now has a Ph.D. in Women and Gender Studies from the University of Warwick.

Albert-Reiner Glaap is Professor of English at the University of Düsseldorf, where he teaches Canadian literature in general and drama in particular. He has made Canadian texts available for German high school teachers.

Konrad Groß is Professor of English at the University of Kiel, where he teaches North American literature and culture. He is a former president of the Association for Canadian Studies in the German speaking countries (GKS).

Gudrun Gudsteins teaches British and Canadian literature at the University of Iceland. She is chairperson of the Icelandic chapter of the Nordic Association for Canadian Studies (NACS/ANEC).

Hans Hauge teaches British, American and Canadian literature, criticism and philosophy at the Department of English, University of Aarhus.

Brian Johnson is a prize-winning University of Manitoba Research Fellow specializing in Canadian literature.

Hartmut Lutz is Professor of North American Studies at the University of Greifswald, where he teaches Canadian and Native literatures and cultures.

Marissa Quie is the Samuel Reichmann Fellow in Canadian Studies at the Faculty of Social and Political Sciences at the University of Cambridge.

Stephen Scobie is a professor of English at the University of Victoria, B.C. where he teaches Canadian literature. He is also a well-known poet, and in 1980 he won the Governor General's Award for Poetry.

Bengt Streijffert is the financial director for the natural sciences at the University of Lund. When given the chance he lectures on Canadian literature and culture. He is President of the Nordic Association for Canadian Studies (NACS/ANEC).

David Williams is a professor of English at the University of Manitoba, Winnipeg, where he teaches Canadian literature; he is also a very talented novelist.

Per Winther teaches Canadian & American literature at the University of Oslo. He is also chairman of the Norwegian chapter of the Nordic Association for Canadian Studies (NACS/ANEC).

Abstracts

Beyer, Charlotte:
From Violent Duality to Multi-Culturalism: Margaret Atwood's Post-Colonial Cultural and Sexual Politics

This article explores the intersection of post-colonial cultural and sexual politics in Margaret Atwood's writing. It focusses on the shift in Atwood's writing in thinking about difference, away from an earlier 'colonial' fiction which was concerned with the problems of defining a specifically Canadian identity and of writing in a colonized space to a 'post-colonial' fiction which emphasizes the provisional nature of all cultures and identities. The article also explores the construction of place as a site for negotiating identity in Atwood's writing, and looks at Atwood's use of the Canadian wilderness, and more recently the metropolis, as literary discourse.

Carlsen, Jørn:
The Story of Canada

The article briefly traces the history of Canada from the earliest days of European contact through to the defeat of the Liberals by the Parti Québécois in the provincial election in Quebec of September 12, 1994. The events selected for attention in this account do admittedly reflect a European/Euro-centric bias, since although Canada is a multicultural country, the great majority of Canadians are white and of European origin. The major schism of the country has so far always been between the two so-called founding nations, the English and the French. However, this history also recognises the importance of the First Nations peoples of Canada, and the article concludes with a glance forward to the founding of Nunavit, the first Inuit territory, due to take place in 1999.

Glaap, Albert-Reiner:
Behind the Scenes, or: What English-Canadian Plays Tell Us about Canada

Increasingly, English-Canadian drama has become a mirror of current issues, though not exclusively Canadian issues. Canadian playwrights think of themselves primarily as writers for the stage about any topic, be it Canadian or universal. In this article, some of the most prominent issues thematized in contemporary Canadian drama are illustrated with reference to eight English-Canadian plays which were written between 1980 and 1993 and which can help us to catch a glimpse of what goes into the making of contemporary Canadian drama. The playwrights considered are Margaret Hollingsworth, Vittorio Rossi, Drew Hayden Taylor, Linda Griffiths, Dennis Foon, Guillermo Verdecchia, Judith Thompson and Raymond Storey; the issues covered in their plays range from immigration to AIDS.

Groß, Konrad:
Identity – Identities: Infamous Canadian Pastime, Venerable Quest, or Trivial Pursuit?

The article examines the issue of a Canadian national identity. All efforts at cementing a pan-Canadian consciousness continue to fail, yet the search for a solution to the problem has not ceased. The stresses and strains within Canadian society, and their origins in the country's history, are discussed. It is noted that Canada has taken well-meant steps towards the creation of a more just society. Yet, it is concluded, the country's multi-ethnic character, together with basic dualism and regionalist disparities, will severely test Canada's ability to stay together as a nation.

Gudsteins, Gudrun:
Wake-Pick Weavers: Laura G. Salverson and Kristjana Gunnars

Alertness to the power of literature in cultural politics and to the vision that destructive dichotomies need to be resolved through constructive acceptance of their binary interdependence characterizes the writing of both Laura Goodman Salverson and Kristjana Gunnars.

Salverson was a Canadian born to Icelandic immigrants. In her works she responded to the pressure on immigrants to assimilate to the Anglo-Canadian cultural heritage during the settlement of Western Canada early in this century. She resisted the idea of unquestioning adoption of the established hierarchy of power and values, on the grounds that freedom and national unity could not be accomplished except by granting equal status to all immigrants and to women and men alike.

A landed immigrant in Canada since 1969, Gunnars was born in Iceland to an Icelandic father and a Danish mother. Both in *Wake-Pick Poems* and in *The Prowler* she picks up themes and motifs from Salverson and lends them a wider application, presenting the tensions arising from the immigrant experience and male/female power politics as essentially exaggerated manifestations of tensions grounded in human nature and existence. Her strategy of resisting divisions is rooted in the outlook on politics and writing that characterizes all of her works. In her own efforts to settle within a Canadian context, Gunnars affirms Salverson's vision yet transcends it to lend it wider application and to emphasize the power of literature to settle and resolve cultural tensions rooted in the duality in human nature but exaggerated by Canada's immigrant history.

Hauge, Hans:
Differences between American and Canadian Studies

The article considers American and Canadian studies largely from an external viewpoint, from that of scholars outside Canada and the USA. There are obvious similarities between the two disciplines, but this article concentrates on the differences: differences, for example, in the origins of American and Canadian studies, in the way they are accommodated within the framework of a European university, and in the attitude of the scholar to the object of study, with the American Studies scholar often taking a more critical stance.

In studying the other, in the final analysis, one is also inevitably studying oneself. In the case of American Studies, one realises differences between the new and the old world; the unique American experience and way, its myths and symbols, can never as such be emulated, shared or imitated. Canadian Studies began as a discipline, it is argued, after a period where serious doubts had been voiced about whether Canada was still a nation. It helped recreate and reinvent Canadian nationality, a national literature, a national political culture. When one studies Canada in that special way which is called 'Canadian Studies', there is a certain reciprocity present as one inevitably begins to reflect on one's own nation, on one's own national literature and on nation building.

Johnson, Brian:
A Bird in the House of Metafiction: Fantasizing Narratological Power in Margaret Laurence's Manawaka Stories

For the fictional narrator Vanessa, as for Laurence, the writing act seems to be a redemptive process that retrospectively and sympathetically connects the older, wiser writing subject with the ghosts of her ancestral past. Significantly, however, this redemptive function of art in Laurence's novel is often marked by a strong anxiety about the authority of the bifurcated narrator and her relation to postmodernism's preoccupation with metafiction. By reconsidering at every level the role of writing in *A Bird in the House* as a modality of power, the article seeks to repudiate – at least in part – the argument that

Vanessa's fiction, to say nothing of Laurence's, is hopelessly fractured. Rather, tracing the development of writing in the novel forces us to ask radical new questions about the origins, practice, and consequences of narratological power in Laurence's fiction.

Lutz, Hartmut:
Contemporary Native Literature in Canada and 'The Voice of the Mother'

Native authors in Canada have access to cultural traditions which have enabled their ancestors to survive under extreme conditions in ways that have not only enhanced the lives of all members of their respective societies, but that have also enabled the co-existence in mutual respect with all their relations, be they rocks, plants, four-legged, winged, finned or scaled. As Daniel David Moses has pointed out, Native traditions honour the environment as a mother. Lenore Keeshig-Tobias, the Anishnabe storyteller, writer, critic and cultural activist from Ontario, has taken up the definition of Native Literature as being the Voice of the Mother in a more down to earth and concrete fashion: it is the voice of the mother which encodes the first and most important exposure of a Native child to the oral tradition.

The literature of First Nations people written down in English or French, or any Native language, is a new mode of expression. Originally, and to this day, First Nations people transmit/ted their history, their myths, fables, philosophy and verbal art forms by word of mouth, passing it on from generation to generation with an accuracy and tenacity that is both admirable and astounding for us who are used to almost exclusively literate (or electronic) forms of information transmission. Since 1960, much Native literature has been written down, with English forming the commonest *lingua franca* for such communication. The article surveys the work of numerous Native writers working in a variety of forms.

Scobie, Stephen:
Double Voicing: A View of Canadian Poetry

The article takes as its theme the idea that two voices are, in one way or another, often evident in Canadian poetry. One type of such 'double voicing' lies in the dual influence of Canada itself on the one hand, and of external literary sources – especially, in the early days, the literature of the colonial power, and more recently of much more diverse origins – on the other. Another type of 'double voice' can be found in Canadian 'documentary' poetry, where the two voices are seen as those of fact and fiction, history and

216

imagination, the documented record and the poetic re-creation. Finally, double voicing is to be found in the Canadian long poem, where it takes the form of a dialogue between the lyric impulse of the short poem and more extended forms of discursive strategy and practice; as the 'long poem' becomes longer, it begins to question itself, and, almost inevitably, to turn back on itself, self-reflexive and self-referential. Double voicing, it is suggested, reflects a profound instinct of Canada's divided society: that nothing can ever be said only once.

Streijffert, Bengt:
Painting Canada

The article aims to provide a brief introduction to the art of Anglophone Canada. The theme is *painting Canada*, i.e. artists working with Canadian motifs, and how Canada and Canadians emerge on the artists' canvasses. The focus is on the English-speaking, European Canada, and not the land of the 'Indians' or the Inuits.

It is argued that it is regrettable, albeit understandable, that art is so little employed in interdisciplinary studies of Canada. There is indeed a branch of art that must be recognized as 'Canadian art'. And it can be employed, even by students who are not primarily interested in art *per se*, as an illustration of the history and development of Canada.

The article discusses the work of artists in Canada ranging from the military art of British army artists in the eighteenth century through to the contemporary work of Alex Colville. Illustrations of six major works are included in the article, which concludes by making the point that with increased international attention being paid to contemporary Canadian art it can now be argued that Canada's art, like its literature, now belongs to the world.

Quie, Marissa:
Cultural and Political Aspects of United States-Canada Relations

The article takes a comparative stance on the analysis of the US-Canada 'relationship'. It focusses much more on the differences between the two nations and the current very noticeable interpenetration of both cultural and political identities than on their formal relationship. In particular, the article discusses multiculturalism and new conceptions of citizenship, democracy and freedom. America has traditionally viewed its society as a 'melting pot' for diverse cultures and peoples in which a new nation could be forged. It is argued that the Canadian policy, as Americans are now recognising, has for a long time been more reflective and innovative on the question of the accommodation of difference within democracy.

Given the demands of the process of globalization, Canada may prove a paradigm for the US of the twenty-first century.

Williams, David:
Re-imagining a Stone Angel: The Absent Autobiographer of *The Stone Diaries*

What is truly postmodern about *The Stone Diaries* by Carol Shields may be its use of the form of autobiography to decentre the figure of an autonomous subject, or to question the metaphysics of identity. In the three decades which have elapsed since publication of *The Stone Angel*, both the structuralist and poststructuralist critiques of identity seem to have altered the usual landmarks of autobiography, making it impossible any more to write unproblematically, or even un-self-consciously, of the self. The most obvious context for explaining this sea-change in the currents of life writing would have to be Jacques Derrida's critique of the metaphysics of self-presence. And yet Shields' novel would seem to shrug off deconstruction as a context for the life story of her autobiographer who is 'virtually absent'.

The article discusses the role of Daisy, 'a woman thinking her autobiography', in *The Stone Diaries*. It is argued that it is only when the book is closed and the autobiographer is at last conclusively absent that she seems most present. For Daisy's inability to rest in peace becomes our own inability to rest in the aesthetic object, or to adopt a romantic faith in beauty as truth, truth beauty. Daisy's quiet distress lives on in the common distress, in our deeply shared sense, finally, of how little we all are allowed to say. Art may not be not enough for any of us; but in the end, there is no place else to go, beyond the organic record traced in stone.

Winther, Per:
The Canadian Short Story in English: An Alternative Paradigm

Serious scholarly attention to the short story as a separate genre is a relatively short-lived phenomenon. In the US, for instance, the short story as a broadly addressed field of critical interest really only dates back to the 1960s. In Canada interest in the short story as a separate genre worthy of critical analysis *per se* has an even shorter history. Nevertheless, as this article sets out to demonstrate, the Canadian short story tradition has had a separate focus and a rhythm all its own. Direct form, for instance, never took on the canonical authority that it did in the United States. Paradoxically, this situation seems to have prepared Canadian short fiction particularly well for the formal flexibility which more than anything else characterizes the contemporary short story and which makes the Canadian short story such a particularly healthy genre, nationally as well as internationally.